LIBERALLY SPEAKING

Why Liberalism Is Right for America

By

Stephen J. Natoli

For Becky!
Stay the course.

Steve Natoli

Library of Congress Cataloging-in-Publication Data

Natoli, Stephen J.
  Liberally speaking : why liberalism is right for America / by
Stephen J.
Natoli.
     pages cm
  Includes bibliographical references and index.
   ISBN 978-0-8283-2571-4 (pbk. : alk. paper) -- ISBN 978-0-8283-
2573-8
(e-book : alk. paper) 1. Liberalism--United States. 2. United
States--Social policy. 3. United States--Politics and government.
I.
Title.

  JC574.2.U6N37 2015
  320.51'30973--dc23

                              2015015721

ISBN 9780828325714 Paperback
ISBN 9780828325738 E-Book

Branden Books
PO Box 812094
Wellesley MA 02482

www.brandenbooks.com

CONTENTS

CHAPTER 1
My Journey to Liberalism

Inauguration, 2013

On January 21, 2013 I stood roughly two hundred yards from the steps of the west front of the U. S. Capitol to see the Second Inauguration of Barack Obama, the forty-fourth President of the United States. There I joined 900,000 of my fellow citizens-the largest throng ever for a president's second inauguration-to be present for history. I had seen many presidential inaugurations on television but this was my first one in person. As the Marine band played patriotic marches and the dignitaries processed in to take their places, the panoply and pageantry of the formal swearing in of our chief public servant was re-enacted according to time-honored tradition. It was a happy crowd, celebrating once again the success of American democracy and congratulating the fellow citizen chosen to lead it.

The occasion was special on a number of levels. First, the re-election of the nation's first African-American president marked an important precedent. Though his First Inaugural four years earlier was a groundbreaking moment, some had tried to minimize it as a nearly accidental convergence of circumstances resulting from the crashing economy of 2008. But now the American people had reaffirmed their choice. They had seen Obama as president for four years and wanted him back. They had not chosen him because he was black or in spite of it; they had made their choice without any regard for it. That may have said more about how far the nation had come along the road to genuine racial toleration and acceptance than many commentators appeared to notice.

Second, this Inaugural was special to me personally because of my own involvement in the process. In 2008 I had become a dedicated supporter of candidate Obama. I had gotten elected to my county's Democratic Central Committee. I did phone banking at party headquarters and walked a precinct for him. I contributed money to his campaign. I had agreed to become faculty advisor for the Young Democrats Club that enthusiastic students wanted to form at the community college where I teach. We registered voters, held rallies, sold Obama gear and got the word out every way we could. Obama was terrifically popular with youth and the excitement was infectious.

Finally, the president's election and re-election represented more than the personal triumph of a young, eloquent and charismatic politician. It also represented more than the collective triumph of those of us who worked for his elevation and reaffirmation as chief executive and titular leader of the free world. It was above all the triumph of a cause, of an ethos, of a belief system based on a set of shared values. President Obama enunciated part of its creed in his Inaugural Address when, referring to the choice at stake in the election of 2012, he stated, "Together, we resolved that a great nation must care for the vulnerable, and protect its people from life's worst hazards and misfortune." The President spoke to it again when he pointed to the lessons learned from the economic crisis he inherited on entering office. He recalled, "Together, we discovered that a free market only thrives when there are rules to ensure competition and fair play."

He made perhaps the most complete explanation in his Address of the choice voters faced between his and his opponent's guiding precepts by saying, "For we, the people, understand that our country cannot succeed when a shrinking few do very well and a growing many barely make it. We believe that America's prosperity must rest upon the broad shoulders of a rising middle class. We know that America thrives when every person can find independence and pride in their work, when the wages of honest labor liberate families from the brink of hardship. We are true to our creed when a little girl born into the bleakest poverty knows that she has the same chance to succeed as anybody else, because she is an American, she is free, and she is equal, not just in the eyes of God but also in our own."

It was this creed that inspired my support, the students' support, and the support of the majority of the American people in two national elections. The election of someone who looks like Barack Obama was made possible by the tenets of this creed; and though he exemplified its beliefs and spoke of them movingly and effectively, it was the beliefs themselves that won those elections by galvanizing the people behind their vision for the future. That belief system is called liberalism.

Why I Have Written This Book

The seed for this book was planted in my mind in the summer of 2012 when I walked into a Barnes & Noble Bookstore in the Rancho Bernardo neighborhood of San Diego, California. My wife and I were visiting our youngest daughter and her husband there for a few days from our home in Visalia, California about 300 miles to the northeast. Visalia lies in the San Joaquin Valley, the Golden State's great agricultural cornucopia. When Borders went out of business our city of 127,000 people, the county seat of Tulare County, a primarily rural area, lost its only full service bookstore, and so when we visit we like to spend some time at a couple of places we don't have around home, the beach and the bookstore.

After looking at the new releases near the store entrance I headed back to the "Current Events & Politics" section. It didn't take long to get the gist of what was there. The section was dominated by the lurid invective of the most inflammatory right-wing authors. Many seemed calculated to appeal to anger, fear and outright hatred. Ann Coulter appeared to see the work of Satan behind liberalism is such titles as *Demonic: How the Liberal Mob is Endangering America*, *Godless: The Church of Liberalism* and *Treason: Liberal Lies about Liberal Treachery*. David Limbaugh adopted a similar line with *Persecution: How Liberals Are Waging*

War against Christianity. Sean Hannity equated liberalism with totalitarian enemies in *Let Freedom Ring: Winning the War of Liberty over Liberalism* and *Deliver Us From Evil: Defeating Terrorism, Despotism and Liberalism.* Glenn Beck's contributions to understanding liberals included the titles *Arguing with Idiots* and *Cowards.* Laura Ingraham charged active disloyalty in *Shut Up and Sing: How Elites from Hollywood, Politics and the Media are Subverting America.* Dinesh d'Souza hinted at the hand of a lunatic on the nuclear trigger with *The Roots of Obama's Rage.* Michelle Malkin generalized that characterization to liberals in general with *Unhinged: Liberals Gone Wild,* and evoked images of an organized crime syndicate with *Culture of Corruption: Obama and His Team of Tax Cheats, Crooks and Cronies.* I saw little balance on the other side. The preponderance of titles seemed to be about a dozen to one in favor of the most extreme conservative ravings, offset occasionally by an Al Franken book here, a Thomas Friedman title there, and an Al Gore title or two. I went up to the counter and asked the clerk, a black woman, why there was such a one-sided ratio of books against President Obama and the liberal viewpoint. "I guess they figure that's what most people around here want to read," she surmised. That may be so. But it's hard to fathom why. California voted overwhelmingly for Obama in a 21 percent blowout. He won San Diego by five percent. The area of which Rancho Bernardo is a part, the 52nd Congressional District, elected Democrat Scott Peters to be its representative in Washington.

No, it seemed to me something very different was afoot here. There is quite obviously a widespread and concerted effort among a strong coterie in the print media to vilify liberalism, not only to extol the conservative world view but much more to paint a caricature of the liberal perspective that is so vile people won't know what liberalism really is. They instead will be trained to immediately associate it with all manner of threat, evil and depravity. The idea is to engender reflexive hate. The very titles and the lurid promotional jackets on these books show a clear focus on whipping up emotions such as fear and outrage rather than appealing to fact and thought. I feel these efforts, together with those of the conservative broadcast media, are having an effect. There are quite a few liberals these days skittish about referring to themselves as such. Rather than echoing the strong liberal affirmations of leaders like Franklin Roosevelt or John Kennedy, they are careful to call themselves "progressives" or even "moderates."

Fortunately, most Americans remain actual liberals or are open to the liberal viewpoint on a host of issues. National surveys show strong majorities of Americans favor Social Security and Medicare and higher taxes on the wealthy. They want increased funding for public education, infrastructure, green energy and jobs. They are for immigration reform, clean air and water, marriage equality and civil rights. They want to see stronger gun controls and foreign policies that promote peace, not war. These are all liberal positions. What is more, President Barack Obama was elected and re-elected by solid margins in both 2008 and 2012.Democrats have registered strong showings in Senate races, gaining the majority in 2006, extending it in 2008, holding it in 2010 and practically running the table in 2012 when they won 25 seats to the Republicans' 8. Even in the House of Representatives where Republicans held their majority in 2012, Democratic candidates actually won one and a half million more votes than did Republicans and fell short of winning a majority of seats only because of the way the district lines are drawn. Republicans made congressional gains in 2014, but even then, initiatives to raise the minimum wage passed in the conservative states of Alaska, Arkansas, South Dakota and Nebraska, and voters on election night cast nearly three million more votes for Democratic Senate candidates than Republican ones. These all show that liberal views remain extremely popular.

But I fear it won't stay that way if people see, hear and read only one side. The vast array of conservative think tanks, authors, radio personalities and television programming churns out immense quantities of invective against liberalism. Faced with a constant inundation from one side without a response, some will begin to fall away. Many who are curious or sympathetic to liberal views might be dissuaded from investigating them. That is, of course, precisely what the long-term conservative vilification of liberalism seeks to accomplish. That's why I have come to feel so strongly there is a need for more sources that present the true liberal outlook to the public, including the motivations that underlie it, what liberals really believe on the issues and why, and the actual records the liberal and conservative philosophies of governance have produced over the years.

The American people deserve to see that liberal values are American values, and to appreciate that much of what has made America free and prosperous is a result of great liberal leaders and great liberal ideas.

In writing this book, I hope moderates will see the wisdom, sense and success of liberal positions, and how they have worked to make America a better, freer and more prosperous nation. Many must suspect the heated conservative invective on the topic, but may not know where to turn to find the truth. This book is meant to be a good place for that. I hope thoughtful conservatives will become more open to the truth about what liberalism actually is and stands for and about its many achievements. I hope that leads to more genuine and respectful dialog and fosters a better chance to get things done together in the common interest.

But most of all I am writing this book for liberals. I believe a lot of liberals are starving for some affirmation of their views and some explanations they can use to defend and promote the principled positions they hold dear. I hope liberals will enjoy seeing some explanations of why we see things the way we do. I will provide these, along with examples of successful liberal approaches and initiatives that have helped people's lives and advanced the peace, freedom and prosperity of America and its people. I believe many will be pleased to have some justifications, arguments and support for their positions readily at hand they can share with friends, the curious, and with those who hold other views.

Most of all, I'd like them to be able to look in the mirror or into the eyes of a conservative friend and say, "I'm proud to be a liberal!"

My Personal Journey to Liberalism

I was not brought up to be a liberal; I am a liberal by inclination and choice. Both my parents were Republicans born in the 1920's who lived through the Great Depression and World War II and moved to California in the great migration west after the war. I was born in Los Angeles but we moved out of the city to the conservative bastion of Orange County when I was just a toddler. It was in this area, resplendent in mile after mile of its namesake citrus groves rapidly being subdivided into suburbia that my first political inklings were aroused in the 1960s.

My father was an executive for a manufacturing company. A great people person, Dad knew the name of every worker on the factory floor and most of their spouses and children, too. He would gladly help any friend or relative. The company, Sealright, made packaging such as plastic cottage cheese and potato salad containers and those glossy paper ice cream cartons. The work force was not unionized and the company wanted to keep it that way. To that end, they gave the workers the same pay and benefits as unionized labor. That could be sold to the employees as a win, since they could make as much as organized workers and get paid vacations and a pension plan without having to pay union dues. For its part, the company avoided the bother of negotiations and the possibility of strikes. Looking back, it's easy to see this as a strong example of what the union movement accomplished for America's working people, not only for union members but also for millions more who were unorganized. Of course, what I got out of it as a kid from my father's influence was that unions are undesirable.

Dad wasn't overtly political but it was clear he was a pro-business kind of conservative. Though he was the son of poor immigrants and his father had his back broken in a mine cave-in, Dad was not sympathetic to unions and believed in an un-intrusive government that pretty much let business do as it pleased. He figured if he could get a college degree then so could others. He felt if the country was at war in Vietnam then the right and patriotic thing to do was to be for the war. He wasn't a big fan of people like Martin Luther King and Cesar Chavez. They stirred things up, and, he felt, therefore, interfered with production. He liked it if everything stayed calm and things ran according to business as usual.

My mother was the overtly political one. She was a big fan of Orange County's most prominent native son, Richard Nixon. He had made his name as a crusading Republican anti-Communist and rode that to congress, the U.S. Senate and the vice presidency under Dwight Eisenhower, all by the time he was forty. Nixon had then lost the 1960 presidential election, a contest of which I was only partially aware at the age of six, by an eyelash to charismatic Massachusetts Senator John F. Kennedy.

My clearest early political memory is of her taking me to the Fullerton train station to see Nixon make a "whistle stop" campaign speech from the back of a train. He was running for governor of California in 1962 to set himself up for a second campaign against Kennedy in 1964.Mother had made a sign that read, "Let's Send Our Pat to Sacramento!" We held that sign up at the rally and it got us on the national TV news. The wit of the sign was that Nixon's wife was named Pat, and he was running against the incumbent liberal Democratic Governor Edmund G. "Pat" Brown, (father of future governor Edmund G. "Jerry" Brown, Jr. elected in 1974, 1978, 2010 and 2014). Nixon surprisingly lost that race, and most felt the defeat had ended his political career. How could he ever think of winning the presidency if he couldn't even get elected governor of his own home state? His frustration boiled over after the results became clear, and Nixon displayed the sense of persecution and pique at the hands of "enemies" that would later lead to his undoing when he lashed out at the press, snarling at them, "You won't have Dick Nixon to kick around anymore!"

Mother's conservatism was based on a little person's sense of not wanting anybody else to get what she didn't get. Her dad had a good job with the railroad but died young. Her mother, my Grammy Moore, was left single with six kids to try to make it through the Depression. She took in sewing and did domestic work. The kids did odd jobs as they could. Times were tough in a way most people today can hardly fathom, and three of mom's five siblings died in childhood. Mother was extremely intelligent, and tough to beat at Scrabble or bridge. She was also a good enough singer to have gotten an audition with the Tommy Dorsey Big Band. She did well in high school and had a remarkable goal for a young woman at the time: to be a doctor. Not a nurse, as would be expected of a woman, a doctor! She took a full schedule at Marshall College, now Marshall University, but also had to work full time to support herself. She had to drop out after one year, unable to get by on three to four hours of sleep a night while working forty hours a week and trying to keep up with a pre-med schedule of classes. With the buildup for World War II now fully underway, she took a job in industry and made pretty good money for the time.

Though she was economically conservative in an anti-welfare kind of way, Mother was ahead of her time as a civil libertarian. She spoke to me about the discrimination suffered by black artists such as the singer Marian Anderson, and expressed her sense of injustice about Japanese-Americans being locked up in internment camps during the war. I remember one incident that showed her basic sense of fairness. As a child, I saw a television news item about an earthquake in the Soviet Union that had killed people and destroyed property. Reflecting the antipathy to Communist Russia that was inculcated so deeply into society during those Cold War days, and my joy as a kid that the "enemy" had been smitten, I exclaimed, "Oh good!" Mother was quick to slap that down.

"Don't you ever be happy when people suffer! Those poor people are not to blame for what their government does."

When I turned 18 in 1972 my mother and I went down to Republican Headquarters in Whittier, the town where Nixon went to college, where I dutifully registered to vote for the first time. I registered as a Republican, of course. I did some phone banking there for Nixon's re-election campaign. I was mostly assigned to call Democrats to find out which ones were for Nixon and to encourage them to vote. There were a lot of them that year. Nixon was way ahead in the polls and on his way to winning in a landslide. I particularly remember calling one fellow with the last name of McGovern, the same as the 1972 Democratic candidate! We both had a good laugh when I asked, "Mr. McGovern, can the President count on your vote this year?" That was one Democratic vote Nixon did not get.

So my basic political outlook, largely inherited from my parents, was that of a loyal Republican and basic conservative. My stance was based on a few grounding principles. Republicans were good and Democrats were bad. Unions caused trouble and were undesirable. Wars we were in were good and loyal people ought to support them. Government ought to try to leave business alone. Government should not be giving much away to people. People deserved to have equal rights, though maybe they shouldn't be too aggressive about asking for them.

Things began to change rather dramatically for me when I went away to college that fall. There were a number of factors involved. National and world events, work, the college environment and my friends all had important impacts on my perspectives on things. The biggest change in national events was the growing scandal enveloping President Richard Nixon and his Administration. The Watergate revelations utterly discredited Nixon. The release of the White House tapes revealed him as racist, crude and vindictive. He and his aides were hip-deep in corruption of all sorts, including bribery, influence peddling and the use of federal agencies to punish and harass political foes, all on Nixon's direct orders.

Nixon had waged an illegal war in Laos and Cambodia, illegal because congress had specifically banned it. The president himself was caught on tape plotting and conspiring to obstruct justice to keep witnesses quiet and the truth from getting out about the Watergate break-in. The impact of the complete and deserved disgrace of a leader who had been held up to me as a great exemplar of public and political virtue was profound.

The ever more obvious foolishness of the Vietnam War was another blow to the old world view. There was no sense in being supportively loyal to an unnecessary and unwinnable war, an intervention into a civil war in a country that presented no threat to the United States, a country in which we had no vital interests at stake. 58,282 Americans died in that conflict, including Philip Day, a kid a little older than I who lived next door to me in high school. I have read his name on the Vietnam Memorial Wall in Washington, D.C. Over a million Vietnamese died in the war too, a number vastly inflated by the U.S. intervention. Our involvement did not change the outcome; it only prolonged the war so that many additional hundreds of thousands of lives were lost. I came to feel that a thinking person need not blindly support wasteful and deadly nonsense to be considered a loyal American. Quite the contrary, a thoughtful and informed patriot should want to spare his country such carnage except for reasons of the utmost necessity.

The college environment itself was enlightening for me. I enrolled in Claremont McKenna College in the fall of 1972. I expected that learned professors would be mostly in agreement about things since they were so smart and informed. Was that ever naïve! Even though CMC has a reputation for conservatism, various professors had views all across the spectrum. That was very good for me to see, for it began to dawn on me that the purpose of education was not simply to fill my head with facts, or even to enable me to find the facts. Both of those were important, but they were not the most important thing. Much more important was to give me the knowledge base and the critical thinking skills to evaluate those facts in context. The purpose of education was not to hand me the facts and my views. It was to teach me to use facts and reason to come to *my own* conclusions and formulate *my own* views. I have never forgotten that lesson with respect to the students in the classes I have taught over the past thirty-two years. It is also the approach that led me to choose a liberal world view.

The influence of friends was also important to the course of my turn to liberalism. At a school where most of the student body lived on campus it was easy to get to know people well and develop real friendships. I bonded with a group of friends who were interested in humanitarian issues. These were young people who wanted to make a positive difference in the world. They were smart, ethical—and Christian. I had some church experience as a child but our family hadn't attended in some years. I did believe in God and thought the basic morality Jesus taught was meant to be taken seriously. And of course, that morality was about love, generosity to the poor and needy, and peace. The more I thought about it the more these values seemed to be at odds with much of the conservative political philosophy I had learned at home. Keep in mind this was before the emergence of the Christian right and Fundamentalist groups like the Moral Majority coming to the fore preaching a fusion of Protestant Christian doctrine and conservative political dogma. What Jesus said about giving to all in need appeared to be at direct odds with a view that held the poor and needy in contempt and was directed toward making sure that none of mine went to them. His pacifism also stood in stark opposition to an outlook that seemed largely to glorify militarism and a "my country right or wrong" mindset.

Coupled with Nixon's disgrace, the lessons of Vietnam turned me against much of my conservative and Republican upbringing. My understanding of Christian morality helped accentuate the change. Finally, my expanding education in history and constitutional law showed that liberal economics had ended the Great Depression and produced tremendous economic prosperity, and that liberal constitutional principles were the reason for the recent triumph of civil and individual rights across the country. By 1974 I had become a confirmed liberal. I re-registered as a Democrat and began proselytizing other students and signing them up as Democrats too. For a Political Science class project I did issues research for Jim Lloyd, a successful Democratic Congressional Candidate. I was glad to vote for Jerry Brown for governor of California.

But that wasn't the end of the story. There were a few more twists and turns still to come. I supported Jimmy Carter in 1976 and remained an enthusiastic liberal into his presidency. He did have some remarkable achievements, including brokering an Egyptian-Israeli peace that has held to this day and beginning on a strategy for energy independence that might have made a huge difference had we stuck with it. But the late 1970s had become a time of economic "malaise." Inflation, high earlier, had exploded into double-digit price increases. It is easier now to see how the economic shocks of the 70's were caused by the 1973 Arab oil embargo which quadrupled the price of oil and the 1979 Iranian oil embargo which doubled it again. Carter's mandatory conservation and push for alternatives is smart in hindsight, as emblemized by his installation of solar panels on the White House roof.

But huge price rises in the nation's basic transportation resource meant suddenly everything had to cost more. Whether you drove or rode the bus or a train, getting to work cost more. Everything that had to be shipped, trucked or flown cost more. Plastics cost more. Fertilizer cost more, which meant food cost more. The economy was bad, Carter was president, and along came Ronald Reagan with a plan to make everything better. While Carter talked about national despair and loss of confidence Reagan exuded an air of sunny optimism and steely resolve. His economic plan, dubbed "supply side" by its supporters, would cut taxes and slash spending, except for the military. The result was a promised economic Renaissance. The idea was supposedly validated by economics professor Arthur Laffer, whose famous "Laffer Curve" said it would grow the economy, balance the budget and help everyone to greater prosperity.

The tide turned Reagan's way, and I was carried right along with it. I voted for Reagan in 1980 and worked the phones for his re-election in '84. His program was like having your cake and eating it too. You could have lower taxes, a good economy and balanced budget and better services. Even so, the reckless Cold War talk was worrisome. So was the anti-environmentalism. The coded "blame the minorities" rhetoric was bothersome too, and some of the deregulation moves seemed iffy, but the former Hollywood actor president sold it all so well. And hey, if prosperity for all could be achieved, it might all be worth it. In spite of mounting evidence, I kept hoping. I cast my last ballot for a Republican presidential candidate for Reagan's vice president, George H. W. Bush, in 1988.

Bush won, but the results that had dogged the Reagan years continued and got worse. By then the verdict was unmistakably clear. The "supply side" theory hadn't worked. The idea of holding humane values in abeyance for economic progress didn't work. The outcome had been bad values *and* a bad economy too, an economy that inflated the deficit, hurt the poor, reduced important services, hollowed out the middle class and helped only the rich. When recession returned and Bush followed the usual Republican mantra that nothing needed to or could be done, my flirtation with conservatism was gone for good.

Nothing I have seen since has changed my view. The Clinton years were a triumphant time of rising employment, wages and freedom that benefitted folks at all levels. We even saw the first budget surpluses in decades. A return to the Reagan style of tax-cutting, deregulatory conservatism and loudmouthed militarism produced not only financial and economic calamity but also needless foreign war under George W. Bush. As I write, much of this damage has been undone by Barack Obama despite unending obstruction by congressional Republicans at every turn. In addition, millions of American lives are being enhanced as they gain access to health care, consumer protection and equal rights that conservatives had spent decades fighting to deny them.

I have often heard the adage that the older people get the more conservative they become. I find that far from the truth in my case, for as I get older I am getting more liberal, not more conservative. That's not only due to liberalism's affirmative democratic and egalitarian values and its acceptance of science, reason and fact as the bases for making decisions. It's also because what I have learned from studying history is that the liberal approach works. It's not only a theoretical ideal; the record shows its practicality. Liberal ideas have been the ones that have made society more just, more prosperous and better for people to live in. In the following chapters we'll find out why and how that is.

CHAPTER 2:
PERSONAL INVENTORY
TEST YOURSELF; ARE YOU A LIBERAL?

Defense/International/Peace

1. World affairs work best for the United States when most countries.

    A) appreciate our friendship B) fear our power C) leave us alone

2. When dealing with stubborn adversaries in the world, the best thing to do first is

    A) try diplomacy B) threaten military intervention C) ignore them

3. Should the United States belong to the United Nations?

    A) Yes B) No

4. Should the U.S. help to fight disease in Third World countries?

    A) Yes, when it can be of help B) Yes, if it earns some benefit for the United States C) No, it should not.

5. Was the war in Iraq worth fighting?

    A) Yes B) No

6. Is it possible to be supportive of the troops in wartime and be opposed to the war itself?   A) Yes B) No

7. Should our intelligence services torture captives to try to get information from them?   A) Yes B) No

8. Should the U.S. support tyrannical governments if they support U.S. policy?   A) Yes B) No

9. Should law enforcement or intelligence agencies be able to hold American citizens without charges or trial for long periods of time if they are suspected of being terrorists?   A) Yes B) No

Political Issues

10. It should be made as easy as possible for citizens to register and to vote.

A) Agree B) Disagree

11. The influence of big money in the political system should be reduced.   A) Agree B) Disagree

12. The President should be elected by popular vote rather than the Electoral College.   A) Agree B) Disagree

13. Illegal immigration should be harshly punished.
    A) Agree B) Disagree

14. Is it more important to follow traditional perspectives or to keep one's mind open to new data and experiences?
    A) Tradition B) Open Mind

Social Issues

15. Public schools should be able to lead children in Christian prayers during class and at assemblies.   A) Agree B) Disagree

16. Public school health classes should teach age-appropriate students about pregnancy prevention and protection against sexually transmitted diseases.   A) Yes B) No

17. When should abortion be legal?
    A) In most cases B) Rarely or never

18. Should tax money go to religious schools?
    A) Yes B) No

19. Should the United States be an officially Christian country?
    A) Yes B) No

20. Women should get equal pay for equal work.
    A) Agree B) Disagree

21. Women should be able to become religious ministers.
    A) Agree B) Disagree

22. Gays and lesbians should be able to serve openly in the military.   A) Agree B) Disagree

23. Same-sex couples should be able to get married.
    A) Agree B) Disagree

24. Drug addicts should be treated more like sick people than like criminals.   A) Agree B) Disagree

25. A private business on its own property should be able to discriminate against people on account of race, religion, gender or sexual orientation.   A) Agree B) Disagree

26. For the most part, does immigration enrich the American culture and economy or does it threaten American society?
    A) Enriches B) Threatens

27. Is it OK for health insurance plans to pay for women's contraception?
    A) Yes B) No

28. Is racial injustice still a problem in America?
    A) Yes B) No

Economic

29. Should Social Security be preserved for the good of senior citizens or cut to save money?   A) Preserved B) Cut

30. The minimum wage should be set at a level that a person can live decently on.   A) Agree B) Disagree

31. Worker's safety should be protected by law
    A) Agree B) Disagree

32. Do you support the idea of government programs to discourage cigarette smoking?   A) Yes B) No

33. Access to good health care should be a human right.
    A) Agree B) Disagree

34. Wealthy people who earn their money primarily from dividends and the stock market should pay a lower tax rate than working people who earn their money primarily from wages.
    A) Agree B) Disagree

35. Wealthy people should pay a higher percentage in taxes than poorer Americans.   A) Agree B) Disagree

36. Should Medicare be preserved for the good of senior citizens or cut to save money?   A) Preserved B) Cut

37. Is it more important to have full employment or balance the budget?   A) Full employment B) Balance the budget

38. Is it more important to preserve infrastructure and vital services or keep taxes low?

A) Preserve infrastructure and services B) Keep taxes low

39. In 1975 the average CEO of a Fortune 500 company made 42 times the wage of the average employee in the company. In 2011 the average CEO made 400 times as much. Does this change seem fair to you?   A) Fair B) Unfair

40. In 1975 27% of the work force was unionized. In 2011 that figure had fallen to 11%. Do you see a connection between reduced union membership and the pay figures in Question 39?

A) Yes B) No

41. Can effective government action improve the economy?

A) Yes B) No

Environmental

42. Global warming is real and largely caused by human activities.

A) Agree B) Disagree

43. Some wild areas are so important they should be preserved in their natural state.

A) Agree B) Disagree

44. Do you support programs that promote clean air and water?

A) Yes B) No

45. Renewable sources such as wind, solar and geothermal should provide a greater share of our energy needs.

A) Agree B) Disagree

46. It is important to protect endangered species of plant and animal life

A) Agree B) Disagree

47. Humans have sovereign dominion over the earth and can do whatever they want with it.

A) Agree B) Disagree

48. Humans are part of the web of life and are dependent on natural ecosystems for their own well-being.

A) Agree B) Disagree

49. Economic growth should be promoted with only minimal regard to its environmental effects.

A) Agree B) Disagree

50. Are you vegetarian or vegan because of your compassion for animals or concern for agricultural sustainability?
    A) Yes B) No

Scoring the Personal Inventory
Count the number of times you answered liberal or conservative.

Liberal answers:

1 A	11 A	21 A	31 A	41 A
2 A	12 A	22 A	32 A	42 A
3 A	13 B	23 A	33 A	43 A
4 A	14 B	24 A	34 B	44 A
5 B	15 B	25 B	35 A	45 A
6 A	16 A	26 A	36 A	46 A
7 B	17 A	27 A	37 A	47 B
8 B	18 B	28 A	38 A	48 A
9 B	19 B	29 A	39 B	49 B
10 A	20 A	30 A	40 A	50 A

Conservative answers:

1 B or C	11 B	21 B	31 B	41 B
2 B or C	12 B	22 B	32 B	42 B
3 B	13 A	23 B	33 B	43 B
4 B or C	14 A	24 B	34 A	44 B
5 A	15 A	25 A	35 B	45 B
6 B	16 B	26 B	36 B	46 B
7 A	17 B	27 B	37 B	47 A
8 A	18 A	28 B	38 B	48 B
9 A	19 A	29 B	39 A	49 A
10 B	20 B	30 B	40 B	50 B

Political Tendencies Based on Respondent Answers

Number of Liberal Answers	Tendency	Number of Conservative Answers

36-50	Strongly Liberal	0-14
29-35	Moderately Liberal	15-21
22-28	Mixed or Middle of the Road	22-28
15-21	Moderately Conservative	29-35
0-14	Strongly Conservative	36-50

Types of Liberals and Conservatives

Some people are liberal or conservative across the board on every issue. Others have liberal views on some issues and conservative views on others.

Types of Liberals

If you chose the liberal answer most of the time, or quite a bit of the time in one or more of the inventory sections, use the guide below to find out what aspects of liberalism most strongly appeal to you.

Peace Liberals: 1 A, 2 A, 3 A, 4 A, 5 B, 6 A, 7 B, 8 B, 9 B.

If you answered 5 or more of these 9 questions as listed above, then you are a particular variety of liberal known as a "peace liberal." Go to Chapter 11 to learn more about liberal attitudes on peace.

Human Rights or Social Liberals: 4 A, 7 B, 8 B, 9 B, 13 B, 14 B, 15 B, 16 A, 17 A, 18 B, 19 B, 20 A, 21 A, 22 A, 23 A, 24 A, 25 B, 26 A, 27 A, 28 A, 32 A, 33 A

If you answered 12 or more of these 22 questions as listed above, then you are identified as a "human rights liberal" or "social liberal." Go to Chapter 6 to learn more about liberal perspectives on human rights and Chapter 15 to learn more about social liberalism.

Economic/Political Liberals: 10 A, 11 A, 12 A, 13 B, 14 B, 20 A, 29 A, 30 A, 31 A, 32 A, 33 A, 34 B, 35 A, 36 A, 37 A, 38 A, 39 B, 40 A, 41 A, 49 B

If you answered 11 or more of these 20 questions as listed above, then you are a kind of liberal known as an "economic liberal" or "political liberal." See Chapter 7 to learn more about economic liberals and Chapter 14 to learn more about political liberals.

Environmental Liberals: 42 A, 43 A, 44 A, 45 A, 46 A, 47 B, 48 A, 49 B, 50 A

If you answered 5 or more of these 9 questions as listed above, then you are an environmental liberal. See Chapter 10 to learn more about liberal environmentalism.

Types of Conservatives

If you chose the conservative answer quite a bit of the time, use the guide below to tell what aspects of conservatism most strongly appeal to you.

Social Conservatives: 10 B, 12 B, 13 A, 14 A, 15 A, 16 B, 17 B, 18 A, 19 A, 20 B, 21 B, 22 B, 23 B, 24 B, 25 A, 26 B, 27 B, 28 B, 32 B, 33 B, 47 A.

If you answered 11 or more of these 21 questions as listed above, then you are a particular variety of conservative known as a "social conservative." Go to Chapter 17 to learn more about social conservatives.

Economic/Political Conservatives: 1 C, 2 C, 3 B, 4 B or C, 10 B, 11 B, 12 B, 20 B, 25 A, 29 B, 30 B, 31 B, 32 B, 33 B, 34 A, 35 B, 36 B, 37 B, 38 B, 39 A, 40 B, 41 B, 49 A

If you answered 12 or more of this group of 23 questions as listed above, then you are a particular variety of conservative known as an "economic/political conservative" or a "movement conservative." Go to Chapter 17 to learn more about economic/movement conservatives.

Defense Conservatives: 1 B, 2 B, 4 B, 5A, 6 B, 7A, 8A, 9A, 13 A, 22 B, 47 A.

If you answered 6 or more of this group of the 11 questions as listed above, then you are a particular variety of conservative known as a "defense conservative." Go to Chapter 17 to learn more about defense conservatives.

CHAPTER 3:

What Liberals Believe

"Some people see things as they are and ask why; I see things that never were and ask why not?"

Robert F. Kennedy

Here is my list of the principles we liberals believe in:

Ethics as the bedrock of our worldview, founded on truth, honesty and love for one another.

Peace with our neighbors and among all nations, beginning with peace within ourselves.

Equality of all people at all times.

Freedom to be, love, do, say and believe as we will, and from preventable wrong and harm.

Community of others whose well-being we foster, particularly those in greatest need.

Opportunity to pursue our dreams.

Meeting Human Needs with compassion, ingenuity and resolve.

Democracy as the foundation of any just political system.

Empathy for our fellows as the wellspring of the causes we champion.

Progress or faith in the improvement of the human condition if we work for it in good will.

Science as a means to discover and employ fact and reason to better our world.

Justice under the law and as the framework for fairness in society.

Security of our persons, rights and dignity, individually and as a nation.

Practicality in the ways we pursue our goals and implement our policies.

Diversity of people celebrated within the **Unity** of the human family.

Civil Rights enshrined and protected.

Service as the means to realize these principles in our society and world.

Love as the source of all the good we do and are.

Being liberal is fun. It's fun to be right on the questions of the day; it's fun to be on the right side of history and it's fun to have a clear moral conscience about human issues. A liberal is motivated out of a sense of love and community spirit, beginning with a belief in the equality and dignity of every human being. That is why liberals have always been the strongest defenders of civil and political rights. A liberal is concerned first with human needs—what do people need to make their lives freer, healthier and more prosperous—and then looks for opportunities to help secure them.

The Merriam-Webster Dictionary defines liberalism as: "a political philosophy based on belief in progress, the essential goodness of the human race, and the autonomy of the individual and standing for the protection of political and civil liberties; specifically: such a philosophy that considers government as a crucial instrument for amelioration of social inequities (as those involving race, gender, or class)."

That means a liberal is an idealist, someone who envisions a better world and wants to help bring it about. Because a liberal is an idealist who wants to make things better in the world, liberals tend to embrace beneficial change, that is, change for the good. Another term for beneficial change is progress and so liberals are often referred to as progressives. At one time there was even a political party in America called the Progressive Party that embodied these ideals.

The word "liberal" itself comes from the Latin word *libertas*, the root of our English word liberty, or freedom. Thus liberals stand for the inherent and universal freedom of individuals to live their lives as they see fit, consistent with the principle that one person's rights extend to the point where they start to infringe on the rights of others. That is because individuals are part of a community, with the natural and, in America, the constitutional right and responsibility to consider and foster the good of the community through the democratic process. Even when it wasn't popular, liberals are and have always been ardent supporters of vibrant, participatory democracy.

As a liberal I am a dreamer. I dream of full employment, of clean water and decent housing, of health care for all, of freedom for the oppressed and equality and respect for the marginalized. Cynics belittle such dreams. "Pie in the sky," they exclaim. Yet how do things ever get better without such dreams? The answer, of course, is that they don't. Margaret Mead once wrote, "Never doubt that a small, committed group of people can change the world. Indeed, it's the only thing that ever has."

Being a dreamer does not equate to being impractical. A good liberal starts with a dream, a compassionate vision for a better future, and then acts to bring it to reality. The Reverend Dr. Martin Luther King stands as a good example. He had a dream of the end of racial segregation, of an American society that lived up to its professed values of liberty and equality. He followed a concerted plan to bring this dream about. It included study and prayer, organizing, training and mobilizing thousands of people. Legal cases were undertaken; politicians were courted; publicity was arranged. Strategies were developed and followed, and the general plan and approach--nonviolent civil disobedience in response to injustice, sometimes even violent injustice—had to be taught to participants. People had to be willing to get arrested and go to jail, to be bitten by dogs, be clubbed, and even to die. The stakes were high but the cause was righteous and inspiring.

This was no starry-eyed, naïve quest. It was hard headed and practical, relying on the innate goodness of most Americans to see the disconnect between the glorious words of the Declaration of Independence, "We hold these truths to be self-evident, that all men are created equal..." and the hypocritical reality of Jim Crow segregation laws. The marchers were ready to be martyrs to prick the conscience of what Dr. King felt to be an apathetic but basically good middle America. The plan counted on the premise that when average people saw raw hate and injustice in front of them on their television sets on the evening news their hearts would be convicted and they would begin to actively support positive change. He was right. Look at a video of the 1963 March on Washington. You will see blacks and whites marching together. That is because Dr. King's message went beyond an appeal to black self-interest and instead appealed to the universal aspiration for an equality based on respect for human dignity itself. That is a core belief of the liberal world view. It started with a dream rooted in the oldest American liberal value--equality. That righteous dream inspired people to engage in a cause greater than themselves, and it called forth a host of ordinary Americans who rose to the status of heroes. Most that joined the movement were subjected to humiliation. Some lost their jobs. Some were arrested. Some were beaten. Some were killed. They were every bit as heroic in service to their nation as anyone who led a platoon; they fought for American freedom right here at home against long odds and in perilous conditions. And the movement succeeded. As Gandhi observed, "First they ignore you, then they laugh at you, then they fight you, then you win." Liberals have that kind of idealism and that kind of persistence.

Another important trait liberals share is empathy—the ability to see and feel the world from other people's perspectives. That is a big part of what Martin Luther King was counting on. I noticed some interesting reactions in mid-March 2013, when Ohio Republican Senator Rob Portman announced his support for marriage equality. The former George W. Bush Budget Director had been a co-sponsor of the 1996 Defense of Marriage Act that defined marriage as only between a man and a woman and prohibited any federal benefits to same-sex spouses. In 1999 he helped campaign for a Washington State law prohibiting gays from adopting children. In 2011 his speech at the University of Michigan graduation ceremony was protested by hundreds of students due to what they called his "openly hostile" record on LGBT rights. So it was quite a surprise when he told CNN Chief

Congressional Reporter Dana Bash that he had changed his position and now supports the right of same-sex couples to marry. The reason? Two years before, Portman's son Will came out to him as gay.

What's interesting to me in the reaction were those, usually supporters of marriage equality, who seemed to regard his new position as tainted because he had only changed his view after having been personally affected. At first I thought, why should that be a surprise, having observed over time that the great gay rights pioneer Harvey Milk was right; the path to equality would be opened most rapidly by virtue of as many LGBT folks coming out as possible. When people actually learn they have friends, relatives and co-workers whom they have known and liked for years, and who happen to be gay, it becomes very difficult to fear and ostracize them. In fact, it starts to become nonsensical. Some are even starting to call the process the "Portman Effect," though you might recall it may earlier have applied to the extremely conservative former Vice President Dick Cheney with regards to his lesbian daughter. And a CNN poll found a correlation between the percentage of people who know someone who is gay and the percentage which supports gay rights. As more people over time have reported knowing someone who is gay, the percentage in favor of gay rights has tracked that increase closely.

But with a little more thought, I became intrigued. What about all those who had moved much earlier on the issue without necessarily having known someone who was gay? I wonder if that might say something about differences between intrinsic liberals and conservatives. Most Americans who are not very young grew up in a society with intolerant attitudes toward LGBT people. Yet those who are generally liberal in their views--pro-immigrant, pro-environmental, pro-social programs, anti-corporate, anti-war, anti-gun--seem to have often been early in supporting the gay rights movement. Many conservatives remain opposed to allowing people of the same sex to marry, but those who know people in that situation seem to be more open to changing their minds.

Might the difference be empathy? When confronted directly with injustice affecting someone they know and love, conservatives show capacity to change. But absent that, they seem reflexively influenced by their background and society's traditional attitudes. When the injustice does not affect them personally, they are often immune to the appeal to change things. I wonder if part of the root of having a liberal spirit may consist in large part of having a greater capacity to empathize with those who suffer without having to personally share in the effect. It would appear to explain a lot in terms of policy positions liberals and conservatives tend to gravitate toward. For indeed, as you will see later, the appeal of modern conservatism is rooted in self-interest just as the appeal of modern liberalism springs from concern for human needs in the wider sense.

Thus, to be a liberal is to be always in search of improvement. A liberal is therefore not afraid of change, and indeed seeks and embraces change when it serves human needs in a positive way. "You must be the change you want to see in the world," is how Gandhi put it. That doesn't mean supporting mindless change just for the sake of novelty. If a long standing way of doing things is working well there may be no reason for wholesale alterations. But neither does it mean we cling to old ways if they are serving us poorly, simply to venerate tradition, or reject out of hand small improvements that can be made even in processes that are reasonably effective. A mindset that refuses to countenance positive change has been responsible for most of the repression throughout history and has no place in liberalism.

Instead, liberals welcome change that works to increase human happiness. That translates into a lot of facets of life. It can mean personal improvement, like learning a new craft or hobby, getting better skills for your job, eating healthier, learning new interpersonal skills for better relationships, mastering new computer skills or gaining expertise in managing your personal finances. It can relate to positive change in your community, be it a recycling center, a dog park, a better bus route, a traffic light at a dangerous intersection, volunteering at a homeless shelter, working in a neighborhood garden or helping start a youth activity to keep kids out of gangs.

The change we are talking about can also relate to national and even international issues. Liberals are concerned about things like clean water and air, humane working conditions, access to education and good medical care for everyone. We believe these matters, along with a decent wage, a dignified retirement, and the promotion of understanding and peace among people and nations are our business and responsibility. We also welcome change because we recognize it is an inevitable part of life. The only state without change is the grave. The only way I progress and improve personally is through change. I have to remember to adapt to difficult change, embrace positive change and initiate needed change.

Part of putting people first is being open to reality. A liberal is committed to seeing things as they are, not sugar-coated to confirm our preconceptions: It means that a true liberal deals in facts. This manifests itself in a willingness to do the homework or research to properly understand an issue in order to discuss, debate and act on it. It means liberals have a respect for science, and see it as a quest for understanding. A liberal is not afraid of what the findings of science might discover. Remember, we are out to improve human happiness, not validate particular conclusions. That means liberals can be flexible about the means to use, provided they are ethical and based on sound social or scientific research. That makes liberals highly pragmatic; we are practical about the best means of putting people first, whether the goal is to eradicate a disease, prevent unwanted pregnancy, increase employment, reduce crime or spread opportunity.

Further, to achieve such beneficial progress, liberals are not shy about enlisting community resources through the democratic process. Yes, it is great to have private charities and foundations to do good works, and liberals provide millions of volunteer hours and billions of dollars in contributions to worthy organizations. But there are issues that are so broad in scope and so important in their effects that only a public program committing community resources and backed by the force of law can accomplish them. Giving women the right to vote, putting America back to work during the Great Depression, ending dangerous industrial child labor and banning the unchecked dumping of sewage and toxic chemicals into the water supply are examples that come readily to mind. These are precisely the kinds of human needs that liberals believe a democratic government, accountable to its citizenry, exists to address.

So let's sum up the principles liberals believe in, and the issues stances those principles lead to:

Ethics as the bedrock of our worldview, founded on truth, honesty and love for one another.

It is curious-curious that physical courage should be so common in the world and moral courage so rare.

Mark Twain

Ethical considerations explain why liberals stand for openness and full disclosure, following the precept first enunciated by Supreme Court Justice Louis Brandeis that "sunlight is the best disinfectant." That's why liberals have always supported such precepts as open government policies, campaign disclosure laws, the Freedom of Information Act and Truth in Advertising legislation. Those who want to do and hide things in the dark usually have good reasons for their secrecy. Liberals reject the Machiavellian assertion that "the end justifies the means." Seeking to bring about a more righteous world, liberals recoil at the hypocritical idea that this can be founded upon evil methods. As Dr. Martin Luther King Jr. put it, "Evil cannot drive out evil. Only good can do that."

Peace with our neighbors and among all nations, beginning with peace within ourselves.

Peace is not a relationship of nations. It is a condition of mind brought about by a serenity of soul. Peace is not merely the absence of war. It is also a state of mind. Lasting peace can come only to peaceful people.

Jawaharlal Nehru

Who needs more strife and contention? The world groans under its continuing burden, and it issues primarily from people who are without peace within themselves. As Jimi Hendrix said, "When the power of love overcomes the love of power the world will know peace." Therefore liberals support all avenues-religious, spiritual, psychological, interpersonal-that help cultivate peace within the human heart and soul, believing that such is the precursor for its extension throughout society and then the world at large.

We further support all good faith efforts to bridge differences between factions, sects and nations to help settle disputes short of the initiation of violence and killing, seeing a resort to military means as truly a last resort. Though enmity, discord, violence and war continue to mar existence on earth, we do not succumb to despair and throw up our hands in resignation. We believe there is a greater purpose in life that requires our commitment and sacrifice, and stand in solidarity with Dr. King's visionary statement, "I refuse to accept the view that mankind is so tragically bound to the starless midnight of racism and war that the bright daybreak of peace and brotherhood can never become a reality. I believe that unarmed truth and unconditional love will have the final word." In the final analysis we realize there is no sensible alternative. As Dr. King put it, "We must learn to live together as brothers or perish together as fools."

Equality of all people at all times.

We hold these truths to be self-evident, that all men are created equal...

Thomas Jefferson, *Declaration of Independence*

The moral foundation of our civic creed is that one person is as good as another. Dedication to that basic principle is the political basis of our rights, to which liberal Americans have always been committed supporters. Yet we are also highly aware that this nation has not always lived up to its professed ideals. There has been legally-sanctioned inequality imposed on Americans of African, Irish, Chinese, Japanese, Mexican and Jewish ancestry, and informal inequality without the explicit force of law imposed on many more. Women and the LGBT community have also suffered under a long history of inequality. These are wrongs liberals are strongly intent on eliminating where they currently exist and preventing from recurring in the future.

But the liberal perspective goes beyond eliminating discriminatory laws. Declaring people legally equal and then neglecting them is no way to achieve actual equality. We support such measures as the enforcement provisions of the Voting Rights Act, which were enacted to keep an eye on states and counties with a history of denying voting rights to minorities and required them to secure federal approval for any changes to their voting procedures. We favor making the exercising of the voting franchise as easy as possible and oppose cynical measures now afoot that throw up difficulties and obstacles in an obvious effort to keep the poor from voting. In order to assure an equal education for children in poor neighborhoods, liberals favor programs helping to mitigate the conditions such children face which sociological data demonstrates prevent them from achieving equally with more affluent kids. That includes programs like Head Start, food assistance, SCHIP for health, additional classroom aides, afterschool programs and the like.

Freedom to be, love, do, say and believe as we will, and from preventable wrong and harm.

Four score and seven years ago our fathers brought forth on this continent a new nation, conceived in liberty...

Abraham Lincoln, *Gettysburg Address*

The very reason for the United States of America was the insistence of its colonial inhabitants that they would enjoy freedom at any and all costs. Our children pledge allegiance every day at school to a flag promising "freedom and justice for all." Our coins are inscribed with the word "LIBERTY." During the darkest days of the Second World War, when tyrannical dictators were on a march of conquest threatening to extinguish freedom throughout the world, President Franklin Roosevelt faced the challenge of leading America at that time of terrible trial, and wanted to crystallize the essence of the values people were being asked to sacrifice for. Liberals are still inspired by his great enunciation of what he called The Four Freedoms. These are freedom of speech, freedom of religion, freedom from want and freedom from fear. Notice that the first two are freedoms *to* and the last two are freedoms *from*. Liberals strongly believe that just as individuals should have the freedom to believe and act as they will, society has a responsibility to preserve its members from harm. And that doesn't just mean criminal and military harm, but also the ravages of disaster, disease, unemployment and a helping hand out of conditions such as poverty and illiteracy as well.

Community of others whose well-being we must consider in addition to our own.

No man is an island, entire of itself; every man is a piece of the continent, a part of the main... any man's death diminishes me, because I am involved in mankind, and therefore never send to know for whom the bells tolls; it tolls for thee...

John Donne

Liberals seek a society in which people live together as brothers and sisters. The "dog-eat-dog" vision of a properly functioning society is not for us. As Franklin Roosevelt put it, "We all do better when we all do better." That's why we want a clean environment, good schools and health care for everyone, living wage requirements and an ethos that fosters cooperation and consideration in an atmosphere of dignity. If it's how we would like things to be for ourselves and our own children, it's how we'd like it to be for others and their children, too. Cesar Chavez reminded us, "We cannot seek achievement for ourselves and forget about progress and prosperity for our community." The sense of community is encapsulated in the Golden Rule that we "Do unto others as we would have others do unto us." Hillary Clinton was right to quote the African proverb, "It takes a village to raise a child," for we are all involved in the community and are all examples for that child, one way or another. True liberals resolve to be good examples for the children and good neighbors to our fellows.

Opportunity to pursue our dreams.

To find out what one is fitted to do, and to secure an opportunity to do it, is the key to happiness

John Dewey

Opportunity is more than removing such things as the intentional roadblocks society used to put in the way of women and people of color and declaring everything even. Those steps, won by liberals against great opposition, were indeed essential, but they are not enough. As the great liberal educator John Dewey reminds us above, part of opportunity entails a process of discovery. Kids can't very well determine what they are "fitted to do" if they arrive at a substandard school cold, hungry or with a learning disability. Society has a responsibility to assist in that process by making sure that all schools are safe, well-staffed and well-quipped. It also needs to see to it that disadvantaged children have some warm clothing and some breakfast in them before they start and some learning assistance if they need it. A single mother may be impeded from preparing for a career because of child care issues, a young adult may not have the financial wherewithal to attend the institution she is qualified for; a veteran may need help with PTSD.

Liberals believe in removing as many of these kinds of restraints as possible, both because it is compassionate and because it will result in a society in which people are able to fulfill their potential and the nation as a whole therefore gets the best from its human capital.

Meeting Human Needs with compassion, ingenuity and resolve.
I believe that, as long as there is plenty, poverty is evil.
Robert F. Kennedy

I have always believed the reason we are on this earth is to do some good in it while we are here. A life well lived is a life that leaves the world a better place than the one it entered. In like fashion, the purpose of civilized society is to provide a better life for its members. If living as a lone wolf without regard to the needs of others was fulfilling and productive then human society would never have developed and people would subsist like wild animals under the terms of the law of the jungle. Liberals reject philosophies based on the glorification of selfishness, and affirm that the highest goal of political society is to meet human needs.

As President Franklin Roosevelt put it, "The test of our progress is not whether we add more to the abundance of those who have much; it is whether we provide enough for those who have little." We are not satisfied while one child endures hunger or one family is homeless. We are not content until everyone who wants a job has one and every student qualified for college has the wherewithal to attend. It is not good enough when one sick person has no means to see a doctor. If there is one imperative that defines liberalism it is the conviction that meeting human needs is our first policy priority. We see it as a calling driven by moral necessity. What are our priorities? Look where you see human misery and there you will find them.

Democracy as the foundation of any just political system.

For us democracy is a question of human dignity. And human dignity is political freedom.

Olof Palme

Liberals believe fervently in democracy. That's because we believe so strongly in equality, in the essential importance and dignity of each individual person. Liberals fought for freedom for America's slaves and, after emancipation, for their full legal equality and democratic political rights. The same cause was pursued with respect to women. Zeal for democracy plays an important part in the liberal commitment to public education, for an informed citizenry is the beating heart of any democratic society. As John F. Kennedy put it, "The ignorance of one voter in a democracy impairs the security of all."

That is also why liberals press for unfettered access to the voting franchise. Voting is integral to democracy, and is democracy's fundamental right, giving life to all the others. It is telling indeed that liberals support all the most open policies that encourage voting and making it easy and convenient, such as vote by mail, extended polling hours, early voting and the registration of teenagers before their eighteenth birthday to become effective once they achieve their majority, while conservatives oppose them.

A liberal commitment to democracy also means that, the will of the people ought to prevail in matters of public policy, under the auspices of the Constitution. The people and their representatives have a right to demand that community resources be used to better the quality of life and provide the securities enunciated in the Four Freedoms. We liberals share the conviction that acting together we can tackle our problems through the democratic process. As Hillary Clinton said, "The worst thing that can happen in a democracy - as well as in an individual's life - is to become cynical about the future and lose hope." In democracy there is always hope, for though special interest, money power and injustice may be strong, in the end they always give way when the people unite for democratic justice.

Empathy for our fellows as the wellspring of the causes we champion.

Our ambitions must be broad enough to include the aspirations and needs of others, for their sakes and for our own.

Cesar Chavez

Liberals do not suffer from an empathy deficit. We want for others and for society in general what we want for ourselves. When we see others in distress, sick, impoverished, denied, denigrated, forgotten or victimized we are motivated at a gut level because we feel what they are going through. It is our empathy that impels us to act in the service of our fellows.

All the great liberal leaders have had this quality in abundance. Bill Clinton used to say frequently at town hall forums, "I feel your pain." He was parodied for it by his political opponents yet was nonetheless elected twice because Americans sensed his empathy and knew it would direct his decisions in their behalf as president. In his Second Inaugural Address the liberal Republican Abraham Lincoln looked forward to a reunited nation "with malice toward none, with charity for all." He exuded empathy for the immense sacrifices made and called on his fellow citizens to join him, "to finish the work we are in, to bind up the nation's wounds, to care for him who shall have borne the battle and for his widow and his orphan..." The key word in this to me is *care*. When people care they can be trusted to do the right thing for their neighbor in need. This is the visceral motive that animates liberalism and gives it its effective force.

Our ideological adversaries like to mock the quality of empathy by calling us "bleeding heart" liberals. They hope their name-calling will make us sensitive to ridicule and cause us to retreat. But think about the alternative to empathetic caring for others. Are you more comfortable with heartless indifference to the hungry, the homeless, the mentally ill, the abused, the trafficked, the addicted, the bullied, the judged and the hated? I never apologize for the quality of empathy; it's what makes us fully human. It is our strongest asset and liberals carry it with pride.

Progress or faith in the improvement of the human condition if we work for it in good will.

You don't make progress by standing on the sidelines, whimpering and complaining. You make progress by implementing ideas.

Shirley Chisholm

Liberals believe in progress, and there is no question this belief in progress is a form of faith. It is closely associated with hope. In simplest terms, we want things to be better and are confident we can bring about the improvement we seek through effort. This positive imagination of what should be and can be is called *vision*, and liberals possess it in abundance. Indeed, everything that has changed for the better in America over the past two hundred fifty years is the result of it.

We are grateful for what is good and right that has been handed down to us. Yet temperamentally, liberals are acutely aware of what is not right and what is not adequate, and have a powerful desire to improve it. The great Thomas Edison understood this when he said, "Discontent is the first necessity of progress." Therefore as a liberal I give due credit to the accomplishments of the past but am clear-eyed about the needs of the future.

Racial and homophobic discrimination, dishonest advertising, rivers so polluted they caught on fire, senior citizen poverty, 45,000 unnecessary deaths a year due to lack of medical coverage and the fourteen-hour work day were all, at various times in our nation's past, considered conditions too ingrained to change. Yet all these ills have been dramatically improved due to liberal vision for a better future and popular progressive action to effect change.

Some folks completely misunderstand and fear the liberal mindset on progress. They opine that liberals point out flaws and try to change things because they are malcontents who "hate

America." Instead, a liberal is like the competitor who runs a 4:08 mile and wants to break four minutes. The hard work of training, practice, changing nutrition, sleep habits, motivation and discipline is not because the competitor hates running and wishes to destroy track and field. It's because of a love for these things and a burning desire to commit themselves to being the best they can be. That is the true picture of how liberals see progress.

Science as a means to discover and employ fact and reason to better our world.

The whole of science is nothing more than a refinement of everyday thinking.

Albert Einstein

So, armed with vision and intent on fostering peace, freedom and progress, liberals set out into the world. By what means are they to proceed? How are they to bring about general economic prosperity? Stop the melting of the Greenland and Antarctic ice caps and the inundation of a billion people's homes? Educate children better? Stop the spread of disease? Improve nutrition and knowledge of healthy eating? Match vocational training with the needs of the coming job market? Spread conflict resolution skills on the individual, family, community or societal levels? Science, that's how. Liberals love science.

Science is simply an organized way of finding answers to the questions we have. It's a *method* of systematizing thought that requires evidence and looks at results through observation, rigorous study of real-world examples or data generated from empirical experiments. It's a *process* that includes the publication of findings so that others can test to verify the results and offer their own explanations for what is discovered, submitting them to the court of informed opinion in order to reach consensus based on objective reality. It's applicable to hard science questions about things like climate change and medicine, but also to more psychological or sociologically-related fields like economics, crime prevention and mental health.

We remember that science is a tool. We already have a general or specific goal in mind, whether it is fewer unwanted teen pregnancies, less gang membership, cleaner air or greater employment. Then we turn to good research to inform how we advocate for what Shirley Chisolm referred to as "implementing ideas." That's because we want to do what works and what serves human needs best. We are open to methods, so long as they are ethical and humane. We look for the consensus of scientists in the field. That's because, as the eminent sociologist Robert K. Merton pointed out, "Most institutions demand unqualified faith; but the institution of science makes skepticism a virtue." We are appropriately skeptical, especially of scientists on the payroll of interests with financial incentives to push self-serving findings such as the tobacco-industry researchers who said smoking was unrelated to cancer or the oil and coal industry researchers who almost alone in their field deny human-generated atmospheric heating. Their contentions have a place, but in our view it lies far behind the credibility of the overwhelming consensus of those not financially compromised. As Upton Sinclair wrote, "It is difficult to get a man to understand something, when his salary depends on his not understanding it."

The alternatives to scientifically-derived approaches are often tradition, prejudice or guesswork. They are no match for good science based on data. The best characterization I've seen came from Carl Sagan, who said in 1987:

In science it often happens that scientists say, "You know that's a really good argument; my position is mistaken," and then they actually change their minds and you never hear that old view from them again. They really do it. It doesn't happen as often as it should, because scientists are human and change is sometimes painful. But it happens every day. I cannot recall the last time something like that happened in politics or religion.

Justice under the law and as the framework for fairness in society.

Rats and roaches live by competition under the laws of supply and demand; it is the privilege of human beings to live under the laws of justice and mercy.

Wendell Berry

Justice can mean the impartial administration of trials and the allotment of punishments commensurate with the infractions of those convicted. But justice in a larger sense means applying the principles of equity and righteousness to the human condition. It is especially to these ends that liberals are motivated to expand justice in society. When Martin Luther King envisioned a day when "justice will roll down like a mighty river" he was not referring to a time when lawbreakers would suffer the appropriate punishments for their offenses. He was envisioning a society in which everyone had a real chance, in which the most humble were not neglected, forgotten or held back.

Liberals work for justice in the sense of fairness. Merriam-Webster defines justice in one sense as "the quality of being just, impartial or fair." Justice is well served in the criminal justice system when people of different ethnicities and socioeconomic backgrounds receive the same sentences for the same offenses. It will be served even better when proven rehabilitative alternatives to incarceration are put into greater use. Liberals are highly concerned with economic justice. The fact that Fortune 500 CEO's used to make 42 times the pay rate of their average employee and now make nearly 400 times as much despite the fact that worker productivity has improved 80 percent since 1979 strikes us as unjust. It is unjust when 95% of the economic gains in the past six years have gone to the wealthiest 1%. Liberals are for changing that to an equitable ratio, through empowering workers by supporting union rights, through the tax structure, through regulation and mandate when necessary. The fact that the federal minimum wage is lower now in inflation-adjusted dollars than it was in 1968 is similarly unjust. Liberals have supported measures like the Lilly Ledbetter Fair Pay Act in their continuing drive to reach the day when pay justice will mean a woman doing the same job with the same performance evaluation as a man will make the same pay, not 77 percent.

But in the broadest sense, liberals are committed to furthering justice by righting the preventable wrongs of the world, particularly when society's efforts to right these wrongs are unequally applied. Merriam-Webster defines justice in this sense as "the principle or ideal of just dealing or right action, conformity to this principle or ideal; righteousness." It's wrong when a toxic waste dump is located too close to a poor neighborhood because the land there is cheaper and the residents are less likely to complain. It's unjust when the small, majority Latino towns in the San Joaquin Valley or the majority African-American towns in the Cotton Belt never seem to get adequate clean water systems, though nearby affluent suburban areas always do. Liberals care about this kind of justice too. We want to be on the side of righteousness. As Bobby Kennedy said:

"Few will have the greatness to bend history itself, but each of us can work to change a small portion of events. It is from numberless diverse acts of courage and belief that human history is shaped. Each time a man stands up for an ideal, or acts to improve the lot of others, or strikes out against injustice, he sends forth a tiny ripple of hope, and crossing each other from a million different centers of energy and daring those ripples build a current which can sweep down the mightiest walls of oppression and resistance."

Security of our persons, rights and dignity, individually and as a nation.

Human beings the world over need freedom and security that they may be able to realize their full potential.

Aung San Suu Kyi

Security is the reason for civilization itself. Society functions because people are interdependent, each playing a part by helping to furnish what others need, and enjoying peace of mind from the knowledge that when we live and work together help is always nearby. Think of all the human institutions that exist to protect our persons, rights and dignity. The family protects and nurtures its members, particularly children and the elderly. Marriage provides a couple with many forms of security, among them emotional, legal and financial. Police are there to protect citizens from internal threats and the military from external ones. The Constitution and courts provide a framework for protecting our rights. A myriad of agencies and industries work every day to protect people from the dangers of life in such realms as transportation safety, disease control, food inspection, pollution abatement, health care, firefighting and emergency services of all kinds. Banks, investment firms and insurers exist to help people with financial security, and government programs such as Pell Grants, Medicare, Medicaid, Affordable Health Care and Social Security are charged with doing the same in regards to education, health and retirement.

Liberals support the institutions and agencies that provide security to people in an uncertain world. We know there can never be complete security from the vicissitudes of life. Accidents happen. Disease strikes. Bad people do bad things. But that doesn't mean we throw up our hands and resign ourselves to misfortune. Instead, we initiate research and implement change to improve things. Safety standards for cars, the workplace and public accommodations have greatly reduced fatalities and injuries due to accident. Medical advances in diagnostics, drugs and treatments have extended the length and quality of life for millions. Scientific policing and technological aids such as DNA have improved law enforcement and innovative correctional programs have reduced criminal recidivism where they have been instituted. We stand firm in our determination to continue making improvements in people's lives along these lines.

A few words are in order about the foundations of economic security. Liberals support people's freedom to start their own businesses. Initiative and entrepreneurship have been the wellsprings of American economic strength. We admire and encourage these. And as we do so, we realize that an essential underpinning of America's great entrepreneurial tradition has always been the powerful work ethic of American labor. America's economic security depends not only on innovative and competent owners and administrators, but also on the remarkable productivity of the American worker. Liberals support not only the freedom of owners to build businesses but also the freedom of workers to organize collectively to bargain for their share of the fruits of the success to which they so greatly contribute, and to enjoy security from preventable health and safety conditions on the job. We do not lose sight of the fact that, as President Barack Obama said:

It was the labor movement that helped secure so much of what we take for granted today. The 40-hour work week, the minimum wage, family leave, health insurance, Social Security, Medicare, retirement plans. The cornerstones of the middle-class security all bear the union label.

We also do not shrink from the people's elected representatives taking a hand in helping that economic prosperity along. Especially in times of serious recession and even Depression, the record has shown that there are a number of proven ways to revive economic fortunes and put Americans back to work. We are mindful of Franklin D. Roosevelt's admonition, "True individual freedom cannot exist without economic security and independence. People who are hungry and out of a job are the stuff of which dictatorships are made."

Practicality in the ways we pursue our goals and implement our policies.

Be practical as well as generous in your ideals. Keep your eyes on the stars, but remember to keep your feet on the ground.

Theodore Roosevelt

The advice of the larger than life, turn of the twentieth century progressive liberal Republican president is as valid today as it was then. As liberals we are visionaries. We are full of ideas for social, economic and environmental improvement. Yet if we try to implement these ideas in unworkable, impractical ways we do great harm to the liberal cause. When that happens our ideological adversaries are quick to attack the intention itself as flawed. One example of this was the school busing controversy of the 1970s. Beginning in 1954 in the *Brown v. Topeka* case, the Courts had correctly ruled that segregation of the schools was unconstitutional. Faced with continued resistance to racial integration, decisions were handed down mandating that children be bused out of their neighborhoods and across towns and cities to achieve racial balance throughout a school district. The consequence was that parents were enraged about their kids having to go to schools miles away while other kids at the same school did not. There was furious resistance to the practice, even in liberal states like Massachusetts. In the process, the underlying principle, the overcoming of segregation in society at large, was forgotten and set back. In many areas today the schools are even more segregated than they were in the 1970s. Medicare and Social Security stand as fine examples of programs that help people with tremendous practical efficiency. According to the Congressional Budget Office and the Center for Medicare and Medicaid Services, the Medicare program operates with an overhead cost of only 2 percent. By contrast, even industry studies such as by the Council for Affordable Health Insurance put administrative costs for private insurers at nearly 17 percent. The Affordable Care Act (Obamacare) set a limit to rein that in by requiring that at least 85 percent of a company's revenue go to actually providing medical care for people. That still allows a private overhead cost of 15 percent. Social Security's record is even better than Medicare's. Its administrative expense has been less than one percent every year since 1989. These are helpful figures to have at your disposal when conservative ideologues make blanket statements claiming that government programs that help people need to be scrapped because they are intrinsically wasteful and inefficient. Compared to their private sector counterparts, they are models of streamlined practicality.

Whether it's retirement, weather forecasting, emergency services, food for the hungry or air traffic control, liberals strongly support the efficient, practical and scientific identification of needs and delivery of services. To do so is good stewardship of the tax payer's dollar. It means a greater share of the funding is there for the primary purpose the program serves. And it protects that purpose from gratuitous political attack. Think of the case of the computer difficulties associated with the October, 2013 rollout of the Affordable Care Act. The website snafus at first made it almost impossible for people to buy health insurance from the federal exchange. The situation diverted public attention from the public's anger at a conservative-engineered government shutdown and fed the narrative that government couldn't do anything right and that perhaps the ACA itself was fatally flawed. Fortunately, the system was largely rectified by the end of December, and the program reached its first-year goals, as 7.1 million people signed up on the health exchanges by the end of March, 2014. Still, the episode underscored the principle that when the implementation of a compassionate program becomes the issue, the principle underlying the program itself can be endangered. In this case that would have meant forgetting the fact that under the former system nearly 50 million people had no health care at all, that tens of thousands therefore unnecessarily died each year and another 1.7 million Americans per year were sent into bankruptcy due to uncovered health bills.

Still, the lesson for liberals is a clear one. To work and be accepted, liberal policy must be implemented with efficiency and practicality. Former liberal California Senator Alan Cranston summed up the twin needs of vision grounded in practicality. He said, "I don't think there's any one definition, but to do effective political work you have to have vision and practicality, and learn how to persuade people that what you feel needs to be done does need to be done." Senator Cranston died in 2000, but his advice rings as true now as ever.

Diversity of people celebrated within the **unity** of the human family.

America is not like a blanket - one piece of unbroken cloth. America is more like a quilt - many patches, many pieces, many colors, many sizes, all woven together by a common thread.

Rev. Jesse Jackson

I am fortunate to live in California, one of the most diverse places on earth. There is no majority ethnicity here. There are people of European ancestry, of many Hispanic origins, and descendants of Africans, South, Southeast and East Asians, the Arab world, Pacific Islanders, you name it. The geography of America's third largest state in square miles produces a wide diversity of lifestyles. South, Central and North Coasters share the Pacific in common but have much that is individually unique. Dwellers in the giant urban centers inhabit cities of strikingly different characteristics within an overall American and West Coast idiom. Anyone who has been to San Diego, Los Angeles, San Francisco and San Jose can comment on their different feels and cultures as variants within quintessential American life. Denizens of the Central Valley, Mojave Desert, Sierra Nevada, Sacramento Delta and Napa wine regions live other parts of the kaleidoscope that is life in the Golden State. The South Bay surfer, San Francisco lawyer, Coachella farmer and East LA auto mechanic are all as Californian as Half Dome and Doheny Beach. And though California may be more diverse than most places in America, it is a microcosm of America writ large and a harbinger of what is to come.

Liberals truly celebrate diversity and thrive in diverse settings. That's because liberals believe everyone has something to contribute, and they are temperamentally open to new ideas. They agree with poet Maya Angelou, "It is time for parents to teach young people early on that in diversity there is beauty and there is strength." One of America's greatest strengths is its diversity. Exposure to various perspectives and ways opens the mind and discourages group think. It encourages us to see each other as members of the human family rather than as separate tribes and sects. As Mark Twain put it, "Travel is fatal to prejudice, bigotry, and narrow-mindedness, and many of our people need it sorely on these accounts. Broad, wholesome, charitable views of men and things cannot be acquired by vegetating in one little corner of the earth all one's lifetime."

This principle evokes not only diversity, but unity. What, then, promotes unity among all this diversity? You can go to quite a few countries in the world today where the roots of unity are plain. The people are overwhelmingly all of one ethnicity. They share the same language, religion and culture. But look at the United States. Go down the main street of most any American city and you will see a dozen different places of worship and restaurants offering delicacies from the food traditions of a dozen different nationalities. Yet surveys consistently show Americans are among the most nationalistic people in the world. What keeps such a nation together?

Indeed it is the shared commitment to rights and freedoms and the acceptance of differences that distinguishes American culture by its unity of purpose coexistent with its diversity of practice. It is not accidental that heavy majorities of people of minority ethnicities, religions and sexual orientations vote for the liberal side in American elections. They recognize whose perspectives exude affirmation and whose policy ideas manifest our longtime unofficial national motto, *E pluribus unum*--out of many, one. Or, as the Father of the Constitution put it:

The diversity in the faculties of men, from which the rights of property originate, is not less an insuperable obstacle to an uniformity of interests. The protection of these faculties is the first object of government.

James Madison

Civil Rights enshrined and protected.
There are those who say to you - we are rushing this issue of civil rights. I say we are 172 years late.
Hubert H. Humphrey, *Democratic National Convention, 1948*

Given the preceding section on diversity as a liberal principle, it should not be surprising that liberals have been the standard bearers of civil rights from the beginning of American history to the present day. Our forebears have been fighting this battle for a long time, and liberals are proud to still be carrying on the fight today. John F. Kennedy expressed the liberal perspective at the root of our civil rights stance in 1963 during a national television address. JFK declared his intention to introduce comprehensive civil rights legislation into congress during a time of vicious repression in the South. He explained, "We are confronted primarily with a moral issue... whether all Americans are to be afforded equal rights and equal opportunities, whether we are going to treat our fellow Americans as we want to be treated."

The concept of civil rights encompasses the concepts central to American identity. The foundational values behind these rights are simple. They derive from the principle of liberty, are applied under the principle of equity, and are carried out under the principle of equality. People are free to do as they wish, so long as their actions do not harm others. The rules and conventions of society must be fair. Finally, opportunities must be offered and prohibitions enforced equally, without respect to person or position. All the civil rights, including the freedoms of religion and speech, the right to vote or be hired for a job, to buy the house we like or marry the person we love proceed clearly from the precepts laid down in the Declaration of Independence. Yet as President Barack Obama said, "Although the principle of equality has always been self-evident, it has never been self-executing."

It is often disconcerting to liberals that Civil Rights even have to come up as an issue. The precepts of freedom, fairness and equality are simple enough, clear enough, and so obviously integral to the founding documents Americans of all views claim to pay homage to that the need to keep fighting to assert and preserve civil rights can seem almost beyond comprehension. And yet every generation of liberals since 1776 has had its own civil rights struggles to wage. There have always been those who could not bring themselves to believe that certain rights were *really* intended for everybody. Liberals have had to fight for the principle that *yes, they are* with respect to one discriminated group after another. Blacks, women, Native Americans, Chinese, Irish, Japanese, Latinos, employees, and now the LGBT (lesbian/gay/bi-sexual/transgender) community have respectively been singled out for the official denial of their civil rights.

As soon as one battle is won, attempts at encroachment begin anew. As soon as one group makes progress, another group gets singled out by another movement to "preserve traditional values," pursue political advantage, or under the guise of some other excuse to treat some people as less than others by denying them such prerogatives as equality, their labor rights, voting rights or the right to make medical decisions about their own bodies. The freedom to voice unpopular opinions always seems to be under assault. Long experience has shown liberals that the fight for civil rights is perpetual. Benjamin Franklin was asked what type of government the Constitutional Convention was creating. The great man answered, "A republic, if you can keep it." Fortunately, every generation of liberals has proven equal to the task, and over time the scope and reach of civil rights has expanded. It is an unfinished task to which liberals remain committed with the fervor of the great French liberal Voltaire, who wrote, "I do not agree with what you have to say, but I'll defend to the death your right to say it!"

Service as the means to realize these principles in our society and world.

At the end of life we will not be judged by how many diplomas we have received, how much money we have made, how many great things we have done .We will be judged by "I was hungry, and you gave me something to eat, I was naked and you clothed me. I was homeless, and you took me in."

Mother Teresa

Service is a revered value in liberalism. The very heart of liberalism is about service to one's community and to others, particularly to those in greatest need. I can personally attest that preparing food at the local soup kitchen or spending Earth Day pulling refuse out of a nearby creek gives me a sense of fulfillment. You ought to try it, or something like it, yourself. Barack Obama was a community organizer in Chicago. Former Secretary of Health and Human Services Donna Shalala was a Peace Corps volunteer. President Obama has said, "The best way to not feel hopeless is to get up and do something. Don't wait for good things to happen to you. If you go out and make some good things happen, you will fill the world with hope, you will fill yourself with hope."

A liberal wants to make a positive difference in the world, and service is how we do that in a tangible way. As Muhammad Ali said, "Service to others is the rent you pay for your room here on earth." Empathy may be the beginning and meeting human needs in some fashion may be the goal, but service is the acid test of whether we are willing to take action to make something happen. Martin Luther King made the case in strong terms: "An individual has not started living until he can rise above the narrow confines of his individualistic concerns to the broader concerns of all humanity." The way we do that is through service.

Love as the source of all the good we do and are.
Darkness cannot drive out darkness; only light can do that. Hate cannot drive out hate; only love can do that.

Martin Luther King, Jr.

The common thread running through liberalism is love. Ask "why?" regarding every item on the list of liberal principles and you will get the same answer: "love." Why do we care about community? Promote peace? Have empathy for others? Why are we concerned with justice, celebrate diversity, insist on equality, and give ourselves in service? At the root, it is because we love. We want to be part of causes greater than ourselves, causes that make a positive difference in people's lives and in the world around us. The motivation behind this is love, the calling to "do unto others as you would have others do unto you."

We believe this force is invincible. People do many things out of love that make no sense from a selfish point of view. They donate kidneys and run into burning buildings. They adopt orphans. They get tear gassed marching for other people's rights. They spend time with Alzheimer's patients. They vote to raise their own taxes for school bonds when they are childless. They persevere in the fight for equal pay for women when they are not women, for immigrants' justice when they are not immigrants, for universal health care when they have good employer-provided insurance. Dr. King taught us that "Love is the only force capable of transforming an enemy into a friend," and assured us that "Everybody can be great... You only need a heart full of grace. A soul generated by love." Liberals care about people; they love, and this quality has been responsible for most of the progress that has been made against long odds in human rights, social equality and economic justice, even in long struggles that at times seemed hopeless. Perhaps the poets sum it up best. As Elizabeth Barrett Browning put it, "Who so loves believes the impossible." When all is said and done, we agree with Virgil: "Love conquers all."

CHAPTER 4:

The Liberal Record of Success

A great democracy has got to be progressive or it will soon cease to be great or a democracy.

Theodore Roosevelt

Liberals have built a proud and successful record in America from earliest colonial times to the present day. They have waged a continuous struggle for human rights and dignity over these long centuries, standing up successively for those denied justice due to their skin color, religion, place of birth, gender, economic status, ethnicity or orientation. They have been on the right side of history, not only in their staunch pursuit of equality but also in their advocacy of open, inclusive and democratic government practices and in their support of policies that have consistently delivered happiness and prosperity to the American people, policies motivated by a philosophy of government that puts service to human needs first. Here is a partial catalogue of their accomplishments and principled positions. I invite you to take some time to fully absorb and reflect on the enormity of the good liberals have done. Consider also that virtually every one of these achievements or positions was faced with strident opposition from conservatives. Quite a few of them still are.

Colonial Period, 1607-1763
Virginia House of Burgesses: First Elected Colonial Legislature
Mayflower Compact Established Democracy and Equality of Citizens in Plymouth
Connecticut Fundamental Orders established citizen rights and the principle that a free people is the source of its government's authority
Zenger Trial Established Freedom of the Press

Revolution and New Nation, 1763-1800
Declaration of Independence
Virginia Statute of Religious Liberty
Writing of U. S. Constitution
Included an End to Slave Trade in Constitution
Won Ratification of U.S. Constitution
Passed and Ratified Bill of Rights
The Nineteenth Century, 1801-1899
Got Rid of Property Qualifications for Voting
Passed Homestead Act
Passed Morrill Land Grant College Act
Passed Pacific Railroad Act
Fought and Won Civil War to Preserve Union and End Slavery
Passed 13th Amendment Abolishing Slavery
Passed 14th Amendment Guaranteeing Citizenship Rights and Equal Protection of the Laws
Passed 15th Amendment Guaranteeing Voting Rights
Opposed Chinese Exclusion Act
Passed Anti-Monopoly Sherman Anti-Trust Act and Interstate Commerce Act

Early Twentieth Century, 1900-1928
Passed Pure Food and Drug Act, Meat Inspection Act, Zoning Laws, Workplace Safety Laws
Established Regulatory Commissions to Monitor Banking, Industry, Insurance, Railroads, Telephone, Public Utilities
Trust Busting Broke Up Monopolies and Cartels, Restored Fair Competition
Passed 16th Amendment Permitting Income Tax Based on Ability to Pay
Passed 17th Amendment: Democratic Election of U.S. Senators by the People
Progressive Reforms: Initiative, Referendum and Recall by Voters
Passed Keating-Owen Child Labor Act

Established National Park Service
Wilson Era: Led Free World to Victory in World War I
Passed the 19th Amendment Giving Women the Right to Vote
Fought for 8-Hour Work Day

Great Depression and World War II, 1929-1945
Roosevelt Administration Brought Relief to Starving Millions in the Great Depression
Employed Millions with New Deal Agencies such as CCC, TVA, WPA, PWA
Ended Great Depression
Ended Prohibition
Passed Glass-Steagall and FDIC, Stabilized Banking
Established SEC, Stabilized Stock Market
Passed Wagner Act to Protect Workers' Rights to Unionize
Enacted Social Security
Passed Minimum Wage, 8-Hour Work Day
Passed War Mobilization Prior to World War II
Desegregated Wartime Defense Industries
Led Nation and Free World to Victory in World War II
Established United Nations
Passed GI Bill

Mid to Late 20th Century, 1946-1999
Truman Era: Successful Transition from Wartime to Prosperous Peacetime Economy
Supported Jackie Robinson Breaking Color Barrier in Baseball
Ordered Racial Desegregation of Armed Forces
Supported Desegregation, Voting Rights, Fair Housing, Equal Opportunity, Interracial Marriage during Civil Rights Era
Kennedy-Johnson 1960s "The Great Prosperity"
Established Peace Corps
Enacted Medicare
Passed Civil Rights Act
Passed Voting Rights Act

Passed Clean Water Act, Clean Air Act, Endangered Species Act
Established Environmental Protection Agency
Supported Women's Contraception and Abortion Rights
Successfully Negotiated Israeli-Egyptian Camp David Peace Accord
Supported Equal Rights Amendment
Developed First U. S. Green Energy Policy
Supported Cesar Chavez and UFW Movement for Farmworker Rights
Opposed Reagan-Era Tax Cuts for Wealthy, Cuts to Public Services
Clinton Era: Longest Economic Expansion in U. S. History
Passed Assault Gun Ban
Negotiated Peace in Northern Ireland
Clinton Era Budget Surpluses

Early 21st Century, 2000-2014
Opposed War in Iraq
Defeated Attempt to Privatize Social Security
Elected Barack Obama, First African-American President
Passed Lilly Ledbetter Fair Pay for Women Act
Ended Torture of Prisoners, Violations of Eighth Amendment
Saved American Automobile Industry
Repealed Don't Ask Don't Tell Military Policy (Gay Rights)
Established Consumer Financial Protection Bureau
Passed Wall Street Reform (Dodd-Frank)
Passed Affordable (Health) Care Act (Obamacare)
Obama Era: Ended Great Recession, Record 57 Consecutive Months of Job Growth
Ended War in Iraq
Won First State Court Decisions and Elections for Marriage Equality
Successfully Fought for Repeal of Anti-Gay Federal "Defense of Marriage" Act
Passed Relief for Hurricane Sandy Victims

The Present Day
Support Separation of Church and State
Support Allowing Women to Make Own Decisions on Contraception
Support DREAM Act for Undocumented Immigrants
Support Marriage Equality
Support Background Checks for Gun Purchases and Ban on Military Style Assault Weapons
Support Eliminating Special Interest, Corporate, Millionaire and Offshore Tax Loopholes
Support Overturning *Citizens United* and *McCutcheon* Supreme Court Decisions which Gave Corporations Rights of Human Beings and Gutted Campaign Spending Limitations
Oppose Cutting Social Security and Medicare
Oppose Cutting Medicaid for Poor, S-CHIP Medical Support for Poor Children
Support Preserving Voting Rights Act
Passed Comprehensive Immigration Policy with a Path to Citizenship in U.S. Senate
Accept Scientific Evidence for Human-Generated Climate Change (Global Warming)
Support Green Energy
Support Federal Job Creation
Oppose Teaching Creationism as Science

Colonial Period: Equal Citizens with Rights
The fundamental political issue in the early colonial period was whether the European aristocratic class system would be established in the colonies. The original Jamestown, Virginia settlement in 1607, for instance was composed heavily of noble aristocrats who hoped to enslave the Native Americans and make them farm and mine gold for their masters' profit. They considered themselves too good to do manual labor. When the Indians refused servility and food supplies ran low Captain John Smith forced

these noblemen into the fields at gunpoint with the admonishment, "He that worketh not, neither shall he eat!" Few English aristocrats followed in their footsteps, and soon most colonists began to consider themselves on a legal peer with their fellows, facing similar dangers and challenges in a new land. The conservative European social class system never took strong root in America.

Far from England's king and parliament, the colonies developed their own elected legislative bodies to deal with local problems the old country's leaders cared little about. They discovered that liberal land policies and freedom of religion provided additional inducements to encourage more immigrants to join them and populate their respective colonies. Another important precedent was set when a colonial jury refused to convict publisher John Peter Zenger of a crime for printing unflattering news and opinion about the royal governor of New York. The jury bought the arguments of Zenger's lawyer that truthful news cannot be libel and that opinion is protected speech, thus establishing a firm footing for freedom of speech and the press in America.

Revolution and New Nation: Revolutionary Principles Inspire a Liberal Constitution

During the Revolution and the establishment of the new United States of America, liberal principles truly gained the upper hand. Before independence conservative opinion favored submission and loyalty to the crown, and after independence it favored the supremacy of the states over the national government and the exclusion, as far as possible, of common people from a real voice in their own affairs.

The Declaration of Independence is one of the most radically liberal documents ever penned. By boldly announcing, "We hold these truths to be self-evident, that all men are created equal..." it established the principle of universal equality as the founding creed of the nation. By asserting that all are "endowed by their creator with certain inalienable rights" it placed those rights out of reach of legitimate abridgement. Finally, by affirming that a government's authority to govern comes from "the consent of the governed" it fixed the people themselves as the source of political sovereignty. It is true that many who signed the document were themselves imperfect exemplars of the liberal egalitarian ethos of the Declaration's precepts, including the principal author, Thomas Jefferson, who owned as many as 200 of his fellow human beings. None the less, the Declaration's import in setting these visions of equity as ideals has guided our national realization of their achievement ever since. The extension of rights to the indentured, men without property, slaves, women, minority ethnicities and now, minority sexual orientations, has advanced and continues to advance as a result of our embarrassment over the difference between actuality and the shining ideal first laid out on Independence Day, 1776.

The writing and ratification of the U. S. Constitution marked the next great step forward for liberal principles by establishing a truly national government with the power to act decisively. The earlier "Articles of Confederation" which the Constitution replaced was less a constitution than an alliance between thirteen separate mini-nations. The Articles declared, "Each state retains its sovereignty, freedom, and independence, and every power, jurisdiction and right," not expressly given to the national government. The states were united only in a "firm league of friendship with each other," without the power to tax or establish national policies on much of anything besides declaring war, making peace, running a postal service, and establishing a uniform system of weights and measures. Consequently, the new nation was riven by disputes between the states, had no coherent national trade or economic plan and no way to pay its bills. The infant United States was becoming a laughingstock.

The Constitution changed all that. Conservatives like to say the Constitution was written to limit the powers of the federal government, but nothing is further from the truth. The main problem under the Articles was a government too weak to unify the states and too weak to get anything done. The Constitution vested the U.S. government with expansive powers, far beyond those in the Articles. The Preamble lays out the six major areas of federal responsibility: "to form a more perfect union, establish justice, ensure domestic tranquility, provide for the common defense, promote the general welfare, and secure the blessings of liberty to ourselves and our posterity..." Article 1, Section 8, the section on the powers of congress, enumerates a wealth of responsibilities in addition to war and peace, of which these are only a few: to "regulate commerce," "lay and collect taxes," "pay all debts," establish and regulate the armed forces, determine copyright and patent law, set up a federal court system, and legislate immigration and naturalization. But in case these specific powers are not enough, it goes on to add, "To make all Laws which shall be necessary and proper for carrying into Execution the foregoing Powers, and all other Powers vested by this Constitution in the Government of the United States, or in any Department or Officer thereof." This last sentence is known as the "elastic clause." That's because it stretches congressional powers, granting ample authority to carry out the six purposes of the Preamble beyond what the specific listing of powers in Article 1 Section 8 provides. In the modern era, for instance, we can have an air force even though the Constitution's wording only mentions the establishment of an army and navy. It is considered part of the overall mandate of the Preamble to "provide for the common defense." The Framers of the Constitution were wise enough to anticipate that new ideas, practices, needs and technologies would arise. Rather than restricting the national government from taking essential steps to deal with problems they could not foresee when the Constitution was written in 1787, they granted wide scope for action, consequences of the lack of which they had seen all too well in the impotent operation of congress under the Articles. What they *did* take care to safeguard were the citizens' civil rights, and these are enshrined in the first ten amendments to the original Constitution, also known as the Bill of Rights.

The Nineteenth Century: Expanding Freedom Under a Government of the People

In America, the great questions of the first half of the nineteenth century (1800's) centered on the issue of slavery. Liberals were in the forefront of the movement to end that detestable and hypocritical affront to human liberty. Conservatives with various motivations opposed them. Most were racist. Some stood for traditional ways. Others valued property rights over human rights. Some fell back on the political argument of "state's rights." There had always been those who opposed slavery on liberal, moral grounds, but the tide of public opinion did not move strongly until William Lloyd Garrison began publishing his magazine *The Liberator* in Boston in 1831. It was the first journal to demand the immediate and permanent end of slavery in America. In 1827 there had been an estimated 130 antislavery societies in the U.S. (106 of those in the South) but by 1836 there were 527. By 1838 the number had grown to 1,300, and in 1838 and 1839 they gathered 2 million signatures on antislavery petitions.

After the Nat Turner slave rebellion in Virginia in 1831 antislavery sentiment was largely silenced in the South, but the cause gained new allies in the women's movement. Garrison joined forces with Susan Anthony, Elizabeth Stanton and Lucretia Mott in calling for liberty and equality for women as well as blacks. The rise of prominent eloquent spokespersons, especially the former slaves Sojourner Truth and Frederick Douglass, brought in new supporters. By 1848 the antislavery Free-Soil third party won 10 percent of the nationwide presidential vote. The movement reached critical mass after the publication of Harriet Beecher Stowe's novel *Uncle Tom's Cabin* in 1852. The smash bestseller personalized the slavery question for millions of readers. By 1854 the Republican Party was founded in direct response to the passage of the Kansas-Nebraska Act, which threatened to allow the extension of slavery into new Northern territories.

The Republican Party of those days was the more liberal party. It stood for human rights over property rights, standing as it did for the restriction of slavery. It stood for the precedence of nationally guaranteed human rights over the idea that "state's rights" permitted localities to nullify national laws or void human freedoms when and where they wished. It stood for the principle of nationally-encouraged economic modernization and development that helped the people. With the election of Abraham Lincoln, many of these ideas were carried out. The Homestead Act, Land Grant College Act and Pacific Railroad Act were passed. During the Civil War an income tax made taxation fairer, and the Banking Acts of 1863 established national standards and a fully unified national currency, the "greenback" dollar. Black army units were recruited. The Emancipation Proclamation ended slavery in the rebelling South; and the Thirteenth Amendment forever ended it throughout the country.

In the second half of the nineteenth century, modern American liberalism began to take shape. The catalyst for this was the growth and spread of industrial society. The emergence of a huge working class and the elevation of a small coterie of the super-rich posed a threat to the democratic ideal itself. The two major political parties had become attentive to the interests of the tycoons and indifferent to the plight of the average person. Mark Twain famously called the late nineteenth century the "Gilded Age" in reference to something with a shiny veneer on the outside that was rotten and corrupt underneath. The late eighteen hundreds saw the spread of enormous inequities of wealth between the titans of industry and finance such as Andrew Carnegie and J.P. Morgan and the surging millions of factory workers and farmers who frequently lived in squalor and privation.

These dynamics helped lead to a new movement called Populism. It started among the farmers of the South and Midwest, who were being charged interest rates of over 100 percent for seed and equipment to put their crop in and had to pay whatever the railroads demanded to ship it out at harvest time. Populist Tom Watson said the Democrats were selling "the liberty and prosperity of the country…to plutocratic greed" and accused the Republicans of being in bed with "monopolists, gigantic corporations, bondholders, and bankers." It was time for the little guys, rural and urban, to get organized and stand up. The Populist platform called for government regulation to protect people from depredations by corporations. They wanted government to take ownership of the railroads, telephone and telegraph systems, and natural resources. Until that could be arranged, the platform called for government commissions to set fair railroad charges and bank interest rates. They called for abandoning the gold standard and greatly expanding the money supply with silver, with the object of lowering interest rates. They demanded women's suffrage, a secret ballot, the direct election of the President and U.S. Senators, and the adoption of the recall and ballot initiative to put the people directly in charge. For industrial workers, they demanded an 8-hour day and the recognition of union rights. In 1892 the Populists elected three state governors, 1,500 state and county officers, five U.S. Senators and ten U.S. representatives. Presidential candidate James Weaver of Iowa won five states and 22 electoral votes.

The situation reached the breaking point for many in the economic depression of 1893-1894, when 500 banks and 15,000 businesses failed and an estimated 17 percent of the work force was unemployed. Jacob Coxey, an Ohio businessman, came up with the novel idea that the government should actually try to do something about this. "Coxey's Army" marched on Washington to ask for a federal program to provide jobs for the unemployed. But it was the era of "laissez-faire," the doctrine that the "free market" should be allowed to operate without impingement. When they arrived, Coxey and his marchers were arrested. Strikes broke out in the coal and manufacturing sectors, and were often violently broken by the police. It became apparent to many that the system was set up to benefit the haves and neglect the have-nots.

The Democrats nominated William Jennings Bryan on a "free silver" platform in 1896, along the lines of what the Populists had campaigned for. This alarmed corporate interests sufficiently that they invented the modern moneyed political campaign to oppose him. Republican nominee William McKinley's campaign manager, Mark Hannah, raised the unprecedented sum of $3.5 million from the movers and shakers, five times the amount Bryan would have at his disposal. Consequently, McKinley's White House effort featured the nation's first mass media election campaign. Newspapers, magazines and billboards were filled with McKinley's advertising, and millions of pamphlets circulated, painting Bryan as a dangerous radical. Numerous paid surrogates toured the country to promote the Republican ticket and views. Meanwhile, McKinley himself ran a relaxed "front porch campaign" from his home in Ohio. At these gatherings, supporters were brought in by rail to stand in front of the candidate's house while he read prepared answers to questions selected for the occasion. Unable to compete with such money and organization, Bryan responded with a similarly unprecedented personal campaign, in which he toured the nation and appealed to the voters directly. In 100 days he traveled 18,000 miles by train and gave more than 500 speeches to untold millions of people. The election was close, but McKinley won.

Early Twentieth Century: The Progressive Era

Though defeated in the ultimate battle, the liberal ideas and approach brought up by the Populists were not dead. They had elected a lot of people at the local levels, and public dissatisfaction with the obvious corruption and unresponsiveness of the political and economic system continued to grow. The greatest triumphs of liberalism since the abolition of slavery were just about to take place. In fact, if you think about it, just about everything the Populists advocated-votes for women, the secret ballot, initiatives and recalls, direct election of Senators, the 8-hour day, union rights, regulation of banking, railroads and industries, taking the money off the gold standard—are now law. Many of these changes were achieved under the banner of Progressivism.

The Progressive Era lasted from about 1900 to 1920. During this time American society was on fire with zeal for positive change.

Progressives wanted to reform and improve American society, and they devoted their energies through democratic political and community action to get things done. There were Progressives of both major parties, including Republican President Theodore Roosevelt (1901-1909) and Democratic President Woodrow Wilson (1913-1921).

"Muckraking" journalists brought abuses to public attention. For instance, Ida Tarbell wrote about the depredations of the Standard Oil monopoly, Lincoln Steffens exposed the endemic corruption of machine politics, Upton Sinclair revealed disgustingly unsanitary practices in the meat packing industry and Lewis Hine's photography aroused public outrage over child labor. The climate shifted from a *laissez faire* attitude that permitted graft, exploitation and double-dealing to run unchecked to a conviction that the public interest required such evils to be controlled by the force of law.

Progressive principles were forthright. Government must operate efficiently and honestly, and reflect the will of the people. Women were entitled to equal rights, including the right to vote. Workers should have the right to unionize, and their health and safety on the job should be protected by law. Child labor was an abomination; children should be in compulsory, taxpayer-funded public schools and their milk must be inspected for freshness and purity. Consumers were entitled to safe and healthy products, and the people's government had the authority to inspect and enforce this. Monopolies, trusts and cartels must be abolished and actual competition restored to the marketplace. The nation's resources must be conserved and its scenic wonders preserved for future generations.

You can clearly see the attitude of modern liberals in the Progressive outlook. If you could boil it down to a bottom line, it would be the principle that the public interest exists and needs protection from the special, moneyed interest. Trust in big business had plummeted because it had been caught in so many incidences of mistreatment of its workers, misrepresentation to the public and corrupt influencing of the political system that the public at large had come to the conclusion that it had to be controlled. The hideous Triangle Shirtwaist Fire of 1911, in which 146 garment workers in New York City burned or jumped to their deaths in a sweatshop conflagration, was for many the last straw. There had been no fire extinguishers or hoses, and the exit doors had been locked. The lust for profit was irresistible to the corporation; its adherence to morality could only be compelled by the force of law.

Look back at the liberal accomplishments listed at the beginning of this section during the early twentieth century and you will see a great many regulations on the conduct of business. There were quality requirements for food, drugs and housing. Regulations on child labor and worker safety appeared. Monopolies were broken up. Workers were allowed to form unions. As Teddy Roosevelt explained, "We are not attacking the corporations, but endeavoring to do away with any evil in them; we are not hostile to them; we are merely determined that they shall be so handled as to subserve the public good. We draw the line against misconduct, not against wealth." Freedom cannot include the "right" of the rich and powerful to abuse, cheat and lie to their workers and customers and then bend the political system through bribery and massive campaign "contributions" to excuse their depredations.

Most of the other great liberal advances of this time were in enlarging direct democracy by the people. The primary, initiative, recall, secret ballot, popular election of senators and women's suffrage were not only to further the ongoing liberal goal of greater democracy but also to take power away from insiders, with their susceptibility to financial or other inducements or threats from the purveyors of special interest. Thanks to these efforts of the early twentieth century Progressives and their two decades of liberal action, the American people were freer and enjoyed greater security than ever before.

Great Depression and World War II: Meeting Human Needs and Restoring World Peace

The national emergency of the Great Depression provided the next crucial test of liberal leadership and principles. The Depression began with the crash of the stock market on Wall Street in October, 1929. Under Herbert Hoover's conservative, do-nothing, business-oriented efforts, the Depression continued to get worse. By the time he left office the official unemployment rate stood at 25 percent, another 25 percent were underemployed, and the output of the national economy had contracted by almost half. Franklin Delano Roosevelt won a decisive electoral victory in November, 1932. He took office the next March with a mandate for change and plenty of congressional support to enact a fully liberal recovery program. The ensuing first Hundred Days of FDR's "New Deal" saw the passage of the greatest concentration of liberal legislation in American history. The New Deal program was spectacularly successful, producing tremendous double-digit annual growth rates and returning millions to the employment rolls.

Progressivism had placed regulations on business to curb its worst abuses, and had made America more democratic. The New Deal also instituted regulations, especially ones intended to correct the banking and stock market deficiencies that helped bring on the Depression. But it went beyond that to provide tangible help to people in need and direct intervention to spur economic growth and recovery. With an eye to the future, it set up ongoing systems that provided for the economic security of the American people. Then FDR had to deal with another major crisis, the Second World War. Once again, a liberal administration and congress came through with flying colors, becoming the second liberal administration in twenty-five years to save liberty by leading the free world to victory in a global war.

The liberal New Deal was successful because it got money directly into the hands of the people who needed it. When the private economy was too weak to provide jobs, FDR and Congress approved a massive public works program. Such agencies as the CCC, TVA, WPA and PWA built needed public works throughout the nation. The millions they hired earned money to spend, which created sales for business and revived the private economy. America's Gross Domestic Product, the value of all goods and services produced in the economy, which had fallen by 45.6 percent in the four years of Depression, grew by an astonishing 62.9 percent in the first four years of the New Deal. Conservatives still try to make the case that the New Deal didn't work, but the figures clearly show their arguments are nonsense. The adoption of a Keynesian (named for British economist John Maynard Keynes) approach of active government spending to replace the lack of spending in the private sector and restore economic vitality was a tremendous success.

New regulations ensured there would be no repeat of the stock market meltdown for over fifty years. The banking system remained stable for another seventy years, until after the New Deal Glass-Steagall protections were foolishly repealed. What's more, liberal policy helped build the middle class and secure it financially. The 8-hour day and minimum wage were enacted. Labor rights were now supervised and enforced by a national agency dedicated to the purpose. Old-age poverty was practically eliminated by the adoption of Social Security. By Presidential order, racial discrimination was banned in the defense industries. At the end of the war, veterans were thanked and rewarded for their sacrifices by the GI Bill, a boon to their higher education and home ownership.

Over the vociferous opposition of conservatives, liberal regulatory, economic and administrative practices had been tried and proved spectacularly successful. The idea of actually getting help directly to those in need and intervening deliberately in the economy to good effect was vindicated beyond doubt. The fascist dictatorships were defeated. America remained a vibrantly free and democratic society. In many ways, this was one of liberalism's finest hours.

Mid to Late Twentieth Century: Civil Rights, Caring for the Planet, and Fostering the Great Prosperity

The years from the end of World War II until the end of the twentieth century further cemented the liberal record of success. In the years 1946-1999 liberal principles advanced on many fronts, to the great benefit of the American people. In particular, liberals achieved major gains in civil rights, inaugurated the environmental movement, and brought tremendous and widespread prosperity wherever their economic principles were followed.

The many milestone accomplishments in civil rights achieved during this time period are still a source of immense pride to liberals. These seminal advances in human equality were achieved often in the face of the most vicious and even murderous violence. Despite these obstacles, liberals fought and won major battles on civil rights, extending the frontiers of freedom and equality over the legacy of segregation and discrimination. The Rev. Dr. Martin Luther King was a liberal, fighting not only for legal equality as a God-given right but for union rights, economic justice and to end the Vietnam War. It was liberal President Harry Truman who desegregated the armed forces by Presidential order. It was liberal President John Kennedy who introduced the comprehensive Civil Rights Act and liberal President Lyndon Johnson who completed his work by shepherding the bill through congress. Johnson and the majority liberal congress continued to enlarge the scope of justice with the Voting Rights Act, Fair Housing Act and the President's Commission on Women. The liberal American Civil Liberties Union brought the case of Richard and Mildred Loving all the way to the Supreme Court, which unanimously ruled laws against interracial marriage unconstitutional. Liberals, led by Senator Bobby Kennedy, gave their support to Cesar Chavez in his fight for equality, justice and union rights for California's largely Latino farm workers. America would be unrecognizable today had it not been for the civil rights battles fought and won by liberals at a cost of much blood and many lives in the middle years of the twentieth century.

This was also the time when liberals brought the environmental movement into the national consciousness. During these years, waves of toxic smog killed 20 people in Denora, Pennsylvania and 200 in New York. The Cuyahoga River in Cleveland, filled with volatile chemicals, burst into flames that rose over fifty feet high. Rachel Carson wrote *Silent Spring*, a book that surmised pesticides and other toxic chemicals in the environment were to blame for drastic reductions in bird and butterfly populations. It raised the possibility that without change the year might come when we would no longer begin spring with the sounds of songbirds, or even our national symbol, the bald eagle, as they would all have gone extinct. President Kennedy set his Science Advisory Committee to work investigating Carson's conclusions, and they reported back in agreement with her findings. A Clean Air Act was in process when Kennedy was killed, and it was passed the very next month. The Water Quality Act, Wild and Scenic Rivers Act and Endangered Species Act, all spearheaded by liberals, were passed over the next few years.

The years when liberal economic ideas reigned supreme from the 1940s through the early 1970s saw the creation of the first great, widespread middle class in the history of the world. Average people had purchasing power, and their buying kept the wheels of commerce humming and spurred the highest level of shared prosperity the world had ever known. Take a look at the figures in Chapter 7 to get an idea just how remarkable that economy was. The administrations of Truman, Kennedy, Johnson and then Clinton in the 1990s saw rising employment and income across the board in American society, a true national prosperity. It's one of liberalism's greatest legacies and achievements, and provides a reliable road map for the future. I can add as a personal note that my own firm conversion to a liberal perspective was cemented by my understanding of the historical record regarding the economy. That record clearly demonstrates the close association between liberal economic initiatives and shared growth and well-being for the American people.

The second half of the twentieth century gave tremendous testament indeed to the great prosperity the American people enjoy when liberal policies are followed. After the passage of the Wagner (National Labor Relations) Act, union rights were safeguarded. Consequently, at the peak, 33 percent of American workers were unionized. The existence of powerful unions meant that workers got a bigger share of company earnings. Rising minimum wages provided a floor and ensured a decent wage for all who worked, raising the pay of those above the minimum wage as well. High tax rates on upper incomes and corporate profits provided revenues that were plowed back into providing opportunity throughout society, including a rapid and massive investment in public education at all levels, from primary grades to low-cost public universities. Combined with the GI Bill for veterans and affirmative action for groups that had historically been subject to discrimination, these efforts began to facilitate upward mobility for a greater number of Americans than ever. Others of these revenues were directed into scientific research such as the space program and infrastructure construction such as water projects to provide jobs and make American industry and the American people as a whole globally competitive. There is no question that a vigorous entrepreneurial spirit is essential to a strong economy. But so is a sense of fairness and a system that allows the fruits of progress to be enjoyed by the broad swath of society as a whole. The record shows that when liberal policies are followed, that's the kind of economy we get. The wealthy, the middle class and the poor all do better.

Early Twenty-First Century: Repairing another Conservative Crash, Expanding Equality, Moving on Health Care

We tend now to think of the early 2000s as a time when liberal movements have taken root, and despite extreme partisan infighting in Washington, liberal social and economic ideals are transforming the country in important ways. But we must not forget that the new century began with liberalism on the defensive thanks to the Supreme Court intervening in the state of Florida's presidential vote recount of the 2000 election. The 5-4 conservative majority in *Bush v. Gore* ordered the Sunshine State to stop counting ballots, effectively declaring the conservative candidate the forty-third president. With a born-again believer in deregulation and tax cuts for the rich as president, an oil industry executive as vice president, military interventionist Neo-conservatives in charge of defense, and Republican majorities in both houses of congress it was a tough time for liberals. Liberals were unable to prevent many of the calamities of the Bush Administration, but had the satisfaction of seeing their principled positions proved right in the long run. Their stands against the Iraq War, the deregulation that led to the housing crisis and Wall Street Crash of 2008, the unwarranted tax cuts that turned budget surpluses into large deficits, and their fight for equality in the face of a slew of ballot measures against marriage rights for gays and lesbians all went down to defeat. Over time though, public opinion changed on every one of these measures and the liberal views were vindicated, not only in the court of public opinion but on the basis of facts and results as well. One issue on which the Bush Administration showed a bit of liberal compassion was immigration. Unfortunately, though good-faith accords with liberals like the late Senator Edward Kennedy were forged, the president's conservative base in congress and the country rebelled and shot down any hope of progress.

A great liberal success of the time was stopping the administration's plan to begin privatizing Social Security. Liberals mobilized the nation against the reckless scheme to enrich brokers and gamble people's retirement in the stock market. Liberals strongly believe in Franklin Roosevelt's original vision that senior citizens' retirement needs begin with a guaranteed income they can count on, not a roll of the dice. Imagine what would have happened to retirees and those nearing retirement age if Bush had succeeded and his plan had gone into effect on schedule just as the crash of 2008 slashed stock values by more than half.

President Barack Obama was elected in 2008 and inaugurated in 2009. His first great challenge was dealing with the Great Recession. Liberal measures turned things around. A $787 billion stimulus package, vigorous action to save the American automobile industry, new Wall Street reforms (Dodd-Frank) and Elizabeth Warren's idea, the Consumer Financial Protection Bureau, were instituted. Job losses of 800,000 a month were turned into gains, and a 9 percent economic contraction was turned back into positive growth, including over five consecutive years of monthly job gains at this writing. Most Americans were hoping Republican leaders would look for common ground to work together with the new president to achieve greater economic progress. Instead, congressional Republicans met privately the very night of Obama's inauguration to promise each other they would oppose any and all of his ideas (and even their own ideas if he started to accept any of them!) and refuse to cooperate with the new president on any matter of consequence. Their strategy was to try to paralyze action, blame him for lack of success and thereby defeat him for re-election. Fortunately, the Democrats had a majority in the House and held 60 seats in the Senate during Obama's first two years in office. This provided just enough votes to overcome obstructive Republican filibusters, which were called more than in the rest of congressional history.

In those two filibuster-proof years from January 2009 to January 2011 an enormous amount of progress was made, adding a tremendous chapter to the liberal record of success. In addition to the economic recovery package and consumer protections mentioned above, liberals passed the Lilly Ledbetter Fair Pay for Women Act and repealed the "Don't Ask Don't Tell" military policy that forced gays to stay in the closet to join the service and discharged them if the truth of their orientation was found out. Despite dire conservative predictions that allowing gays and lesbians to serve openly would cause a disastrous decline in military morale, equality has gone extremely smoothly. When it comes down to it, most Americans these days get that equality really does mean everybody, and they are supportive of this fundamental national value. The tide has now turned regarding gay rights, and at this writing 36 states and the District of Columbia have adopted the liberal, American view of equality and repudiated this latest vestige of conservative bigotry. Few now doubt that this latest civil rights cause will end with equality triumphant in all 50 states.

Speaking of military matters, one of the liberal president's first acts was to end American torture of enemy prisoners, a shameful practice antithetical to American values and an actual war crime that had been instigated and strongly defended by the previous administration. He was able to wind down the unnecessary war in Iraq and is well on the way to doing the same thing in Afghanistan. Under his direction many more top Al-Qaeda leaders have been eliminated than under the previous administration, including 9/11 mastermind Osama bin Laden himself in a daring raid into Pakistan on the president's direct orders. Once again, liberals showed they can defend the nation and do so within the civilized standards established under international law (standards the United States pushed very hard to get the world to adopt in the aftermath of the horrific abuses of the Second World War) and commensurate with the values of a free constitutional democracy.

There has been tremendous progress on the environmental front, including expanded vehicle gas mileage standards, requirements to make power plants 30 percent cleaner by 2030, and a rapid acceleration in the development of clean solar and wind power spurred by a combination of incentives, environmental regulations, and direct investment under the stimulus. The health savings from reduced pollution are estimated at $93 billion a year. All this has been accomplished while the U.S. has greatly reduced its reliance on foreign energy.

No summation of the liberal record of success of the early twenty-first century would be complete without mention of the

Affordable Care Act, also known as Obamacare. Despite problems with the initial computer rollout, the first 6-month enrollment period saw 15 million people get access to health care thanks to the program. That included 8 million who enrolled in the exchanges, 3 million young adults covered on their parents' insurance until age 26, and 4 million lower income folks who newly qualified for Medicaid. The number served by expanded Medicaid would be much larger except for states with spiteful Republican governors who blocked this health access to their own constituents. It is only fair to point out that the plan wasn't everything liberals wanted. Most would have preferred a "single payer" system along the lines of Medicare. Many fought to at least include a "public option" choice, a government-offered plan to compete with the for-profit policies offered on the exchanges. But the Act needed some conservative Democratic votes to pass, and their price was that provisions like those had to go. Yet we cannot lose sight of the transformational success the ACA has been for the liberal cause. The vision of such liberals as Franklin Roosevelt and Harry Truman, of health care as a universal in American life, is well on its way to being established in the United States of America. And that's a very good thing. The liberal ideal of a responsive society acting to improve people's economic, health and personal security and freedom has been alive and well these past few years.

The Present Day: A Liberal To-Do List

Liberals today continue the fight to make America and Americans more free, secure and prosperous. They know that much more needs to be done. On several issues, recent progress has been made but is not yet complete. For instance, a majority of states still do not have full equality for people of minority sexual orientations, or specific laws mandating true equality for women in the workplace. A comprehensive immigration bill passed in the Senate, but has been stymied in the Republican-controlled House. A great deal more urgently needs to be done with respect to environmental security against climate change, including increased efficiency and investment in renewable energy sources.

The continuing trend of growing economic inequality is a development liberals feel strongly about. Much more needs to be done to return progressive taxation and substantial increases in minimum wages to the front burner of policy debates. Seattle's recent decision to raise its minimum wage to $15 an hour over the next few years will be an excellent test case. Liberals are confident it will prove a great spur to widespread prosperity and set a groundbreaking national example. In addition, local and national infrastructure projects are sorely needed to increase societal efficiency, safety, global competitiveness and to provide jobs. The way to broad prosperity is not more tax cuts for the rich, it is more jobs at better pay for the working and middle class folks who make up the vast center of American society. Liberals will have to fight and plead their case for these projects.

Health security will have to be maintained and improved, and the safety net will have to be defended against the attacks of conservative zealots intent on instituting a "law of the jungle" society. To this end, liberal efforts to roll back the corrosive and corrupting influence of big money in the political process will have to remain an ongoing priority. The recent *Citizens United* and *McCutcheon* Supreme Court decisions in particular must be reversed. This will have to be accomplished either through a constitutional amendment or through the election of liberal presidents who, over time, will replace conservative justices with liberal ones. Until that happens, special interests will continue to have the biggest influence over lawmakers and the loudest megaphone with the public in their unending campaign to protect and expand their profits by confusing and deceiving the American people on topics like the environment, food nutrition, health care, education, clean elections and war.

Liberal defenders of civil liberties have their work cut out for them. They will have to find a way to restore the protections of the Voting Rights Act and get rid of Republican-imposed voter suppression laws that have been passed in a number of states. The revelations of widespread NSA intelligence-gathering on American citizens shows a system run amok that must be reined in. Threats to net neutrality present a real danger of compromising the freedom of the internet and threaten to turn it into an unequal system with corporate users and the well-heeled in the express lane and everyone else stuck in cyber gridlock. Finally, the increasingly intrusive and intimate targeting of people by advertising, especially online, is another personal liberty issue where people should be able to set limits.

The bottom line for us is that these issues pit the liberal vision of an egalitarian society of shared opportunities against a two-tiered society of the haves with special privileges and the have-nots without them. Liberals are disgusted with the dynamics of too big to fail, special tax havens for millionaires and billionaires who ship jobs overseas, public funding for private academies while public school teachers have to buy classroom supplies with their own meager salaries, public subsidies and tax breaks for huge corporations while food stamps and Medicare are cut over supposed concern about budgets. Liberals will have plenty to do as long as there are interests intent on pushing inequity and injustice and on gaming the system to make themselves even wealthier by taking away the basic rudiments of security from average working people, the 99 percent. There will be more advances and liberal successes to add to the proud record of our past, but as has always been the case, only to the extent that people of vision and commitment work for them. The basic liberal premises, that human needs come first, and that people acting together through the democratic process have a role to play in ensuring fairness and opportunity for all in society, remain as true and foundational as ever.

CHAPTER 5
Where Liberal Ideas Come From

Liberalism, above all, means emancipation.

Hubert H. Humphrey

Liberalism and Freedom

Liberals introduced Social Security in the 1930s. They were out front in the civil rights struggles of the 1950s and 1960s. They supported the expansion of low-tuition public universities. Today they fight for such causes as marriage equality, universal health care, a living wage and immigration reform. How are these causes and issues connected? The answer lies in one word: freedom. Liberals believe in freedom from discrimination, freedom to love and make our own choices, freedom from sickness and crushing poverty, and freedom of opportunity.

The great liberal President Franklin D. Roosevelt summed this up when he enunciated the "Four Freedoms." During the desperate struggle against the fascist dictatorships of the Second World War, FDR made it clear America would fight to preserve the Four Freedoms at home and to restore them to a "suffering humanity" groaning under military oppression abroad. The Four Freedoms are Freedom of Speech, Freedom of Religion, Freedom from Want and Freedom from Fear.

The basic philosophical thrust of liberalism is thus the promotion of human freedom. Liberals believe in the basic premise that people should be able to live their own lives. In order to accomplish this, liberals feel that personal rights must be safeguarded and that institutional obstacles standing in the way of people's freedom need to be removed. These two drives, the safeguarding of rights and the removal of impediments standing in the way explain what animates the liberal movement.

Safeguarding people's rights are strongly included in the first two freedoms, of speech and religion. These are "freedoms to." Liberals believe people have the right **to** do, feel, believe, and express themselves as they wish. There is also a component of this in the fourth freedom, the Freedom from Fear. FDR and liberals agree people should have freedom **to** live their lives without fear of oppression. Certainly in President Roosevelt's mind were the oppressions of tyrannical regimes of the kind exemplified by the Nazi, Fascist and Japanese militarist enemies FDR was leading the fight against in World War II.

So liberals, as defenders of freedom, stand and have always stood strongly for these freedoms. But what about the "institutional impediments" working to try to deprive people of these freedoms? It is one thing to say you agree with these freedoms, but may be another to actually guarantee them when some are trying to deny people their rights. What was to be done when African Americans were being lynched for exercising their freedom of speech by asking for equality? What is to be done when a city that routinely approves plans for the projects of most religious groups refuses to allow the construction of a Muslim mosque? Liberals would say such actions require enforcement. For these rights to stand and have any meaning, the community as a whole, even the nation as a whole, through its elected government, must be empowered to protect these rights and enforce their observance by individuals and localities who would deny them.

But the freedoms **to** do things (provided they do not infringe on the rights of others in the community) is only half the picture. The last two of the Four Freedoms, Freedom from Want and Freedom from Fear, are primarily freedoms **from** things, and their inclusion in the list sheds great light on the liberal tendency to tackle human problems proactively.

Consider Freedom from Want. That means freedom from things like hunger, ignorance, and lack of clothing, shelter and medical care. It may be a fine thing for some to say they support people's freedom to eat, go to college and be attended by competent medical professionals. But liberals go farther. We believe it is the obligation of the community to foster the availability of these essentials of life. There needs to be a sufficient supply of food for people to be able to eat, schools for people to be able to learn and medical professionals and facilities in order for people to receive the care and treatment they need.

That's why liberals support effective action to foster food production, education and medical care. Such action may take the form of agricultural research or building irrigation systems. It can mean support for schools and colleges, including medical schools and for hospitals and clinics. But it can also take the form of such things as raising the minimum wage, so people who work full time for a living can make enough to be able to put food on the table, pay the rent and keep the heat on in the winter. It can mean financial aid and scholarship help so students from families with limited means will have a chance to go to college too. And it can take the form of Medicare, Medicaid, SCHIP and President Obama's Affordable Care Act so that the aged, the poor, children and indeed everyone can go to the doctor when they are sick. The "right" to do something necessary to live and thrive is not much of a right if you can't afford it. And when millions of people who work or who are willing to work cannot afford to take care of the basic essentials like being able to buy food, pay rent, go to the doctor or get an education, it says something intolerable about the way things are. In this regard, liberals take their cue from the late South African freedom leader Nelson Mandela, who said, "There is nothing more powerful than the words, 'This is not right.'"

A host of sociological studies show that poverty and want are strongly correlated with innumerable negative social outcomes. According to the Princeton University study "The Future of Children" by Jeanne Brooks Gunn and Greg Duncan, the infant mortality rate is 75% higher for poor families. Children in poverty are twice as likely to be in poor health and are hospitalized at twice the rate of those who are not poor. They are 6.8 times more likely to be the victims of neglect or abuse. Teen girls in poverty have 3.1

times more out-of-wedlock births. Poor families are 2.1 times more likely to be the victims of violent crime. According to the study, "For low-income children, a $10,000 increase in mean family income between birth and age five was associated with nearly a full year increase in completed schooling." Liberals do not just accept such statistics as the operation of inevitable fate or the "free market." Liberals believe in using government action where it can help to make conditions better so people can thrive.

Finally, we turn to freedom from fear. Part of that means freedom from criminal predation. One of society's most important obligations is to provide the security apparatus we are all accustomed to, including police, courts and jails. But liberals know that issue goes far beyond police and jails. The statistical evidence is clear: crime thrives in low-income, low-wage, low education areas. The surest way to enhance freedom from this kind of fear is to provide the kind of real opportunity that transforms communities and ameliorates the conditions that spawn antisocial dysfunction.

Another part is freedom from fear of foreign attack, and that is the reason for having intelligence services to ascertain the capabilities and intentions of potentially threatening individuals, groups and nations, and a military and other security services to directly respond to them when needed. But in addition to these, effective diplomacy and constructive humanitarian intervention in world trouble spots can do much to lessen the need for military operations. Recent experiences in Iraq and Afghanistan make clear how illusory the promises of quick and decisive results from military interventionism can often be.

But another major component of freedom from fear is its application to our own society and to those very institutions set up to provide oversight and security itself. That's why liberals are serious about bullying. People, especially kids, should not have to worry about being maliciously humiliated, threatened and extorted. Such experiences can be as damaging as physical harm. Firm laws and standards have to be passed and enforced to keep people from living in fear of dangerous conditions at work and dangerous products at home. There have always been greedy and unscrupulous people willing to jeopardize the well-being of others to increase their own profits.

But those charged with safeguarding society need to be answerable as well. That's why liberals insist on holding police and all law enforcement agents to a high standard of professionalism and scrupulous adherence to the rights of the accused. It's why liberals seek changes when we see that a much higher percentage of minority defendants are subjected to harsher sentences than majority defendants are for the same convictions. It's also why liberals stood against the Bush administration's practices of arresting people without charges and subjecting them to torture, and continue to fight to rein in surveillance of citizens without warrants in violation of the Constitution's Fourth Amendment. The recent revelations of NSA leaker Edward Snowden have been helpful in this regard. The perversion of governmental power into oppressive power is always a danger and must be restrained by an informed and vigilant citizenry. On this topic the great liberal Supreme Court Justice Louis Brandeis was on point when he said, "Sunlight is the best disinfectant."

So the liberal perspective begins from a platform of compassion. We want the four freedoms for ourselves and because of empathy we want them for others as well; indeed, for everyone in society. The foundation of this view is ethical. But it is also practical. Societies that operate this way are prosperous, safe and happy. This contention is not merely theoretical. Columbia University's Earth Institute surveyed people in 156 countries in 2013 for its World Happiness Report. It found that Denmark, Norway, Switzerland, the Netherlands and Sweden are the world's five happiest countries. These are also countries where the minimum wage is $19 an hour, none of whom have been at war in over 65 years, that enjoy excellent national health care and retirement provisions, universally strong educational systems, comprehensive national infrastructures under responsive democracies devoted to civil liberties in which private interests are not allowed to bankroll political campaigns. In short, the happiest countries in the world are the ones governed under liberal principles.

Freedom In Society: The Social Contract

The end of law is not to abolish or restrain, but to preserve and enlarge freedom. For in all the states of created beings, capable of laws, where there is no law there is no freedom.

John Locke

The question of freedom is an important one. Freedom is a cardinal value in America, and much of our civic debate centers on what should be regarded as inviolable freedoms and what can or should be subject to limitations. The question has an important bearing on our conception of civilization itself, its standards and its bounds. Must we give up any freedom in order to live in society? And if so, how and where should we set the limits?

The English philosopher Thomas Hobbes began thinking and writing about these ideas in the seventeenth century. His great treatise *Leviathan* (1651) hearkens back to a time before organized society when humans had perfect freedom. Imagine a nomadic Stone Age type of existence before either law or government. Without institutional restrictions on behavior there was perfect freedom. Hobbes refers to this life as the "state of nature." Yet at some point people decided to abandon this perfect freedom and live under the rules and restrictions of society. Why? That is because though there was perfect freedom there was no security. In the state of nature the prevailing mode of human intercourse was "the war of all against all," resulting in a life that was typically "nasty, brutish and short." If I enjoyed perfect freedom to kill you and take your food I stood under similar threat from you to do the same to me. At some point, Hobbes surmised, people decided to put an end to this dog-eat-dog existence by setting up a leader with the authority to enforce order.

Thus was born what Hobbes called "civil society" under what is now termed the "social contract." The Leviathan would protect the persons and properties of the citizenry and punish evildoers. In return the people would obey his laws. People would not be as absolutely free as before, but they would be more secure. They would enjoy general liberty to conduct their own affairs so long as they refrained from preying on others or disturbing societal order. It was an arrangement freely entered into, Hobbes felt, and unbreakable once formed.

So Hobbes taught that civilization required a bargain between people and government wherein citizens give up some freedom to do as they wish and live under legal authority in order to enjoy some security. The ruler enforces order and the people obey the laws. Once such a civil society is established, he believed, the bond is irrevocable. Thus was established the intellectual foundation of constitutional monarchy and liberty under law. It wasn't perfect but it was a start.

John Locke accepted the premises of Hobbes' argument for the necessity of giving up some freedom in exchange for security but came at the question from a little different angle. In his *Second Treatise of Government*, written in 1690, Locke asked some new questions. What interests would have been so essential to a people that they would have yielded some of their freedom of action in order to see that these were protected? Locke came up with three such interests, which he termed the "natural rights." He identified life, liberty and property as these three rights.

But where Hobbes saw submission to lawful authority a one-time event which bound people to obedience thereafter, Locke saw a reciprocal social contract. In his view the governmental authority was established to safeguard the three natural rights. The government was responsible for protecting the citizens' lives from foreign armies or murderers, their liberties from oppressors or kidnappers and their property from thieves. The citizens were obliged in return to obey laws against murder, kidnapping and thievery. Now if a citizen "broke the contract" and stole, then the government could rightfully take away that person's rights by imprisonment, for instance.

That was as far as Hobbes went. But Locke asked: what if the government was the one taking or failing to preserve its people's lives, oppressing their liberties or despoiling their property? In that case, he declared, it was the one breaking the contract and the people would have the right to replace it and establish a new one to better preserve their natural rights. Locke thus made the social contract mutual and reciprocal. The check on the people was to obey the law and the check on the government was to serve the people's interests.

Where Hobbes' one-sided social contract served as a justification for constitutional monarchy, Locke's formulation instead promoted liberal democracy as the preferred structure to protect liberty under law. That is liberal in the original sense of liberal meaning freedom, a democracy in which civil liberties are protected.

It is in the Lockean sense, of course, that the founding ethic of the United States was established. In the Declaration of Independence Thomas Jefferson echoes Locke in the "inalienable rights" of "life, liberty and the pursuit of happiness" and in holding that, "when a long train of abuses" has proven the government remiss in its part of the bargain that the citizens may of right, "erect new safeguards for their future security." In other words, they may change it or even overthrow it violently if there is no other recourse.

Thus we have the basis of social contract theory as introduced by Thomas Hobbes and further developed by John Locke. Their view of freedom under law, particularly in the case of Locke, with his "life, liberty and property" formulation of natural rights, restated by Jefferson as "life, liberty and the pursuit of happiness," was integral to the founding ethos of the United States.

As we look at the concept of freedom in action there are always gray areas and special considerations to take into account. For example, Jefferson's "freedom is not license" and, Justice Oliver Wendell Holmes' famous "freedom of speech does not give one the right to shout 'fire' in a crowded theater" exemplify the principle that it is inadmissible to exercise one's own rights by denying them to others.

That is why one person's right to enjoy loud music in the middle of the night gives way to his neighbor's right to enjoy quiet during normal sleeping hours. That is also why the property owner's right to the labor of his slaves was eventually overturned in favor of the rights of the slaves to their liberty. To liberals, the general principle is that human rights trump property rights.

These principles lie at the heart of many controversies in contemporary society. If the data show that talking on one's cell phone while driving is equivalent to driving drunk then do the people have the right to legally ban the practice? In other words, does the state's responsibility to protect the lives of its citizens carry greater weight than a driver's freedom to talk on a hand held phone, just as it does with the drunk's freedom to drive a car? I and most liberals would agree with the eighty percent of Americans who say yes, it does.

The same consideration is at the heart of environmental disputes. When a certain level of air pollution is shown to cause a certain number of cases of asthma, heart disease, stroke and the like, is there a point at which the need to protect people's lives and well-being outweighs the right of drivers, fireplace owners or industries to pollute the air without restriction? Of course it does. The question is where to draw the line.

Similarly, we maintain a military defense to protect citizens' lives against foreign enemies. The property right some might prefer to control all their money is superseded by the need to collect taxes to pay for this defense. Is it so much different to hold that the need to protect citizens' lives against disease is an issue of the same kind? It is difficult to see why one is accepted by practically all while the other is styled an alien concept by some. The under girding principle is the same, that the people acting together through the democratic process have the right and duty to protect the life, liberty and pursuit of happiness of society's members.

So let's sum up with a reminder of the reason government exists. In Western thought it is part of a social contract whereby the citizens institute an authority with the mandate to protect their natural rights, those of life, liberty and property, or their pursuit of happiness, to phrase it the way Thomas Jefferson expressed the third natural right. It is a compact in which the peace-loving and law-abiding seek security against the predatory and destructive.

We have seen that there are frequently tradeoffs to be made when conflicting liberties collide. It has long been recognized, for instance, that freedom of speech does not include the right to incite deadly panic and that property rights no longer confer an "owner" with the right to bind fellow human beings to unpaid service and deprive them of their liberty. One's freedoms become limited when they begin to detract from those of others. That is why liberals have a strong preference for the little guy, the downtrodden and the marginalized. So often they have been, and still are, unfairly preyed upon and exploited by the selfish, the powerful and the greedy.

The level of essential protection and necessary restraint is in the eye of the beholder. These are often questions to be determined by the political process. In the times of the Robber Barons of the late nineteenth century, for instance, a laissez-faire understanding of freedom meant that the strong and powerful had license to employ and house workers under appallingly unsafe and unsanitary conditions and to keep them in such penury that many felt forced to risk sending their young children into mines and factories to earn a few extra pennies a day. The rise of the Populist and Progressive movements, however, led to the adoption of child labor laws, building codes and the Pure Food and Drug Act of 1906. The "right" of the bosses to cruelly use their laborers and tenants and bilk consumers ran into the countervailing rights of life, liberty and the pursuit of happiness of their victims.

So it is today. We see extremists who hold that their right to property means the government has no authority to tax them. Others maintain they have a right to bring loaded firearms to political events. Others yet contend that while a national program to defend citizens' health and lives against foreign enemies is warranted a national program to defend citizens' health and lives against disease and infirmity is impermissible. And there are those who say that rights to things like fair trials with evidence must be dispensed with in certain cases to be determined by them.

These arguments are not new; there have been such since the early days of the republic. The boundaries have always been a bit fuzzy, and the voices of the extreme and the self-serving have usually been the loudest and always the better funded. Yet over time the advocates of decency have advanced nonetheless. As Dr. King put it, "The moral arc of the universe is long but it bends toward justice."

The liberal conception of freedom under law means people's right to autonomy in their own personal choices, under a government responsive and accountable to their will and subservient to the transcendent principles of justice. Freedom does not mean the right of the cruel and unscrupulous to take advantage of the honest and innocent. It does not mean the right of business owners to impose their religious or sexual views on their employees. Quite the contrary, it entails the right of the latter to defend themselves against the former. Liberals can always be counted on to support these principles as a matter of justice, and to advocate through the democratic process that they are similarly supported as a matter of law.

How did these liberal ideas originate? Secular thought: History, Facts and Reason

If I have seen further it is by standing on the shoulders of giants.

Isaac Newton

To see how the ideas that motivate liberalism came to be, you have to go back in history several centuries. The key societal development in the formation of the liberal view was the rise of the idea of individualism. In Europe, during the Middle Ages, people lived in a society that strongly repressed individualism. People were seen as part of an order of society. Those in the noble and religious orders had various rights and privileges. But the 97% who were commoners had no rights, only obligations and duties to perform in the service of their social superiors. Most people were ignorant rural peasants, un-free "serfs" bound to the land to perform manual labor for those born to the upper-class aristocracy.

For most people, life was hard, poverty-stricken and short. Their hope was directed to the afterlife. If they worked hard, kept quiet, obeyed their earthly "betters" and followed the prescriptions of the church, they might hope for happiness in the life to come, at least after they had put in a few centuries of atonement in purgatory. The idea was to keep the lower classes quiet, obedient, and hard at work taking care of the needs of the lords and the clergy. This strategy worked most of the time. On those occasions when it didn't and the peasantry got too vociferous or, at times, even rebelled, they were rapidly put back in place by the most vicious repression. Neither thumbscrew, the lash, the hangman's noose or burning at the stake were spared for those who dared question the ordained order of society and their assigned place in it.

Over time, food production improved and barbarian attacks lessened. Towns began to arise, providing opportunity for people who could escape from serfdom to go into crafts and trade and become their own bosses. Kings began to consolidate their political power, and in order to effectively administer their realms they needed trained and educated bureaucrats. This gave rise to the establishment of the first universities. Most of these began by concentrating on training the officials needed to run the bureaucracies of crown and church, but little by little the academic environment began to foster an atmosphere of discussion and the investigation of knowledge in a broader sense. A rising middle class paired with a rising level of education began producing that most dynamic of human conditions: a growing population of people thinking for themselves. And, as the defenders of the *status quo* would learn, there is nothing more dangerous to the maintenance of a class-based social system than that!

What followed was the dynamic period called the Renaissance. Renaissance is a French word meaning "rebirth," a term that aptly described a time when the growing practice of thinking for one's self led to an explosion in things like personal opportunity and creative and artistic expression. It was the rebirth of cities, trade, intellectual curiosity and art that had lain dormant since the fall of classical Greece and Rome. Great artists like Michelangelo, Raphael and Leonardo da Vinci painted and sculpted in a new style based on a strikingly beautiful realism that captured the individual personalities of their subjects. Think of Leonardo's "Mona Lisa" as an example. The developing tendencies toward personal initiative and creativity in trade and the arts spread to other walks of life. A new spirit of questioning and change had been unleashed.

Religious figures like Martin Luther began questioning the doctrines and infallibility of the church and scientists like Galileo began questioning ideas that had been handed down without proof for centuries. This new process of looking for evidence to determine the truth was a direct challenge to the old practice of accepting received wisdom based on the pronouncements of ancient scholars or the officially promulgated interpretation of ancient scripture. It was the forerunner of the scientific method and the spirit of questioning and testing to achieve progress that animates the liberal movement even today. Great dramatists like William Shakespeare explored humanistic themes emphasizing that people's destinies were in their own hands and that the human heart is the source of our greatest strength. Sick of fanatics fighting wars of religion, philosophical thinkers like Michel de Montaigne spread a view based on a humble acceptance of our own imperfections, tolerance for the views of others, and a skeptical and open-minded approach to learning from life, science and other cultures. This outlook began to displace dogmatism and raise suspicion against the acceptance of stubborn attempts by monarchs and the church to enforce conformity and adherence to the old ways and understandings.

The new spirit of inquiry spawned a Scientific Revolution. The old ideas that the Earth was flat and the center of the universe were proven wrong, and those who had tied their authority to the maintenance of such beliefs lost credibility. When Isaac Newton formulated the theory of gravity complete with calculations that completely explained the movements of the planets, the usefulness of reason became too clear to ignore. The universe operated according to natural laws. And if there were natural laws governing the physical universe might there not be such principles at work in human society as well?

The quest to find and develop this knowledge for the good of society was called The Enlightenment. Natural laws in physics equated to natural rights in society. People were already moving out of serfdom, exhibiting their intelligence and drive. The conviction grew that the old class system was faulty, that one person was intrinsically as good and deserved the same rights and opportunities as another. The concepts of liberty, equality, and a citizenry with a voice took root and bloomed. They led to the ideas of free speech, voting and a government responsible to those it governed. These are the founding principles of political liberalism and of America.

Economic liberalism took shape as political liberalism confronted the circumstances of modern industrial society. The Scientific Revolution of the 1600s and 1700s began to drastically transform society in the 1800s. It produced tremendous technological advances-factory machinery, the steam engine, steam boats and railroads to name a few-that spawned a new industrial economy and a new urban way of life. A vast gap opened between the few wealthy industrial and commercial magnates and an enormous new class of wage workers. Although this mechanization produced goods in previously unimaginable quantities it drove hordes of hand crafters out of business and obliged them to enter the factory economy. In many ways they were forced into an existence similar to that suffered by the serfs of medieval times. They typically worked 12 to 16 hours a day, six days a week for a dollar a day. They lived in firetrap tenements without running water or sewage systems.

The working people wanted a bigger share of the profits they were generating for their employers and to get this they wanted freedom. They wanted freedoms like the right to vote, the right to form unions to bargain for things like reasonable pay, humane hours, safe conditions and benefits. They wanted their elected representatives to have the authority to establish legal requirements like reasonable housing codes, minimum wages and workplace protections. They sought public benefits like schools for their children, clean water supplies, paved streets, city transportation systems, pure food inspection, and old-age retirement assistance. They were fought every step of the way as they pursued these goals. Conservatives argued that if they couldn't afford these things for themselves they didn't deserve to have them. Liberals countered that providing decent and humane standards of living for all is one of the cardinal purposes of society and of a government responsive to the people, the whole people.

The liberal movement was joined by people motivated by compassion, faith, peace and hard-headed realism. Scientists, social scientists, educators, economists, civil libertarians and criminologists joined after seeing that the liberal perspective was the one that best fostered freedom and equality in society. They also joined because they saw from the statistical or historical record that liberal policies produced the best results: a stronger economy, longer life spans, and a happier nation.

One after another, the roadblocks have fallen. Liberals have overcome conservative efforts to restrict rights by race and sex, to repress union organizing with armed force, to subject workers to hazardous working conditions and provide hazardous products to consumers without restriction. They have had to struggle endlessly with those who maintain that the pre-eminent purpose of government is to safeguard the wealth of the wealthy and make sure their taxes are low. Liberals believe that in order to have a thriving society there are basic necessities and basic opportunities that must be provided and funded, and that taxes on the well-off must be sufficient to make these investments a reality. As Franklin Roosevelt said:

There have always been those who did not believe in the people, who attempted to block their forward movement across history, to force them back to servility and suffering and silence. The people have now gathered their strength. They are moving forward in their might and power--and no force, no combination of forces, no trickery, deceit, or violence, can stop them now. They see before them the hope of the world--a decent, secure, peaceful life for men everywhere.

Famous Liberal Thinkers and Doers

But if by a "Liberal" they mean someone who looks ahead and not behind, someone who welcomes new ideas without rigid reactions, someone who cares about the welfare of the people -- their health, their housing, their schools, their jobs, their civil rights, and their civil liberties -- someone who believes we can break through the stalemate and suspicions that grip us in our policies abroad, if that is what they mean by a "Liberal," then I'm proud to say I'm a "Liberal."

John F. Kennedy

Here are some of my personal favorites among those who have contributed to a more just, humane and reasonable world down through the ages. All of them have made a difference and furthered the values of liberalism. Any list of liberal giants is bound to be incomplete; I am sure the reader can come up with many more. Here is mine, in order from most ancient to most recent.

Thales is credited with initiating the idea that the world works according to rational principles.

Socrates originated the concept that the road to excellence proceeds along the path of questioning accepted ideas.

Plato taught that we should strive toward the ideal in all our endeavors. He believed that people could intentionally improve human society through education and deliberative community choice.

Aristotle formalized logic and emphasized the systematic development of knowledge.

Jesus, Mohammed, Maimonides and *Buddha* all taught ethical spirituality based on compassion for others.

Galileo Galilei withstood persecution and torture in defense of reality-based science against the demands of imposed dogma.

Michel de Montaigne stressed humility, tolerance and an open mind as the keys to social peace and progress.

William Shakespeare taught that our destiny is in our own hands. "The fault, dear Brutus, is not in our stars, but in ourselves."

Thomas Jefferson wrote history's greatest defense of freedom and encapsulation of liberty under law in the Declaration of Independence.

Alexander Hamilton spurred the writing of the Constitution and successfully made the case for a strong, proactive and unified American government.

Edwin Chadwick pioneered enlightened public action to improve the lives of the poor in England through reform of the Poor Law and the implementation of the Sanitary Commission.

William Lloyd Garrison uncompromisingly attacked American slavery through his publication *The Liberator*.

Susan B. Anthony made the constitutional case that American women were entitled to the right to vote.

Dorothea Dix initiated the movement that led to humane, science-based mental institutional care in the United States.

Abraham Lincoln emancipated the slaves, preserved the Union and showed that liberal government could further the prosperity of the people through such innovations as the Homestead Act and the Morrill Land Grant College Act.

Samuel Gompers led the establishment of America's first successful labor union organization, the American Federation of Labor, ushering in an era that would transform the standard of living of the American people.

Robert La Follette was the first to implement a fully liberal program as Wisconsin Governor from 1901 to 1906, including the minimum wage, workers' compensation, women's suffrage, progressive taxation, open government and protections against corporate power.

Theodore Roosevelt as president used the Sherman Antitrust Act to break up monopolies, started the environmental movement by protecting two and a half million acres in monuments and parks and another 148 million acres as national forests, and approved many consumer protections such as the Pure Food and Drug Act.

John Dewey was a lifelong innovator in education, leading the movement away from rote to hands-on experiential learning, and stood as an uncompromising advocate for an open-minded, free-thinking democratic society.

Woodrow Wilson passed the greatest liberal reform package up to his time. His "New Freedom" agenda included a graduated income tax, 8-hour workday, anti-monopoly and union rights under the Clayton Antitrust Act, the Federal Reserve and the first child labor protections. He belatedly but decisively gave his support to the at-long-last successful campaign for women's voting rights.

Franklin Roosevelt did more than any U.S. President to ensure that average Americans benefited more fairly from the hard work they did in building up the nation. His "New Deal" provided millions of jobs and saved the country from the Great Depression, established minimum wages, fostered union protections and brought electricity to the nation. His Social Security program ended the destitution of old age and provided relief for the disabled and unemployed. His G.I. Bill repaid millions for their service and revolutionized college education in America. The result was the creation of the largest and most prosperous middle class in world history.

John Maynard Keynes was the British economist who showed how to get out of a recession or depression by increasing government spending to make up for the shortfall in the private sector. Such "countercyclical" spending was successfully used in ending America's Great Depression and in innumerable cases around the world since.

Harry Truman pushed Congress for a civil rights bill. When it failed to act, he courageously desegregated the U.S. Armed Forces by Presidential Order, even though it appeared to be an act of political suicide. Campaigning as a strong defender of equality and the New Deal, he confounded expectations and won re-election.

Earl Warren won over his colleagues on the Supreme Court to achieve a unanimous decision in the *Brown v. Topeka* case of 1954, which declared racial segregation in the schools unconstitutional.

Martin Luther King, Jr. combined steadfast faith, inspiring oratory and nonviolent resistance in leading the Civil Rights Movement to triumph over the legacy of racism. One of the truly great men of the last millennium, he died a martyr to the causes of justice and equality.

John F. Kennedy inspired a nation to achievement and service with initiatives such as the space program and Peace Corps. His Inaugural Address and definition of liberalism stand as unsurpassed explications of the liberal ethos.

Mother Teresa reminded a fractious world through a life of service that every human being deserves love and care, even the homeless, the destitute and the forgotten.

Lyndon Johnson advanced social justice immensely through his "Great Society" measures, including the Civil Rights Act, Voting Rights Act, Head Start, Office of Economic Opportunity and Medicare.

Nelson Mandela exemplified through his life's story his irrepressible thirst for freedom and unconquerable spirit in the face of injustice. As President of South Africa he then used the power of love and forgiveness to effect reconciliation between former enemies. His path shows that doing the good thing is also doing the right thing.

Harvey Milk became the face of gay rights in America. The first prominent openly gay public official was elected County Supervisor in San Francisco and then tragically murdered within a year of being sworn in. By urging LGBT Americans to come out of the closet, he showed straight Americans that gays and lesbians were their children, co-workers and friends. He thus began the human side of the process that now sees equality sweeping the nation.

Barack Obama passed the Affordable Care Act to begin the path toward the security of universal medical coverage in America. He expanded civil rights by passing equal pay legislation for women and ending discrimination against sexual orientation in the military. His encouragement and support helped marriage equality spread across the nation during his tenure. The passage of his stimulus package helped avert a second Great Depression, saved the American auto industry and spurred the most rapid expansion of green energy in American history.

Elizabeth Warren stands as a tireless advocate for the rights and needs of regular Americans. She successfully lobbied for a Consumer Financial Protection Bureau in the Obama administration to defend people against manipulative and predatory bank and credit card practices. Elected to the U.S. Senate from Massachusetts in 2012, in the true liberal tradition she remains a thorn in the side of crony capitalism and a powerful fighter for a fair shake for the 99 percent.

Religious Thought

My Christian religious faith is a big part of my liberalism. Much of my own liberal transformation came from my growing conviction that liberal perspectives were in accord with the ethics and behaviors Jesus taught and demonstrated throughout his life. As we have seen in the preceding pages, you can also think your way to liberalism, and many atheist and agnostic people do. I don't have a problem with that, and indeed feel liberalism is quite justifiable and supportable on rational and philosophical grounds quite apart from the religious angle. In my case, I find the rational support for the liberal case can either stand on its own or serve as a powerful multiplier. The clear economic and social success of liberal ideas and policies was the other part of the equation in my own acceptance and adoption of liberalism. I discuss the reasoning behind this in Chapter 4. It makes complete sense to me to use both faith and reason, since my concept of God is in complete accord with the idea that a perfect, loving, omnipotent divinity would at the same time be logical and make sense. If you have religious dictums and teachings that hold certain things that are consistently disproved by real world experience, then that raises some rather serious issues about your theology. Faith and reason ought to be complementary.

I am a Christian, and I see the basic message of Christianity, that is to say, Jesus' message, as profoundly liberal in the modern American sense of the term. Make no mistake, I do not for a moment believe that if Jesus came back today he would belong to a political party or run for office. His focus and mission were not political; they were spiritual. "My kingdom is not of this world," he said.

Yet even so, we as concerned humans and as citizens are called upon to operate in the world. In doing so, we are each guided by our world view. Our morals, ethics, ways of thinking, upbringing and experience all go into forming what that world view is. And if we have a religious persuasion, it will certainly play a strong role. Mine certainly does. And my sense of the Christian message is that it deeply supports a liberal social and political worldview. That is because it calls upon the believer to live in service to society as a whole, and especially those in need, rather than to be solely self-serving. And of course there is no finer example of this than the life of Jesus himself.

I know, a lot of right-wingers say they base their political views on their Christian beliefs. I just wonder whether they have ever actually looked at the Gospels when they say something like that. Jesus advocated a radically liberal social welfare program. He commanded his followers to heal the sick, feed the hungry and help the poor in every way possible. He wasn't materialistic. He advised one questioner, "If you would be perfect, sell all you have, give to the poor, and come, follow me." He wasn't militaristic, saying, "They who take up the sword shall perish by it," and, "Blessed are the peacemakers; they shall be called sons of God." He told his disciples to forgive "seventy times seven" rather than avenge. He was no respecter of the social pecking order of his day. The poor widow who put two pennies in the collection was worthier than the rich man who contributed a large sum because "she gave all she had." This social message was to be the result of a change of heart. The punctilious, legally observant religious scribes were not his model of conduct. They aridly followed the letter of the rules but their hearts were not engaged. "Do unto others as you would have others do unto you," since known as the "Golden Rule" was his defining moral standard. "Love your neighbor as yourself," was its encapsulation, as love itself was its foundation. To, "Love God and love your neighbor as yourself" would, as he stated, be to fulfill the whole of the law and all the commandments.

Perhaps most illustrative of Christian social morality as explained by Jesus himself is found in the Gospel of Matthew, chapter 25 verses 34-40. From the New International Version:

"Then the King will say to those on his right, 'Come, you who are blessed by my Father; take your inheritance, the kingdom prepared for you since the creation of the world. For I was hungry and you gave me something to eat, I was thirsty and you gave me something to drink, I was a stranger and you invited me in, I

needed clothes and you clothed me, I was sick and you looked after me, I was in prison and you came to visit me.'

"Then the righteous will answer him, 'Lord, when did we see you hungry and feed you, or thirsty and give you something to drink? When did we see you a stranger and invite you in, or needing clothes and clothe you? When did we see you sick or in prison and go to visit you?'

"The King will reply, 'Truly I tell you, whatever you did for one of the least of these brothers and sisters of mine, you did for me.'

Jesus lived the message he preached. He was constantly among the poor, the unequal, and the sick. He spent most of his public ministry taking care of people's human needs. He healed all who sought his aid, always without charge. He provided food for the hungry, sometimes for thousands at a time, again without charge. He fought against the rampant commercialization of religion, overturning the stalls of the vendors and money changers at the Temple. He spoke out for better treatment for workers, for gleaners, for foreign immigrants (strangers), for widows, in short, for all the poor and needy. He hung around more with prostitutes and thieves than with the well-born and the rich, against whom he told parable after parable, warning them of the judgment they faced for failing to improve the lot of the needy. He corrected those who maintained that misfortune in this life is deserved and a result of divine punishment, frequently correcting this view with regard to illness and then again in the case of accident when a tower fell in the town of Siloam, taking many lives. He famously told people to pay their taxes, using the example of a coin bearing the Roman Emperor's face to enjoin his listeners to, "render therefore unto Caesar the things which are Caesar's and unto God the things that are God's." For Jesus, human needs always took precedence over ritual obligation. He was always in trouble with the authorities for healing or feeding people on the Sabbath, a day when legalisms forbade any labor. "The Sabbath was made for man, not man for the Sabbath," he stated. Then Jesus said to them,

"I ask you, which is lawful on the Sabbath: to do good, or to do evil, to save life or to destroy it?" He cut through the legalistic foolishness by concluding, "Therefore, it is lawful to do good on the Sabbath."

From a moral and political sense these questions are more than mere dry controversies from twenty centuries ago. They go to the very heart of much that animates present American debate. In a country where belief in God is very high (92%, according to the Gallup Poll in 2011, including 85% of liberals) and much of that identifies itself as Christian belief (78.4% of all Americans, according to a 2013 Pew Poll), the Christian right has attempted to seize the mantle of the moral high ground as the true bringers of Jesus' political and social message. This they do, of the very Jesus who said to give to all in need and to all who ask, and to do so without thought of recompense. Let's look at the supreme irony of their position.

The Christian right and its allied political conservatives rail against help for the poor, yet the Lord they claim to worship constantly gave help to the poor himself and commanded time and again that his followers do likewise. Conservative Evangelicals were among the most prominent advocates who launched the frenzied and ridiculously exaggerated campaign against a national health care plan, even though Jesus himself healed all comers, commissioned his disciples to do the same, and told his followers to "heal the sick." They overwhelmingly supported a candidate for president, Mitt Romney in 2012, who ran on a platform against universal health care even though he had implemented it in his own state, claiming that what was good on a state level was evil on a national level, all remindful of how the Pharisees tried to maintain that healing people on a Tuesday was fine but on a Sabbath day a sin. Many of these same Christian rightists champion unrestricted and increasingly lethal weapons in society and aggressive wars around the world, despite the fact that the founder of the faith they claim to espouse wholly rejected both. They turn apoplectic at the idea of taxes to raise money to help ameliorate the injustices and serve the needs of society, when Jesus himself said to pay them. For years they have denigrated immigrants and stood in the way of accepting them into society, when Jesus said to welcome the stranger and assured that the worker was worth his pay. They have fought against equality first for racial minorities, then for women, and even now today for women, gays and lesbians, and this despite the egalitarian New Testament injunction that "all are one in Christ Jesus." It is a strange logic of the Evangelical political right that purports to follow the ethical precepts of Jesus Christ and incorporate them into American political issues but does so by siding against what he actually had to say on the matters in question.

I recently saw a post on *Facebook*; it consisted of two pictures side by side: a Holy Bible and a rifle. The message read, "Like and share if you support both!" Someone who has actually read the New Testament and thought about it for more than a minute or two realizes the inherent contradiction there. When he spoke of war, weapons and killing Jesus was crystal clear. "They who pick up the sword shall perish by it." "Blessed are the peacemakers." "Turn the other cheek." "Love your enemies and pray for those who persecute you." Conflating the Holy Bible and a lethal weapon as if the only choice is to support both or oppose both (If you're not for guns you're not a good Christian) is simply ignorant. The attitude of the religious gun lover is far more cultural than religious. Those who are thoughtful and support the rifle in addition to the Bible do so as a necessary evil, believing Christ's pacifistic injunctions to be lofty though unrealistic ideals in a sometimes unfortunately dangerous world, not as something to enthusiastically celebrate.

To take the matter a bit further, Christianity is not the only religion concerned with social and economic justice. There is a rich tradition along the same lines in all the major faiths, including for instance Judaism, Islam, Hinduism, Taoism and Buddhism. All enjoin believers to treat others honestly and fairly, protect the vulnerable and innocent, help the needy and liberate the oppressed.

All have a counterpart to the Christian Golden Rule, instructing followers to treat others as one wishes to be treated. All demand an active engagement in working to make the community a better place for all its members; none says to stand aside and let "the market" decide who has to wallow in misery, and none says it is evil for people in a democratic society to insist that their government actively supports these principles by setting up policies and programs that actually help people. The world's spiritual traditions form a great source of strength and provide a solid moral foundation for untold millions of religious liberals.

To close this section I'd like to encourage you to engage in some personal reflection. If you belong to a liberal religious group or have your own liberal religious perspective, what role does your own religious belief play in your approach to liberalism? Does it change how you see certain issues? Which issues, and in what ways? Do your religious beliefs play a part in how you prioritize which issues are most important to you? Do you feel motivated to make a difference in helping people or furthering solutions to these issues? Consider how you might be able to translate your calling into action.

Quotes from Famous Religious Liberals

Human rights are not only violated by terrorism, repression or assassination, but also by unfair economic structures that create huge inequalities.

Pope Francis

A nation that continues year after year to spend more money on military defense than on programs of social uplift is approaching spiritual doom.

Martin Luther King, Jr.

We are prophetic interrogators. Why are so many people hungry? Why are so many people and families in our shelters?

Why do we have one of six of our children poor, and one of three of these are children of color? 'Why?' is the prophetic question.

Jim Wallis

Love and compassion are necessities, not luxuries. Without them humanity cannot survive.

Dalai Lama

The nonviolent technique does not depend for its success on the goodwill of the oppressor, but on the unfailing assistance of God.

Cesar Chavez

We must restore hope to young people, help the old, be open to the future, spread love. Be poor among the poor. We need to include the excluded and preach peace.

Pope Francis

None of you will have faith till he wishes for his brother what he likes for himself.

Prophet Mohammed

We spoke out, committed civil disobedience, and went to jail because the peace hangs senselessly and precariously upon weapons costing billions to build and billions to improve — weapons which become more useless as we add to their destructive force. With this money we could have fed the world's people. Half the children on earth go to bed hungry — millions more have retarding and stunting protein deficiencies. Instead of building the peace by attacking injustices like starvation, disease, illiteracy, political and economic servitude, we spend a trillion dollars on war since 1946, until hatred and conflict have become the international preoccupation.

Father Daniel Berrigan

However many holy words you read, however many you speak, what good will they do you if you do not act upon them?

Buddha

The Seven Deadly Sins are: Wealth without work, Pleasure without conscience, Science without humanity, Knowledge without character, Politics without principle, Commerce without morality, Worship without sacrifice.

Mohandas K. Gandhi

CHAPTER 6:
Human Rights

"Power concedes nothing without a demand. It never did and it never will. Find out just what any people will quietly submit to and you have found out the exact measure of injustice and wrong which will be imposed upon them, and these will continue till they are resisted with either words or blows, or both. The limits of tyrants are prescribed by the endurance of those whom they oppress."

Frederick Douglass

Does it bother you when you hear someone say gay people shouldn't be allowed to get married or adopt children? That somebody who was brought to America from a foreign country by their parents as an infant and can remember no other home should be deported to that foreign country?

That it's OK to deny people medical care if they are too poor to afford it?

That demonstrators can only exercise free speech in fenced, restricted areas designated and kept under surveillance by the police?

That companies can be allowed to hide things in fine print that let them share your personal information and commit you to things you are not aware you are agreeing to?

That kids from wealthy neighborhoods in your area go to modern, well-equipped schools while kids from poorer areas go to ramshackle, poorly-equipped schools?

That it's all right to torture a suspect if someone thinks they might be a terrorist?

That women, on average, still earn only 77% of what men earn doing the same job with the same number of years of experience and similar performance evaluations?

If your consistent answer to these questions is yes, you are likely a liberal. Liberals have always been in the forefront of extending and expanding human rights because liberals are imbued with a set of principles that promote freedom. These principles include equality, fairness, personal autonomy, security, community, and a priority system that places human needs first because it is infused with empathy.

Equality

Liberals believe in equality before the law, and they believe it for real rather than just paying lip service to the concept. The Declaration of Independence famously states, "We hold these truths to be self-evident, that all men are created equal…" Liberals like Abraham Lincoln believed that meant slavery was inconsistent with the principles of freedom. "No man is good enough to govern another man, without that man's consent," he said. Conservatives looked for reasons to create exceptions. Surely, they felt, equality, though a good concept for white, Christian, property-owning men, could not apply to blacks, people of other non-Caucasian races, slaves, Jews, Hindus, women and the landless. All couldn't really mean "all," could it?

The Fourteenth Amendment avows, "No State shall…deny to any person within its jurisdiction the equal protection of the laws." Liberals like Elizabeth Cady Stanton believed that meant women, as well as men, deserved the right to vote. It took 72 years and a constitutional amendment, the Nineteenth, to accomplish that. Some, such as conservative Supreme Court Associate Justice Antonin Scalia, still don't think the equal protection clause of the Fourteenth Amendment requires equal rights for women. Here is what he said about it: "In 1868, when the 39th Congress was debating and ultimately proposing the 14th Amendment, I don't think anybody would have thought that equal protection applied to sex discrimination, or certainly not to sexual orientation. So does that mean that we've gone off in error by applying the 14th Amendment to both? Yes, yes. Sorry, to tell you that." So, we still have people, even prominent ones, looking for reasons to deny equal rights.

Liberals, on the other hand, take the wording at face value. No one can be denied equal rights, period. In proposing legislation to end the racial discrimination against African-Americans in his day, President John F. Kennedy observed, "We are confronted primarily with a moral issue." Kennedy based his views on strong sources. Where should we search for the right answer to this issue? He said, "It is as old as the Scriptures and is as clear as the American Constitution. The heart of the question is whether all Americans are to be afforded equal rights and equal opportunities, whether we are going to treat our fellow Americans as we want to be treated." His answer, based on both, was an emphatic "Yes!" Modern liberals are proud to emphatically agree.

The uncompromising liberal view of equality has therefore been applied in a wider and wider circle over the centuries. The principle was clearly enunciated in the beginning of the country, but was not realized in many people's daily lives. The pursuit of the dream to bring Jefferson's words to fruition continues in our own time, concentrating now most urgently on the LGBT community. This unfinished work shows liberalism at its best. Carved over the entrance to the Supreme Court building are the words "EQUAL JUSTICE UNDER LAW." The views of certain retrograde Associate Justices notwithstanding, that is what liberals continue to strive for.

Fairness

Liberals also support human rights because of an innate sense of fairness. Liberals understand that legal equality does not mean equality of condition or results. Some people will always be wealthier or smarter, some are good artists or athletes and others are not. Not every student who applies will get accepted for enrollment into the college of their choice. But what liberals really want to foster is a society where everyone has an equal opportunity to try, and a fair chance to acquire the tools for success.

That's why liberals always fight so hard to get better funding for poorer school districts, or poorer areas within a school district. That's why they are in favor of keeping college tuition as low as possible, with plenty of scholarship help available. The statistics strongly show that kids from poorer families and families in which English is not the primary language do worse in school, have lower graduation rates, lower college attendance and graduation rates and lower lifetime incomes. They also have higher incidences of unwed pregnancies, incarceration, chronic health problems and shorter life expectancies. Part of the reason liberals are concerned and want to do something about these problems comes from empathy and compassion. It doesn't feel right to send kids into the struggle of life with two strikes against them due to the financial conditions of their parents. The other reason is pragmatic. If equalizing school funding will help reduce crime, the dropout rate, the prison population, health care costs and result in more qualified students going to college and becoming successful members of the middle class, liberals wonder why would anyone not want to do it?

The fairness issue goes beyond this to many facets of life and policy. It's why liberals favor a graduated income tax rather than the "flat tax" idea wealthy conservatives push. In the early twentieth century Liberals and Progressives, including Republicans and Democrats, passed the Sixteenth Amendment authorizing a federal income tax. The principle was to make wealthier folks pay a higher rate of tax, based on the idea that first, they could afford it better, and second, they benefit more from what the taxes buy.

How so? Why not collect everything from, say, a sales tax, where everyone would pay the same percentage? Well, the poor have to spend just about everything they earn just to get by.Rent, groceries and the essentials of life take up almost the entire income. So the poor would pay taxes on everything they earn. The wealthy have a bigger cushion. They don't spend all their income, so they would not have to pay taxes on the part they invest or put away for things like college and retirement, things the poor person can scarcely do. The rich also benefit more from the services government provides. Police and fire protection guard the tycoon's mansion, worth millions, from harm, conferring a much greater benefit than the same service provided to the average person's humble house or apartment. Consider also that the same city street is worth different amounts to different interests. Suppose a bank teller needs the street to get to work, and makes $30,000 a year. Without the street this worker couldn't get to the job, costing him or her $30,000 in earnings. But the same street is worth a lot more to the bank. Suppose the bank has 1,000 customers and $50,000,000 on deposit. If the city doesn't keep the street up and customers can't get to the bank, they will likely take their deposits somewhere else. The street, maintained at taxpayer expense, is worth $30,000 to the teller but $50,000,000 to the bank owner. Is it fair to assess them the same amount for its upkeep? Based on their relative abilities to pay and the relative value they get back, the liberal would say, "Definitely not! That's not fair."

Personal Autonomy

Liberals place a high value on personal autonomy, the principle that people should have the right to decide most things about their lives for themselves. This pillar of freedom is the basis of a number of issues liberals have fought for and still fight for today. Some of these include freedom of conscience about religion and from an imposed religion, women's admission to college and to many career fields formerly restricted to men, the right to divorce, and reproductive rights such as to decide for one's self about contraception and abortion. It also applies to the liberal stance on consensual sexual relationships including the right to interracial and same-sex relationships and marriages.

It may seem hard to imagine, but all of these practices were at various times forbidden by those who wished to impose their social and moral views on others through the force of law. Freedom from state-sponsored religion was made unconstitutional in 1791 by the First Amendment's clause against any "establishment of religion." Even so, "blue laws" were passed in most states that restricted commerce or various activities like playing baseball on Sundays under the premise that people ought to be in church instead. Though most of these laws have been repealed, some still persist. In thirteen states, for example, it is illegal to buy or trade a car on a Sunday!

Women were completely excluded from higher education until 1837, when Mary Kellogg, Mary Caroline Rudd, Mary Hosford and Elizabeth Prall were the first women admitted in to Oberlin College in Ohio. Sixty-three years later, in 1900, most colleges still accepted only men, and just 2.8% of women went to college. As late as 1970 only 9% of college graduates were women. Today they constitute the majority of college graduates. This progress over time is not only a testament to the triumph of liberal egalitarian ideals over those who fought to keep women in their traditional subservient roles but also an example of what can happen when obstacles to personal autonomy are removed. Just think how much more vibrant every field of endeavor is today, with America making use of 100% of its brain power instead of only half!

The slow but inexorable movement of women into professions once limited to men is still going on. It began with secretaries and teachers, continued with police officers and firefighters and finally spread to doctors and corporate executives. The military is now about to open the combat arms to women volunteers. It's about time. Will some women wash out because they will prove unable to carry an 80-pound pack on a 25-mile hike? Doubtlessly so. Then weed them out on their inability to perform the physical demands of the job, not because they are women. There are some women who relish the challenge and *will* be able to do it, and our experience with law enforcement and firefighting tell us it will be more than many expect. Leave it up to equality and personal autonomy, the values America was founded on, and marvel at the results.

Bans on divorce or the requirement of an adversarial judicial process to determine "fault" were another vestige of the attitude that the state had an obligation to impose conditions on people's personal lives. It eventually became apparent to all but the most stubborn that trying to force people to stay in a marriage against their will was not working. Common sense and the principle of personal autonomy won out. Divorce laws were liberalized in the 1970s beginning with California, with the concept of no-fault divorce. An interesting statistic is the higher incidence of divorce in conservative-voting states and lower incidence in liberal-voting states. The Wall Street *Journal* conducted an analysis of census data and came to the conclusion that, "Overall, the report shows that people living in northeastern states have lower marriage and divorce rates. And while those in the southern states are more likely to get married, they also have higher divorce rates." It's ironic that the very same socially conservative states that trumpet their commitment to "family values" and tried to prevent easily obtained divorce are the very states whose citizens have been the ones to most utilize it.

Reproductive rights are another facet of personal autonomy. The Supreme Court, in the case *Griswold v. Connecticut* in 1965 struck down the state's authority to outlaw birth control, basing their ruling on the right to privacy. The Court extended that ruling in 1972, deciding in *Eisenstadt v. Baird* that Massachusetts could not deny access to birth control pills to single people. There was another big dust-up over the provision of birth control pills under President Obama's health care law. Conservatives and some religious organizations tried to make a case that people's employers and churches should get to decide whether they get access to contraception. The liberal view prevailed, as it should. Anybody is free to give advice, but the decision is up to the person involved, not their boss or church. That is what freedom is. If my boss is a Jehovah's Witness I should not be denied a blood transfusion I need because he doesn't believe in it. It's my life. I get to decide, not him. The famous case *Roe v. Wade* in 1973 held that a woman's right to an abortion in the first trimester of a pregnancy, until the fetus is viable, is also protected. The basic principle underlying all these, whether it is called privacy, personal autonomy or some other name, is that people are entitled to make their own decisions regarding these personal matters. They are nobody else's business.

The same idea holds true with liberals when the subject is personal relationships. Conservatives imposed and then fought to maintain controls on interracial and same-sex relationships for many years. Though most states had repealed or had never enacted anti-miscegenation (against racial mixing) laws, all the former slave states except Maryland still had them on their books when the Supreme Court ruled them invalid in the 1967 case *Loving v. Virginia*. At that time only 20% of Americans approved of interracial marriages according to the Gallup Poll. By 2011 the liberal view had largely swept the country, with 86% supportive of marriage between people of different races.

The same is momentously underway with regards to same-sex marriage equality, support for which has surged from 27% in the late 1970s to near 60% today. Acceptance of the principle of personal autonomy is largely behind this change, along with a better understanding that sexual orientation is biologically determined. The American Psychological Association, for instance, stopped categorizing homosexuality as a disorder back in 1975 and unanimously endorsed same sex marriage equity in 2011. With "Don't Ask Don't Tell" in the military repealed, marriage equality the law at the time of this writing in thirty-six states and the District of Columbia, and the Supreme Court having ruled the federal Defense of (straight only) Marriage Act unconstitutional in 2013, it now seems we are on the threshold of seeing the liberal position on this great human rights movement become universally enshrined across the land. This is a struggle in which liberals, as allies of the LGBT community, can take special pride. Once again, personal freedom is triumphing over age-old prejudice thanks to those who have stood up for human rights and fought the good fight.

The principle of personal autonomy has also played a part in other issues. One is the right to conscientiously object to military service during those periods when America has had a military draft. Another is the ongoing liberalization of marijuana laws in fifteen states, where possession is treated like a minor traffic infraction, or even full legalization, voted in by the electorate in Washington state and Colorado. The failure of the Eighteenth Amendment in trying to enforce the Prohibition of alcohol from 1918 to 1933 is probably the strongest example of the futility of unduly trying to restrict personal autonomy in this way. The basic liberal perspective on human rights is therefore to favor personal autonomy, limiting it primarily when an action harms or interferes with the rights of others.

Security

Liberals have an expanded idea of human rights that includes a reasonable level of security from the adversities of life. We feel it is part of the community's responsibility to its own members, a basic function of our democratic government, to afford protection and safety to people in time of need. To an extent, conservatives agree with us on some of the basic human rights such as freedom of speech and trial by jury. They are big on the freedoms "to" do this or that. They agree that government should protect people, but apparently only from military or criminal attack. Where we often part company is in our desire also to achieve some insurance and freedom "from" the negatives life can send our way, negatives like disaster, disease and unemployment.

Liberals have used government to provide security for people in many ways. Franklin Roosevelt got congress to pass the Social Security retirement program for senior citizens in 1935. Seniors went from the most to the least impoverished age group as a result. It provides a majority of their retirement income to 70% of American seniors, who earned it by paying into it their entire working lives. Social Security also provides survivor aid to orphans, disability assistance to those with handicaps and unemployment assistance. Medicaid, for the poor, and Medicare, which people also pay into while they work so it will be there when they reach 65, were passed in 1965 under Lyndon Johnson so that medical care to the needy and the elderly (over age 65) would be assured. Liberals tend to think of medical care as a human right. Everyone needs it at some time or other, but the working poor were not getting it with their employment. Among the elderly, only a very few could afford to pay the mounting medical bills of old age out of their own pockets or the inflated rates private insurers needed to charge the oldest and sickest members of society in order to make a profit.

Rather than leave the poor and elderly to sicken and die without hope, a liberal president and congress acted. Conservatives were mortified. Conservative icon and future President Ronald Reagan wailed, "It will be the end of freedom in America!" Instead, Social Security and Medicare remain the most popular and among the most effective federal programs ever instituted, saving, prolonging and improving the quality of millions of lives at a cost far below that provided by private insurers. Along with Medicaid, they strongly fit Abraham Lincoln's prescription, "The legitimate object of government, is to do for a community of people, whatever they need to have done, but cannot do, at all, or cannot, so well do, for themselves in their separate, and individual capacities." People's retirement and health security are every bit as important to them as security against fire, flood, crime or military attack. They are essential for life, and are necessities people cannot so well secure on their own. So, just as firefighters, flood control, police and armed forces are part of securing human rights, so are making sure society's health needs are met. That's how liberals see it.

We collectively take action as a society to insure ourselves in innumerable ways against harm. Think of air and water quality controls, meat inspection, weather satellites, the air traffic control system, workplace health and safety regulations, car, plane, bus and ship safety requirements, inoculations against illnesses, engineering requirements and inspections for roads and bridges, residential and commercial building standards, and the testing of drugs, medicines, toys and consumer goods of all sorts. Would you like to see any of these protections curtailed? Liberals support these efforts to provide security for public health and safety.

Community and Putting People First.

A sense of community is a core liberal value. It is based on, as President Barack Obama is fond of saying, "We are not a red America and a blue America; we are one United States of America." Bill Clinton likes to say, "We believe that 'we're all in this together' is a better philosophy than, 'you're on your own.'" Or, as Martin Luther King put it, "We may have all come on different ships but we're in the same boat now."

The impulse to put people and their needs first is a liberal imperative. Dr. King said, "Whatever affects one directly affects all indirectly. I can never be what I ought to be until you are what you ought to be. This is the interrelated structure of reality." The liberal heart cannot stand idly by in the face of human suffering, want and need. Franklin Roosevelt electrified the nation in the depths of the Great Depression by promising to *do something* about poverty and unemployment. In his Inaugural Address he affirmed, "This nation asks for action, and action now!" He promised to give it to them, making the people's government their partner in recovery in a New Deal that would directly create the jobs they needed. He inspired confidence with his ringing exclamation against his predecessor and those minds shackled by ideology and inertia, those too timid to act, when he assured the American people, "The only thing we have to fear is fear itself." Afterward, these bold words were backed up by programs that put millions of Americans to work and ended the Great Depression.

Liberals do not believe the responsibilities of the people's government end with defending the frontiers, arresting lawbreakers and enforcing contracts. To ignore solvable problems and preventable human suffering is intolerable to liberals, because to us, human needs come first. An ideology based on what size government ought to be is nonsense to a liberal. It ought to be whatever size it needs to be to fix those problems the people need fixed and cannot fix so well in their individual capacities. When the flood waters rise, the fire spreads or the epidemic grows people need help, not ideologies. Liberals want to make sure that help is there.

Where do these impulses come from? Liberals are attracted to the insight of the English philosopher Jeremy Bentham, who wrote, "The greatest happiness of the greatest number is the foundation of morals and legislation." In the spiritual realm, Jesus of Nazareth commanded, "Do unto others as you would have others do unto you." Mohammed echoed this in Islam. The Qu'ran states, "No one of you believes until he loves for his brother what he loves for himself." The wellspring of all these statements is empathy, the ability to place one's self in another's shoes and want what is best for that person. All politicians pay lip service to this quality. How else could they get people to vote for them? But to real liberals it is not something that has to be affected; it is part of their core.

The Affordable Care Act is a fine example of values reinforcing practicality. Liberals believe it is immoral to deny human beings a basic necessity like health care. Obamacare saves not only lives but also money compared to the previous system. Liberals supported even more effective measures, such as giving the government stronger authority to use its massive purchasing power to negotiate lower drug costs from manufacturers, and by having a "public option" insurance plan as an alternative to those provided by for-profit companies to put some real competition into the mix. Unfortunately, Representatives beholden to the pharmaceutical and insurance industries managed to defeat those provisions, but the Act even still is a major step forward for the American people, some 15 million of whom became insured in its first year of operation and some 32 million of whom will eventually added to the rolls of the insured through its provisions.

These principles underlie the many other liberal positions on human rights. For community and "people first" reasons, liberals look at education as a human right, not a privilege. They believe small rural communities deserve clean water supplies as much as large urban ones do. It's why they support the Violence Against Women Act, fight so hard against human trafficking and predatory clergy, make a big deal out of bullying, and call out demeaning and derogatory speech. Some conservatives decry this as unwarranted "political correctness," as though insulting people and battering women are positive goods that need to be protected. Liberals remember that the basis of political correctness is empathy for the feelings of other human beings. You don't use racial slurs and epithets. You don't go to the synagogue and tell jokes about the Holocaust. It's a form of bullying and fails the test of treating others the way one would like to be treated.

The same goes for voting as a human right. It is the foundational right upon which democracy itself stands or falls. Liberals are consistently for making it as easy as possible, such as by encouraging voting by mail and making early voting widely available. Conservatives, on the other hand, continue to raise obstacles and make it more difficult, following their age-old practice of trying to restrict voting to "the better sort of (wealthier) people." It is nothing but a sham designed to exclude liberal voters from the polls. The first priority should be to facilitate people exercising their right to vote. A secondary concern is to guard against fraud, which the actual facts show to be extremely rare. If they are truly worried about this, I have often thought the way to go about it is to require the state to provide people with an ID card, at its trouble and expense, not the citizen's. Most people in states with these requirements just use their state-issued driver's license, but those without a driver's license tend to be older folks who no longer drive and poorer people who have no car. These are precisely the people for whom going through a lot of expense and trouble like taking time off from work, finding a bus or hiring a cab is a real impediment to exercising their right to cast a vote.

Liberal opposition to the awful 2010 Supreme Court ruling *Citizens United v. Federal Election Commission* is also about human rights and putting people first. The idea of declaring an entity like a corporation a "person" and allowing it to electioneer with unlimited and anonymous funding is a perilous step indeed. This ruling on a razor-thin 5-4 vote by the Court's conservative majority overturned forty years of sensible limitations imposed and agreed upon by both parties in the wake of the outrageous Watergate corruption scandals of the 1970s. Liberals oppose this egregious miscarriage of justice and support overturning this decision. The people of Montana, Colorado, the legislatures of 16 states, and the councils of dozens of cities across the country have voted against it.

Hillary Clinton's longstanding public practice stands as a good example of the liberal imperative to keep an unerring focus on human rights. I invite you to go to the liberal website *Daily Kos* at (http://www.dailykos.com/story/2013/10/18/1248523/. You won't see Hillary Clinton in the same light ever-again#. There you will find a 2013 article scratching the surface about the tremendous difference Hillary Clinton has made in the world over the past couple of decades since she went to China as first lady and raised a diplomatic stir when she spoke out for women, saying, "Women's rights are human rights." In it, actress Meryl Streep introduces Clinton and calls attention to the consistent advocacy she has done as a matter of course as first lady, senator and secretary of state. The site also includes video segments from Streep and Clinton.

Because of her efforts to call attention to courageous individuals who have stood against their governments, many of those individuals are alive who would not otherwise be, such as Nobel Peace Prize winner Aung San Suu Kyi of Burma. Her efforts on behalf of education, voting rights, small business ownership, and protection against female sexual mutilation and rape have made a difference in many places around the world. Studies again and again have demonstrated that societies that empower women are more prosperous, peaceful and free.

Often times, changing societal perspectives can be even more important than enacting policy, passing legislation or negotiating a treaty. When attitudes evolve, the legal changes become possible. Witness our own history about extending rights in the examples of slavery, women's suffrage, racial segregation and marriage equality. The movement of minds was the necessary precursor to the progress made in every case. And most often, the movement of minds happens after hearts are changed first. That and her own personal conduct have been the foundations of Mrs. Clinton's contributions over these years.

To sum up, whatever the issue, you can always count on liberals to support communities and put the needs of people first. Liberals value human rights, including equality, fairness, personal autonomy, security and community for their own sake. The underlying principles behind this stance are a firm belief in those rights, compassionate empathy, a practical approach and the courage to pursue justice in the face of selfish and self-interested power. As Martin Luther King taught us, "We must rapidly begin the shift from a 'thing'-oriented society to a 'person'-oriented society. When machines and computers, profit motives and property rights are considered more important than people, the giant triplets of racism, materialism and militarism are incapable (of) being conquered."

CHAPTER 7:
The Economy

"There are those who believe that if you just legislate to make the well-to-do prosperous, this prosperity will leak through on those below. The Democratic idea has been that if you legislate to make the masses prosperous their prosperity will find its way up and through every class which rests upon them."

William Jennings Bryan

There is no clearer barometer for the effectiveness of liberal ideas than the American economy. Just look at private sector job creation. From 1961 to 2013 Republican presidents governed for 28 years, and in that time the economy produced 24 million private sector jobs. In that same period Democratic presidents governed for 26 years and the economy generated 46.7 million private sector jobs. That's 857,000 new jobs a year under Republicans and 1,796,000 a year, more than twice as many, under Democrats. And that's not just a brief snapshot of results; it's a record compiled over 54 years by nine separate presidential administrations. That story is the same on the state level. Eleven of the top thirteen states in median household income are liberal states with Democratic majorities that vote Democratic for president. Of the twelve states with the lowest poverty rates, nine are liberal states and only three are conservative. Eleven of the twelve states with the highest poverty rates vote conservative.

You would think if conservative economics were so great, poor states that have followed the conservative line for thirty years like Oklahoma and Mississippi would move up the prosperity ladder. But they don't. And if liberal economic ideas were so terrible you would expect wealthy states like Massachusetts and Washington that have stayed liberal for decades would be falling apart by now. But they aren't. The two biggest states in population and economics, California and Texas, are often held up as examples of the two philosophies. Liberal California's median family income of $67,700 is 15 percent higher than conservative Texas's $58,900. California's poverty rate of 13.2 percent is 19 percent lower than the Texas rate of 16.2 percent. Thirteen percent of Californians don't have health insurance, compared to 23.9 percent of Texans. The Texas rate is an amazing 84 percent worse! We need to take a careful look at how the economy works to see how and why it works differently and better under the liberal philosophy.

What exactly do we mean when we talk about economics? *Dictionary.com* defines economics as *the science that deals with the production, distribution, and consumption of goods and services, or the material welfare of humankind.*

Economics can therefore be looked at in two ways: the mechanical nuts and bolts of the "production, distribution and consumption" of what people want and need, and the moral perspective of ensuring that the economic system is fair and just to society and its members, that it indeed contributes to "the material welfare of humankind." To a liberal, the two aspects, both mechanical and moral, are inseparable. An economic system that churns out production but leaves many of its people in poverty is seriously deficient. An economy that produces but exploits and degrades people, or despoils the ecosystem they and the natural world need to survive is similarly deficient. But so is one that is caring and well-intentioned but unable to produce enough to meet its people's basic needs. Are we stuck with an either/or choice about this? Happily, no, because the liberal approach to economics succeeds on both counts.

When I was in the conservative camp I was willing to swallow their assertions that "pro-business," low tax, anti-worker, anti-consumer, anti-environmental policies were needed to foster a prosperous and growing economy. It might be unfortunate, but these were purported to be the necessary prices that had to be paid for national wealth. It was even contended that this ideology and its policies were better for the workers and society at large in the long run.

But these claims turned out to be completely wrong. Once I lived through an actual application of the conservative approach (in the Reagan and George H. W. Bush years), became aware of the facts such as in the first paragraph of this section, and investigated the economic results of the past, the historical record made crystal clear that the American people have consistently enjoyed much greater prosperity during liberal administrations than conservative ones. My realization of these facts played a major role in my permanent conversion to liberalism. We didn't have to put up with mistreatment of workers and the environment and live in a dog-eat-dog world as the price of a good economy. An active public care for people and the tools of scientific and proactive public investment in the economy produce far better results than a laissez-faire neglect of public investments and human needs.

One of the greatest attributes of the liberal philosophy is its emphasis on fostering an economy that benefits all the members of society as a whole. The goal is to fulfill what President Kennedy was getting at when he said "A rising tide lifts all boats." So the two questions to ask when talking about an approach to economics are first, does it work, and second, is it moral.

There is no doubt experience has shown an economic system does well when there is wide scope for innovation and entrepreneurship. But it is equally clear that the good operation of an economy depends on firm and reasonable rules and laws. That's because whenever there are financial rewards at stake there are strong temptations to lie, cheat or mistreat other people. As James Madison wrote, "If men were angels, no government would be necessary." But men are not angels, particularly when their prime motivation is money.

How Does the Economy Work?

Republicans claim rich people and big corporations are job creators, so their taxes must not be raised. This is baloney. In order to create jobs, businesses need customers.

Robert Reich

Let's get down to basics here. The economy works because people buy stuff. According to the World Bank, the American Gross Domestic Product (GDP) in 2013 stood at $16.2 trillion. The GDP is the total market value of all the goods and services produced in the country in a year, and the American economy is the biggest in the world by far. Yes, China is catching up, but the U.S. is still number one.

The American economy is mainly driven by "consumers," that is, by the people, who spend their money on everything from mortgages to cars, groceries to haircuts, movie tickets to fortune tellers. These purchases can be anything, either tangible goods like a pair of shoes or an I-phone, or intangible services like legal advice or getting your nails done. This consumer spending accounts for 70% of the U.S. economy. A bit less than 20% is spent by the various levels of government. The remaining 10% comes from business spending.

Prosperity

We all do better when we all do better.

Paul Wellstone

Consumer spending, at all levels, is crucial to economic performance. It's what makes prosperity possible. While saving for the future-for retirement, for a planned purchase, or just for a rainy day-is a good idea for individuals, and a certain amount is good for the economy as a whole, the main thing that keeps the economy humming along is spending. This spending, based on the desire and ability to buy the goods and services that produce prosperity is called "demand," and it drives good economic times. If people aren't buying, then companies and individual purveyors are not making sales and nobody has an income.

If people are buying homes, for instance, then real estate agents, appraisers, mortgage lenders and insurance brokers are all doing well. Home builders and all the contractors, like carpenters, electricians, cabinet makers, roofers and plumbers are busy and making money. As the new homeowners move in and need to furnish and equip their new places, sales boom at furniture, appliance, drapery, hardware, carpet and garden stores. All these providers, with more customers to serve, have to hire more workers to keep up. It all creates what economists like to call a "virtuous cycle" of prosperity. More business means more people employed. More people earning good money means more spending and sales across the economy. The cycle builds on itself and prosperity expands. Times are good.

The biggest ingredient in national economic prosperity-remember, about 70 percent of it-is thus whether the great mass of Americans have money to spend and are spending it. For about 40 years, from the time America climbed out of the Great Depression in the late 1930s until the early 1970s, the nation enjoyed strong prosperity. That is because wages grew strongly and across the board. People had a rising standard of living and the expectation that increasing prosperity would continue. People bought homes, cars, boats, RVs, televisions and new clothes at unprecedented rates. They went on vacations.

Liberal social and economic policies had a great deal to do with this magnificent improvement in the American people's standard of living. The liberal perspective was (and is) that if average people are doing well, the economy as a whole will do well. Public policy helped foster this great surge. Here are some of the ways it did so.

Strong unions, their rights protected for the first time by supportive labor laws, represented 33% of all workers. They were able to bargain successfully for a greater share of business profits to go to the workers. Minimum wage laws made sure low wage workers made enough to live on and provided a wage floor for the rest of the work force. Tax laws made it more attractive for companies to re-invest profits back into the firm than to send them offshore or into inflated bonuses for top executives. Social Security made sure those too old to work did not sink into destitution. Medicare kept millions of senior citizens from being bankrupted by illness, as well as their adult children who in previous years would have had to bear the cost after their aging parents' money ran out. These folks would now have more money left to spend in the economy.

The GI Bill provided educational opportunities and thus, after graduation, access to upper middle class, white-collar careers for the millions of World War II, Korean War and Vietnam War era veterans. Pell Grants and other federal scholarship aid allowed millions of others to pursue higher education too. Concurrent with this, state governments massively expanded their public university systems, making advanced degrees available at reasonable cost to many more Americans. The success of the liberal civil rights and women's rights movements and the establishment of liberal federal scholarship assistance thus opened more jobs and educational opportunities to people who had previously been excluded due to their race, gender or poverty. America began using a greater share of its human capital than before; and much more than many other countries did. The U.S became the most educated nation in the world, and, not surprisingly, led the world in invention and innovation.

The Interstate Highway Program, the biggest construction project in the history of the world, tied American ground transportation together and provided millions of jobs. The space program led to incredible technological advances in aeronautics, physics, jet and rocket propulsion, solar energy, metallurgy, electronics, communications, and computer technology. These spawned entire new industries. American universities were the envy of the world, and American scientists dominated the Nobel Prizes for Physics, Chemistry and Medicine. Note that these were all government programs that invested in America's intellectual and technological development, provided for its infrastructure needs, directly created millions of jobs, and made sure that substantial benefits from the growing economy were shared by the working and middle classes. Liberals support the role of the democratically-elected representatives of the people making these kinds of wise investments by developing policies and programs that "promote the general welfare" of the nation's people and economic well-being. In the mid twentieth century, corporations and wealthy individuals paid high tax rates to support these public investments. Corporations paid effective rates over three times as high as today and rich individuals paid more than double. Yet economic growth continued at a much higher pace than since those rates were lowered.

The great expansion of public education spread opportunity and prosperity widely throughout the whole American economy. Millions of families moved out of poverty and into the middle class, and with good new disposable income to spend they bought the homes, cars, televisions, swimming pools, recreational vehicles and what-not that kept sales and employment high and the economy humming. This underscores the importance of consumer spending to the economy. If wages are too low, credit is too tight or unemployment is too high, spending will go down. When people are worried about their future prospects, spending goes down too. Thus when there is bad economic news, like the stock market crash of 1929 or the financial and housing crash of 2008, people reflexively cut back on their spending. They reasonably worry that if the economy goes bad their jobs may soon be in jeopardy. They figure they had better start saving in case they lose their jobs or have to take a pay cut. So they stop buying.

This lack of spending sends the national economy into a tailspin. The more people cut back the more sales drop. When sales fall companies cut back on employee hours. Then they start shedding jobs. They cancel expansion plans: The more the layoffs, the more spending throughout the economy slumps. Not only the jobless, but those who fear they may be next in line for a pink slip cut back on their spending, too. Less spending makes the economy worse, which means layoffs and less spending by the unemployed and everyone else who fears their job may be next. Instead of a "virtuous cycle" we know have a "downward spiral." When this leads to two consecutive quarters of a year in which the economy shrinks, economists consider it to be a "recession." When the nation's total output goes down a lot it may be referred to as a "Great Recession," like the one beginning in 2008, when GDP (Gross Domestic Product, the measure of all goods and services produced in the country during a year) contracted by about 5.1 percent. This caused unemployment to double to 10 percent and caused the loss of nearly $16 trillion worth of value (22 percent) in assets like homes, property, stocks and businesses. A really terrible downturn is called a "depression," like the Great Depression that started in 1929 and resulted in an almost 50 percent fall in the American GDP by 1933.

How to Get Out of a Recession or Depression

So, first of all, let me assert my firm belief that the only thing we have to fear is...fear itself — nameless, unreasoning, unjustified terror which paralyzes needed efforts to convert retreat into advance.

Franklin D. Roosevelt

When the economy sinks into a recession or a depression there is a proven way for the government to take action and help start the nation on the road to recovery. It's by spending money. Yes, spending money. If that seems against common sense to you, consider what a recession is: a time when sales are down because people are not spending enough. That is what sets off the downward spiral of dropping sales, production cuts and job layoffs. The 70 percent of the economy based on consumer spending is down, and the 10 percent based on business spending goes down too, because what business is going to buy more equipment, hire more workers or give raises when sales are falling?

If consumer and business spending are down, then who is left to restore demand for the goods and services that entrepreneurs and professionals of all kinds are offering for sale? The government: that's who. Government can help in all sorts of ways. It can buy surplus farm production and store or distribute the food to the needy. It can increase its orders for equipment and supplies. It can go on an expanded campaign of infrastructure construction and repair by building or fixing the roads, bridges, dams, energy grid and so on to provide revenue to companies and jobs for their workers. It can even directly provide jobs to those out of work by expanding community service, maintenance and reclamation projects of all kinds. People with jobs and money buy goods and services; those without do not.

The steps described in the previous paragraph are exactly what the great liberal President Franklin Roosevelt and a supportive liberal congress did to overcome the Great Depression in the 1930s, with spectacular success, an *average* annual economic growth rate of over 10% for his entire 12-year term! British economist John Maynard Keynes wrote the book that established the formal theory of why this works. His *The General Theory of Employment, Interest and Money*, published in 1936, established the basis for modern liberal economic theory. It supports a vibrant private sector economy, but understands and recognizes the crucial role government can play in keeping the system fair to all in society and in taking action to head off the unnecessary suffering and economic cost of widespread unemployment during severe downturns. The basic idea is to borrow and spend when times are bad, and pay down the debt when times are good.

Liberal and Conservative Stewardship of the Economy

I believe in a relatively equal society, supported by institutions that limit extremes of wealth and poverty. I believe in democracy, civil liberties, and the rule of law. That makes me a liberal, and I'm proud of it.

Paul Krugman

Here's the record of all the presidents from 1929 to the end of 2013. The growth, inflation and unemployment figures in this table come from the Department of Commerce and the Bureau of Labor Statistics and are percentages per year.

President	Years	Growth	Inflation	Unemployment
Hoover (R)	4	-14.2	-6.6	18.5
Roosevelt (D)	12	10.4	2.2	11.7
Truman (D)	8	1.4	5.3	3.9
Truman (D)*	5	4.8	3.6	4.3
Eisenhower (R)	8	2.5	1.4	5.4
Kennedy (D)	2.8	5.7	1.2	5.5
Johnson (D)	5.2	5.4	3.0	4.2
Nixon (R)	5.6	2.7	5.9	5.1
Ford (R)	2.4	2.9	7.5	8.1
Carter (D)	4	2.8	9.7	6.5
Reagan (R)	8	3.6	4.7	7.5
Bush I (R)	4	2.0	4.4	6.3
Clinton (D)	8	4.3	2.6	4.9
Bush II (R)	8	1.6	2.8	5.8
Obama (D)	6	2.3	1.9	8.2

(*) Much of Harry Truman's first three years was spent having to make a drastic conversion from the wartime economy of World War II to peacetime. There was tremendous dislocation as war production orders were cancelled at the same time millions of servicemen returned home looking for work. The last five years of Truman's tenure represent a more normal measuring stick.

So let's compare and sum up the economic results of the past 80-plus years under Republican and Democratic administrations. First: the Republicans. From Hoover to George W. Bush Republican administrations produced an anemic average growth rate of only 1.68% a year, with an unemployment rate of 7.3% and an average inflation rate of 3.9%.* Under the Democrats from Roosevelt to Obama economic growth averaged 5.1% a year, unemployment averaged 7.2% and inflation averaged 3.5%.The Democrats, the more liberal party, outperformed the Republicans, the more conservative party, in all three areas, as you can graphically see in the chart below.

All Administrations, 1929-2013, including the Great Depression.

	Years	Growth	Unemployment	Inflation
Republicans	40	1.68%	7.3%	3.9%*
Democrats	46	5.12%	7.2%	3.5%

*(In the Republican results inflation rates are not included under Hoover because they are not comparable to normal times. With farms, homes, businesses, cars and all manner of personal property being sold at auction for pennies on the dollar, prices went down drastically, but not in a good way. This deflation was part of the overall disaster of the Depression's effect on falling wages, prices and values which wiped out people's financial well-being. Prices fell an estimated 9 percent in 1931 and 9.9% in 1932, but no one was arguing that this was a positive development. It reflected desperate people losing their property and impoverished consumers unable to pay the cost to buy the goods and services they needed.)

But what if we exclude the Great Depression as an anomaly? Even without Hoover, the other 36 years under GOP control from Eisenhower to George W. Bush have produced the following stats: an average growth rate of 2.53%, unemployment rate of 6.1%, and inflation rate of 3.9 %. If you don't count the first four years of Roosevelt's time in office, when the country was digging out from under massive unemployment figures accumulated by his Republican predecessor, the Democrats averaged a 4.27% growth rate (and remember, we're not counting the excellent growth rates Roosevelt compiled in the New Deal years) with only 5.1% unemployment and a lower 3.8% inflation rate than under the Republicans. Put another way, for the last 77 years, the economy has grown 68.8% faster and unemployment has been 19.6% lower when a Democrat ran the country. Whichever way you slice it, liberal policies have produced consistently and decisively better results for the American people over a very lengthy period of time. The chart below makes it clear.

Administrations, 1942-2013, not including the Great Depression.

	Growth	Unemployment	Inflation
Republicans	2.53%	6.1%	3.9%
Democrats	4.27%	5.1%	3.8%

Another simple presidential rating system could be based on two criteria. Did the economic growth rate exceed the inflation rate? And did the Administration in question reduce the unemployment rate it inherited from its predecessor?

There were no Republicans who did, none at all! In fact, only Eisenhower of the seven Republican presidents had a growth rate above the inflation rate. And consider, if inflation is growing faster than your income, then you are losing money. And even in Eisenhower's case the unemployment rate increased. George H. W. Bush also rates better than a complete failure because even though his growth vs. inflation rate was more than two-to-one to the negative, he at least brought Reagan's high unemployment rate down a little bit.

Of the Democrats, six of the seven, all but Carter, had a growth rate above the inflation rate. And all but one, including Carter, had a lower average unemployment rate than the one inherited from his predecessor. Obama had unemployment rates as high as ten percent persisting into the early months of his Administration as a result of the George W. Bush recession. He had brought that down to 5.8% before midway through his second term, an improvement of more than 40%. Over the past 80-plus years the evidence is clear: the economic prosperity of the American people flourishes under Democratic governance and stagnates under Republican governance.

In the table below, "Success" is an administration in which the growth rate was better than the inflation rate and unemployment improved from the situation inherited. "Failure" is defined by an administration in which inflation was higher than growth and unemployment went up. "Mediocrity" entails growth above inflation but with higher unemployment (Eisenhower) or inflation higher than growth but an improvement in unemployment (Carter and G.H.W. Bush).

	SUCCESS	FAILURE	MEDIOCRITY
Republicans	0	5	2
Democrats	6	0	1

So, political spin doctors can make their cases and argue until they're blue in the face to tout their preferred stances on managing the economy. Conservatives can cite reason after reason why low taxes, spending and regulation and a minimum of government help and intervention are good for the economy. Liberals can give just as many reasons why higher taxes, especially for the wealthy, more services, stricter regulation and more proactive intervention are good for the economy. That's all well and good, but argument pales next to results. The actual record of these approaches in the real world provides the most conclusive argument, and the verdict is clear. The liberal approach preferred by Democrats has consistently produced better results for the American people than the conservative nostrums instituted by Republicans. Those are just the facts, and they are a big reason why I became a liberal and remain proud to be one.

Deficits, Taxes, Prosperity and the National Debt

Traditionally, the way deficits have been cut is you hold expenditures more or less constant in real dollars and then let growth come in to fill it up.

Phil Bredesen

When the federal government spends more money than it takes in through taxes, it is running a deficit. It "borrows" the difference primarily by selling treasury bonds that bring in money now and pay investors back over time with interest. A deficit is a term that says a budget did not balance in a particular year. We use the term "national debt" to describe the total accumulated amount the national government owes to its creditors altogether. Deficits are not always bad, especially when an economic recession necessitates increasing spending to create demand in the economy in order to keep businesses afloat and employees at work. If the growth outpaces the deficit then the nation and its people are coming out ahead.

During the Great Depression the federal government under the liberal direction of President Franklin Roosevelt ran deficits of about $3 billion a year, equivalent to 6% of the 1933 American economy at the depth of the Depression. As usual, conservatives railed against deficit spending, but the spending produced tremendous growth rates that put millions to work and grew the national economy. By 1939 the economy had grown by 63.4% and was producing nearly $36 billion per year more than in 1933. Is it worth it to invest $3 billion a year to increase national prosperity by $36 billion a year? Liberals certainly think so.

In the recessions beginning in 1981, 1990 and 2001 the federal government increased its own government hiring and provided assistance to states to do likewise. Government employment grew by 3% as part of the recoveries from the 1981 and 1990 recessions and 1% in the 2001 recession. Once you have strong employment and a good economy, tax revenues increase as a result of more people working for better pay which means more customers which means more companies turning a profit. Government expenditures go down too, since there are fewer needy getting unemployment, food stamps and Medicaid. Then the budget deficit naturally is reduced, as it was in the late 90s in the last years of the Clinton presidency, and is now in the last years of the Obama presidency. In fact, strong economic growth was actually producing a budget surplus in Clinton's last three years of up to $230 billion per year. The $787 billion Obama stimulus of 2009 (about 4% of GDP) helped turn job losses of up to 800,000 per month into private sector job gains that have gone on for an all-time American record 60 consecutive months at the time of this writing. Other countries that have studied the historical record also understand the value of stimulus spending for reviving a sick economy. For example, when the Great Recession hit, China initiated a $578 billion stimulus (6% of their GDP at the time) which was followed by annual growth rates of 7% to 9%.

The comparison to budget "austerity" measures could not be more painfully clear. In the late 90s recession Japan decided to cut back and rein in public spending in an effort to balance its budget. It cancelled building projects and laid off workers, expecting to save money. Instead, the economy remained depressed. In actuality, the Japanese growth rate for the past twenty years has averaged a negative -0.3%. Their GDP in real terms is lower than it was over two decades ago! In addition, even with spending cuts, because of falling revenues the national debt has ballooned from 20% of GDP to over 200%!

Europe's experiment with austerity after the 2008 recession has produced results similar to Japan's. After slashing spending in budget-balancing schemes, the depressed economies of Italy, Spain, Portugal, Ireland and Greece saw their deficits grow. Soon after the imposition of these austerity measures, Europe's economy went back into recession, and four years later the GDP and employment figures of major countries like Britain and France have still not recovered to pre-recession levels. In fact, they have taken longer to do so than they did in the Great Depression of the 1930s, when liberal expansionary spending policies were followed.

Conservatives remain fixated on deficits and the national debt. Yet if one looks at the record, it has been under conservative administrations that the debt has soared. In 1981 Reagan inherited a $59 billion deficit for the year from Carter. After Reagan's tax cuts it more than tripled to $180 billion a year. It grew to $220 billion a year under his successor, the elder Bush. After Clinton got rid of the red ink, two new rounds of tax cuts for the wealthy under the younger Bush turned $230 billion annual surpluses into $450 billion dollar-a-year deficits. Then the Great Recession, triggered by lax conservative regulation schemes, pushed the deficit up to an incredible $1.4 *trillion* in 2009. By 2014, Obama had been able to reduce that by two-thirds, down to $492 billion.

So the evidence is clear that the liberal policies are the ones that work. The conservative theories of deregulating business and cutting taxes for the rich and corporations while getting rid of help for the needy and investment in the nation's infrastructure has always led to economic inequality and recession, which push up the very deficits they claim to abhor. In fact, more than half of the entire national debt in the history of the United States was compiled in just the last three Republican administrations of Reagan and the two Bushes. Liberal policies that make the wealthy and profitable corporations pay their fair share and use the revenues to promote education, opportunity, and provide lots of jobs are the ones that make for prosperity, deficit reduction and social peace.

For instance, in the mid-1960s there was tremendous prosperity under the liberal governance of Presidents Kennedy and Johnson and a liberal congress. In those days, personal income tax rates for earnings above $1.5 million in today's dollars were taxed between 77 and 91 percent. At the same time, the top corporate tax rates were between 48 and 52 percent. The capital gains rate, the tax paid from turning profits on stocks and bonds, made primarily by the rich, stood at 40 percent. As a result we had new and expanding schools and university systems, a new national highway system, new water projects, a vibrant space program spinning off new technologies, and our roads, bridges, ports and facilities of all kinds were well-maintained. These projects provided millions of jobs and average people had money to spend. Consequently the economy was expanding, and inflation, unemployment and crime were low.

As I write these words, riots have been taking place in Ferguson, Missouri just outside St. Louis, where a black teenager was shot and killed by a white policeman. Two-thirds of Ferguson's residents are black and half of its young people are unemployed. Is it any wonder that despair, anger and dysfunction are rampant in such communities? Where the private sector is not doing so, liberals believe the federal government needs to step in and provide the jobs that give people an income, their self-respect and the incentive to be responsible citizens: That is what hope is all about. Liberals agree that conservative President Ronald Reagan was right when he said, "The best social program is a job." Where we disagree with him and other conservatives is in their insistence that somehow it is wrong for the people's government to help provide those jobs. Let's restore some of that tax burden to the wealthiest individuals and corporations. The cuts over the past thirty years have not trickled down and produced prosperity for the average person. Then let's use that revenue to put *all* Americans back to work.

There is so much in America that needs doing, and liberals believe we can and should put people to work doing it. To cite a few examples, the National Park Service has a $12 billion maintenance backlog. Only 37 percent of American roads are in "good" condition, and states are falling behind by $30 billion a year to keep their roads in repair. President Obama has increased funding greatly for solar power, yet it still provides only 0.3 percent of America's electricity. Germany, by comparison, has been going at this issue aggressively and recently passed 50 percent, with 23.1 million gigawatts of their power coming from solar. The Transportation Department finds that there are 66,405 structurally deficient bridges in our country. The Administration on Aging projects that our senior citizen population is in the process of doubling between 2000 and 2030 to about 72.1 million and will constitute 19% of the population by 2030.

A lot of those older folks are going to need care. Every community can identify worthwhile projects, and there are still far too many people without a job. Skeptics say we can't afford it, but the opposite is true. We can't afford not to give our people worthwhile employment and we can't afford to have young people out of work with no hope. They are fodder for crime and gangs, which end up costing society and budgets a lot more than jobs. The newly employed will spend their earnings right back into the economy as well, providing sales for local companies and contributing to a virtuous cycle of community development, job creation and overall economic prosperity.

There is another reason to promote opportunity and reverse income inequality, a reason made chillingly clear in a thorough international study of the United States and other countries in January 2014 by Oxfam, the poverty-relief organization. The report, *Working for the Few: Political Capture and Income Inequality*, found a pervasive tendency in nations where income inequality was growing for the wealthy to find it easier and easier to bend the system ever further to their benefit. And the United States was the country in which income inequality was growing the fastest. According to Nick Galasso, co-author of the report, "High levels of inequality actually corrode democratic processes. What we have seen across the globe and what the report documents is how wealth concentration is used to influence the political process to create laws and regulations that benefit the rich over everyone else." Liberals agree that is a primary reason why the economy has been so good for the top few percent and so tough for everyone else for the past few decades. We want to see that dynamic ended. However it is done, through unionization, wage requirements or the tax system, or ideally a combination of all three, the proportion of national income going to average working Americans has to go up, at least to where it was during the Great Prosperity. And the tax burden on the wealthy and profitable business has to go up some to provide the national services and social safety net that have been rolled back under misguided conservative doctrines over the past three-plus decades.

The hard truth that many do not want to see is that corporations do not WANT to create jobs. They want to make profit, and if they can do that without hiring they will, for that will make profit higher yet. They do not WANT to provide health care or contribute to society. To a corporate entity these are costs. They did not, and still do not when they can avoid it, WANT to pay workers a living wage, give them a forty hour week, vacations, lunch breaks, ventilation, safe working conditions or any other humane terms of employment until they were forced to do so by workers united together in strong unions and by labor and consumer legislation rammed down their throats by politicians more worried about losing the votes of an aroused populace than about losing corporate money.

Former Clinton Administration Labor Secretary Robert Reich sums things up cogently in this summary:

The real reason small business owners and struggling whites haven't done better is the same most of the rest of America hasn't done better: Although the output of Americans has continued to rise, almost all the gains have gone to the very top.

Government is implicated, but not in the way wealthy Republicans want the other members of their coalition to believe. Laws that the GOP itself championed (too often with the complicity of some Democrats) have trammeled unions, invited outsourcing abroad, slashed taxes on the rich, encouraged takeovers, allowed monopolization, reduced the real median wage, and deregulated Wall Street.

Four decades ago, the typical household's income rose in tandem with output. But since the late 1970s, as these laws took hold, most Americans' incomes have flattened. Had the real median household income continued to keep pace with economic growth it would now be almost $92,000 instead of $50,000.

That is the kind of economy, an economy of the rich, by the rich and for the rich that liberals are dedicated to getting rid of.

Liberals do agree there is a time when governments can think of pulling back on spending. That is when the economy is prosperous and growing, when there are plenty of opportunities for people to find work in the private sector and when business is investing in projects that promote both growth and employment. But laying people off and cancelling government orders and projects during a recession does nothing but contribute to demand decline and make the recession worse. Common sense and the real historical record have made that apparent to those who put real-world results and the mitigation of human suffering ahead of blind adherence to discredited ideology.

Unions, and Why the Union Shop is Fair

In our glorious fight for civil rights, we must guard against being fooled by false slogans, such as 'right-to-work.' It provides no 'rights' and no 'works.' Its purpose is to destroy labor unions and the freedom of collective bargaining.... We demand this fraud be stopped.

Martin Luther King Jr.

Liberals support the union movement because it is the main countervailing power workers have to improve their pay and working conditions. Strong unions provide a voice and a means for the average American to live a decent middle-class lifestyle. Before the success of unionization, workers toiled in squalid conditions for starvation wages. It is only because of the freedom to unionize, won at the cost of many lives and many more broken bones, that most workers have a five-day forty-hour work week, paid holidays and workplace safety protections. Social Security, employer-based medical coverage, the Occupational Safety and Health Administration and the end of child labor would likely never have happened without the labor union movement pushing for them.

Fighting for labor rights and benefits against corporate might has never been easy. Today a powerful campaign led by business interests does everything it can to discredit the labor movement and try to convince workers that unionization runs against their own self-interest. Its primary goal is to weaken labor's effectiveness so that corporate management and wealthy investors can take an even greater share of company profits than they already do, while forcing wages, benefits and humane working conditions down for average workers. The Republican Party is in strong sympathy with these anti-worker views. One of its tactics is to make illegal the practice of permitting workers to establish a closed union shop at places of employment. These restrictions, often called "right to work" laws are, as the quote from Martin Luther King at the beginning of this section states, anything but pro-worker. Below is a blog I wrote on the topic on December 13, 2012.

"Why the Closed Union Shop Is Fair"

Last week the Republican-controlled Michigan House and Senate passed legislation banning the closed union shop. What it basically does is make it illegal to require someone to belong to the union in order to work at a unionized employer. I'd like to touch on the reasons why the closed shop is reasonable and justifiable.

The most often-cited justification is to stop the unfair practice of "free riders." Since negotiated wages, benefits and safe and healthy working conditions are enjoyed by all the workers, it is unfair for some to reap the rewards without contributing through their membership and dues to the cost and support of bargaining for them.

A second reason comes from the idea of the corporation as a cooperative endeavor in which management and labor each have roles and responsibilities to the organization. The company cannot operate without both. Opponents of union shop often say they stand for the freedom of workers to choose. They like to call such laws as recently passed in Michigan "right to work laws." A better frame of reference might be "corporate servitude laws." When a person hires into a firm there are always a number of requirements involved. The prospective employee doesn't get the freedom to tailor everything to his or her own personal wishes. A host of such issues as hours, pay, breaks, vacation policies, sick leave, retirement benefits, discipline procedures, scheduling and the work to be performed are all part of the package. When you hire in you are accepting all of the above. To say that the worker has no freedom with regards to what management wants but freedom only in what their fellow workers want smacks of the authoritarian mindset toward which that view is slanted.

Finally, the union shop can only exist where it is democratic and contractual. Unlike the corporation, the union is a democratic organization. It must be voted in by the workers and the contracts it negotiates for them must be democratically approved by their votes. When union shop arrangements are in place they exist because they have been **negotiated and accepted by both sides** and ratified by a vote of the workers. The result is a contract, a binding agreement on both sides with the force of law. Consequently, to pass laws like Michigan's is to restrict the freedom of labor and management to negotiate conditions of employment, to subvert the force of a contract and to obviate the democratically expressed voice of the workers.

Regulation

It's all very well to run around saying regulation is bad, get the government off our backs, etc. Of course our lives are regulated. When you come to a stop sign, you stop; if you want to go fishing, you get a license; if you want to shoot ducks, you can shoot only three ducks. The alternative is dead bodies at the intersection, no fish, and no ducks. OK?

Molly Ivins

Liberals are in favor of sensible economic regulations to require transparency, protect people's safety, fight corruption and make sure a sufficient share of the economy's proceeds goes to the average worker that he or she can actually live on it. Unlike the ridiculous exaggerations pro-business conservatives throw around, true liberals do not want to impose regulations just to grow government or to make it harder to conduct business. Liberals want to establish regulations when they are necessary to protect people's lives, safety and well-being, and to insure an honest, just, open and free society.

We established the Environmental Protection Agency because air pollution was so bad it was killing people and water pollution was so bad rivers were catching on fire and killing all the fish. The minimum wage was established because businesses were colluding to pay people starvation wages they couldn't support their families on. Anti-trust laws were passed because corporate cartels and monopolies were fixing prices, to the detriment of consumers. The Securities and Exchange Commission was set up because Wall Street firms were not telling investors the truth and their reckless practices had crashed the stock market and caused the Great Depression. Depression-era banking regulations were imposed because over 5,000 banks had failed in the Depression and took everyone's savings down with them. The recent Dodd-Frank legislation and the Consumer Financial Protection Bureau were passed to restrict the unsound practices that led to the 2008 major economic meltdown.

No true liberal is for regulation for its own sake. Conservatives complain about regulation in the abstract, but when they are asked to name specific regulations that simply burden business but do not protect people's health, safety or well-being or promote the honesty of the marketplace they usually have nothing to say. Any time they can name such regulations they will find only cooperative allies among true liberals. We want to get rid of such regulations too. After all, practicality and efficiency are two of our cardinal guiding principles. But we do not support getting rid of regulations that save people's lives and health just so someone else can make a few extra bucks.

Some of the regulations liberals feel most strongly about are the ones that foster economic fairness. We need an economy that encourages innovation and entrepreneurship but also one that makes sure a reasonable share of the profits gets to the workers. We did that in the Depression and "Great Compression," as Nobel Prize winning economist Paul Krugman referred to the prosperous and growing years from the 1940s to the 1970s. From the liberal perspective that is moral and the historical record proves it's effective. It worked and it's even good for rich people. Increasing economic inequality is a characteristic of unregulated capitalism, or at least the way it most often is regulated, that is to the benefit of those on top. Historically, when we fostered the minimum wage, benefits, unions and a tax structure that made sure a reasonable chunk of the profits was recycled back into society in ways that improved opportunity for the rank and file, or gave incentives for companies to plow money into the company and their people, all boats did rise.

As an example, the federal minimum wage today is $7.25 per hour. Yet in 1968 the minimum wage in inflation-adjusted dollars was worth $10.06 in today's money. A worker working a full-time job at the minimum wage in those days could support a family of three over the poverty line. That same worker toiling at the minimum wage fell below the poverty line in 1983, and has only lost ground since.

The contention that a hands-off or "laissez-faire" approach to society and the economy is "moral" is clearly refutable. Human slavery was the clearest example. The history of child labor, dangerous and defective products, quack medicines, unsafe workplace conditions, killer hours, and the exposure of workers and the environment to toxic pollution like asbestos and PCB's are only a few of the abuses that had to be restrained by sensible and humane regulations in the public interest. Individualism exists in civilization within the framework of the community. We don't practice laissez-faire with regard to preventable diseases, crime, floods and so on. We take action as a community to protect society and its members. As such, we promote conditions that increase prosperity and restrict people from doing things that harm others. These are the cardinal purposes of law and government itself.

Make no mistake, it takes a lot of hard work and guts to start and run a small business. The majority don't last a year. I have great respect and admiration for people who launch their own ventures. The numbers say that while the number of jobs at large employers has remained stagnant since the 1980s, *all* the net job creation since that time has come from small businesses.

But with that said, we can't forget that small concerns can often be tempted to cut corners in any number of ways. The results can compromise quality, consumer protection, the environment, and the safety and well-being of their workers. Here are some reminiscences about summer jobs from my college roommate Tom Reardon, now a Professor of Developmental Economics at Michigan State University and Rinmin University in Beijing.

"The key is to get worker safety regulations in place and truly implemented. I recall when I was a manual worker in the 1970s... I was crop dusted by planes at the potato farm (I complained and they said, fine, we will fire you, and I went back out); on roofs, tarring, I was made to climb three and four stories on long ladders, no safety belt, 2 x 25 pound cans of tar in each hand, scared totally shitless... inching up on my chest, shaking like a leaf; I can feel and see it today; I complained, and the man said, fine, you can walk off the job and we will just keep your pay... I stayed... over and over I was in these dangerous situations (I was a jack hammer man on the streets, no safety goggles, no breaks...) and when I complained I was always humiliated. That is what it was like before our law, and/or before it trickled down to the small firms, the independent operators. I grew to hate small enterprises at that time, oddly, because the many I worked for, they all seemed ravenous and unbridled, unwatched, uncaring... it is surely not that way for all or even many at that time, maybe... I say that now just to not think of the rapes, the dustings, the dangers, the humiliations, of the many workers over time. Now in the emerging economies, quickly industrializing and urbanizing, the wheel is again turning. I wish them only to move quickly through the hard stage we tarried so long in."

The sad truth is that such exploitation still takes place. Farm workers continue to die from heat stroke every summer at a rate over 20 times that of other workers. A recent PBS Frontline report, "Rape in the Fields," found that rape of female farm workers is "common." It pointed to a survey of 150 female California farm workers in 2010 that found that 80 percent had experienced sexual harassment. A survey of 100 women, mostly immigrants, at Iowa meat packing plants found that 84% reported being subjected to sexual harassment.

Detractors like to charge that liberals "harp on" such problems unnecessarily or are out to impede the conduct of normal business out of hatred for free enterprise. These tend to be the charges of industry lobbyists, professional spin doctors and knee-jerk conservatives who don't really understand the liberal world view. Liberals put people first. People don't deserve to be raped, poisoned or subjected to life-threatening danger in the course of trying to earn a living. Apply the Golden Rule. Is that the way you would like to be treated? If not then it isn't right to treat others that way. According to the Bureau of Labor Statistics, the efforts of Progressives and liberals to protect the American worker have made a difference. Fatalities on the job went from 61 per 100,000 workers in 1912 to 4 per 100,000 by the end of the twentieth century. Much of this can be attributed to the establishment of the Occupational Safety and Health Administration in 1970. There is still work to be done effecting improvement in dangerous occupations. The death rate in mining is still 30 per 100,000 workers, in the category of agriculture, forestry and fishing it is 20 per 100,000 and in construction it is 15 per 100,000.

Perhaps the greatest testament to the necessity of intelligent regulation is the conversion of Alan Greenspan, Chairman of the Federal Reserve from 1987 to 2006. This doctrinaire laissez-faire conservative honed his anti-regulatory perspective as a young man in regular attendance at salons hosted by "Objectivist" author Ayn Rand. As the Fed Chair nominated by conservative icon Ronald Reagan, Greenspan preached a doctrine of "self-regulation," assuring congressional committees that America's major financial institutions would certainly, for the good of their industry, be able to restrain themselves from following recklessly risky practices in pursuit of short-term profits on their own, without regulatory oversight from government-imposed laws and regulations. He championed the dismantling of the important banking and stock market restrictions that were imposed in the wake of the Great

Depression and that had prevented another one ever since. Early in his tenure the removal of Savings and Loan laws resulted in the S & L Scandal of the late 1980s that required a $125 billion bailout from the American taxpayer. In the middle of his term the relaxation of stock market standards helped usher in the Dot Com Bubble that kicked off the recession of the late 1990s. Finally, the removal of Glass-Steagall banking restrictions and the Fed's refusal to regulate such risky instruments as derivatives, subprime loans and securitization led directly to the Financial Crash and Great Recession of 2008, which destroyed $16 trillion of American assets and caused financial ruin for millions. At long last, Greenspan admitted the folly of his disastrous 19-year stewardship over America's financial system. In an interview on National Public Radio on October 18, 2013, Greesnpan said, "Self-regulation is not the way the world works. The premises I held prior to 2008 I had to discard because the evidence definitely said I was wrong." Our basic premise is this: The economic system exists to serve humanity, not the other way around.

What does the Constitution say about the Economy and Government's Authority Over It?

I imagine an America that can actually change. That we become a nation that prospers again but without pillaging the resources of nations that make their people hate us. That we become a nation that, as the constitution says in its preamble; the very first paragraph, 'promotes the general welfare' of its people

Richard Schiff

Liberals believe the people have strong authority to regulate economic matters in the public interest. To accomplish this, they believe the people's representatives in government can and should act to promote a just and inclusive prosperity that improves the lives of the American people as a whole. Everyone willing to work and contribute is entitled to reasonable compensation, safe and humane working conditions, life-sustaining benefits and the prospect, after many years of productive labor, of a retirement in sufficiency and dignity. Liberals see things this way because of our commitment to justice and our empathy for human beings. As such, we are in strong accord with Nobel Prize-winning economist Joseph Stiglitz, when he says, "The only true and sustainable prosperity is shared prosperity."

The U.S. Constitution specifically lays out in its Preamble the federal government's responsibility to "promote the general Welfare." Article I, Section 8 goes on to enumerate some of the ways it is empowered to do this. It authorizes the authority to "lay and collect Taxes," "pay the Debts," "borrow Money," "regulate Commerce with foreign Nations, and among the several States," "coin Money, regulate the value thereof" and "to promote the Progress of Science and useful Arts," by "securing for limited Times to Authors and Inventors the exclusive Right to their respective Writings and Discoveries." In case these are not enough, the "elastic clause" at the end of the section grants the authority "To make all Laws which shall be necessary and proper for carrying into Execution the foregoing Powers, and all other Powers vested by this Constitution in the Government of the United States, or in any Department or Officer thereof."

Economics is an exceedingly complex field of study, dealing as it does with the decisions of 7 billion people over practically all aspects of their material lives. To underscore this fundamental reality, try guessing how many of the leading banks and investment houses correctly and accurately forecast the Crash of 2008. If your guess was "none" you would be absolutely correct. So, here's what we can say with pretty strong confidence. The financial geniuses can't seem to predict when a crash is coming. We have also seen how they can't seem to control themselves and stick to safe and sane investment patterns without sensible requirements in place to restrain them. We do know that every major crash of the past 90 years has come after a period of conservative deregulation has removed important economic safeguards. We also know that when crashes come, millions of people who had nothing to do with causing them lose their jobs and homes. And we also have seen that strong action by a responsive government to create jobs can mitigate a recession's effects, preventing bankruptcy for thousands of companies and destitution for many millions of citizens.

The Constitution gives clear and obvious fiscal powers to the government to "promote the general welfare" by spending and borrowing money, controlling its value and regulating all commerce. Never anywhere does it say it is forbidden to provide jobs, to assist with training, to help people stay in their homes, to set up retirement and medical services, or to promote business expansion and hiring. Yet many conservatives decry such actions as "unconstitutional." If they believe what they are saying, they don't know what they are talking about, for the Constitution forbids none of these things. It is not a constitutional question but a policy question. Politically, they are against the idea of a compassionate and active government that takes direct action to help people. The liberal view is precisely the opposite. When people are hurting and the private sector has no jobs to offer, human needs come first. We have proven and effective ways to achieve prosperity, and not to use them is not only economically foolish and wasteful but unacceptably inhumane. We believe we are on this earth to help people, not watch them suffer. Count on liberals to promote an economy that puts people first and leaves no one behind.

CHAPTER 8:

Health

Let us be clear about our choice. When we raise taxes on the wealthiest Americans, no one dies. When we cut Social Security and Medicare, people die.

Annabel Park

Let me share a blog I wrote on health care back in 2009. "Another Unnecessary Death" 2/27/09

I talked to a woman today who's losing her daughter to breast cancer. We'll soon have another preventable death and another set of motherless kids.

I'll call the daughter Holly. Holly has four children. Holly got divorced. Holly had no health insurance. So when she felt a lump in her breast, Holly didn't go to the doctor. There would have been the visit, then referral to a specialist, then all sorts of tests. That kind of stuff is expensive. She'd had a lump that wasn't malignant before. Maybe she would get lucky again, she hoped. Maybe she could save some money she and the kinds really needed.

But maybe didn't happen this time. When Holly's mother finally found out she told her to go; she would pay for it. By then several months had gone by. The news was bad. The cancer is in both breasts and the lymph system. Holly was told she had only weeks to live, no more than a month.

But Holly is a fighter. She's a former top high school athlete and still has a competitive streak. Her mother is going to borrow money for a desperate operation. They're going to remove both breasts, a lot of skin, and many lymph nodes. Then she'll have massive radiation. There will be a lot of sickness and excruciating rehab. The prognosis: This will probably delay her death by two or three years. As extensively as the cancer has spread there's almost no hope of getting it all. It's probably in her thoracic organs. But there might be a 1% chance of longer-term survival. And a couple of more years for the kids to have a mother will be good, too. After all, the youngest is only three.

On a national news show yesterday I saw a wealthy attorney whining about the Obama proposal to let income taxes for those earning at least $250,000 a year return to their pre-Bush levels, going up 4% to fund a $600+ billion reserve to get a national health insurance program off the ground. He complained it would "destroy my American dream." Cry me a river, bub. Take one more DUI case a year if you're so down about paying an average extra $1,100 in taxes after deductions out of your $300,000 income. What about Holly's American dream? What about her kids? What about the 50 million (and rising) other Americans in the same boat? How many more thousands must die for no good reason? I often wonder what planet people like that attorney come from.

When it comes to health care liberals have no ideological axes to grind. They don't care whether it's fully private, fully government-funded or a mix of the two. All they care is that it works and people get the medical care they need. Kids should get inoculations. Expectant mothers should get prenatal care. Older folks should get regular checkups. When people are sick or injured they should be able to go to the doctor. When someone has a serious condition that requires surgery or expensive treatment in order to get well, they should be able to get what they need without facing bankruptcy. The noise put out by people with ideological preconceptions to defend or financial interests to serve does not interest us. Good medical care does.

That is why we should cut through the fog and take a stark look at health care in America. If our system worked well for all our people liberals would be more than satisfied. But it does not. The figures are quite clear on this. 17.9% of the American Gross Domestic Product is now spent on health care. The average for OECD countries is 10%. (Thirty-four countries belong to the Organization for Economic Cooperation and Development, a group that started with the U.S., Canada and the European countries receiving Marshall Plan aid and that now comprises much of the rest of Europe plus other nations such as Japan, Korea, Australia, Mexico and Turkey.) 16% of our people are completely without health coverage, about 49 million in total. No one in any other OECD nation is. Average life expectancy in our country is 75 for men and 80 for women. The OECD averages are 78 and 83. The infant mortality rate in the U.S. is the highest and the maternal mortality rate is the third highest. We have the second lowest hospital beds per capita and the fifth lowest number of physicians per capita. These results are not acceptable.

There are many people in the United States who like mindlessly to chant, "USA! USA!" and, "We're number one! We're number one!" They feel it is reflexively patriotic to so believe. They do not like to hear news that contradicts their ignorance.

There are others who believe that an unfettered "free market" is always the best solution to every problem. When evidence demonstrates otherwise on a particular issue they are quick to offer a myriad of excuses. They do not like to hear facts that do not fit their ideological preconceptions.

There are others yet who feel their profits depend on maintaining arrangements as they are, and many others they pay to advertise, advocate, and legislate to protect these arrangements. They like to pretend, and may in some cases even believe, that their personal interests and the national interest are one and the same. They do not like to hear anything that questions this.

The bottom line is that we are paying much more and getting much less for our health care dollar than comparable countries. The Canadian, French, British, German, Japanese, Italian and many other plans work better than ours at far less cost. If we spent what they do per person on health care we would have an additional $1 trillion, a thousand billions, a year to devote to other things. And these costs had been going up by nearly 8% a year. The economy could not sustain a bubble like that anymore than it could sustain housing prices annually going up at that rate. This is not about politics or ideology. It is about practicality being applied to keeping people well.

The passage of the Affordable Care Act, or Obamacare, was long overdue and is a case in point. During the election year of 2008 surveys showed health care was the number three issue in voters' minds, behind only the economy and the war in Iraq. In the United States in 2011 a Harvard University study found that 62% of the 1.6 million bankruptcies that year—almost one million families-- were due to "overwhelming medical expenses." Duke University found, for instance, that even the 78% of cancer patients who had some form of insurance still averaged $1266 per month in out of pocket medical expenses. The U.S. was the only advanced country in which anybody ever went broke because of medical bills, because it was the only such country that didn't have a program to make sure all its citizens' health needs were provided for. Even worse, according to Harvard Medical School, 45,000 Americans were dying needlessly every year because they lacked access to health care, even though America spent nearly twice as much per person on its health care system as any other country.

With these needs in mind the Obama Administration and congressional Democrats passed the Affordable Care Act in 2010. As President Obama said at the time, "We have now just enshrined, as soon as I sign this bill, the core principle that everybody should have some basic security when it comes to their healthcare." Quickly dubbed "Obamacare," the program, which began enrolling customers in 2014, will provide a means of insuring 32 million Americans. Many of the terms of the Act may be familiar to most Americans by now. Among these are that people can no longer be denied coverage due to having pre-existing conditions and adult children of the insured are covered on their parents insurance until age 26.The 85% rule requires insurers to spend at least 85% of the amount collected in premiums on actual patient care. Moderate and low income people who make too much to qualify for Medicaid, are not old enough to qualify for

Medicare, but do not have insurance through their work will get help to pay for premiums on a sliding scale. There are requirements for future efficiencies such as by establishing an electronic medical records database. The health care cost increases have been cut by two-thirds since Obamacare passed, to 4% in 2012 and 3.6% in 2014. That represents a promising start to a program that is not fully phased in yet.

Consider that when nearly three thousand Americans died in the terrorist attacks on 9/11 the conservative administration then in office initiated two wars and suspended important parts of the Constitution. Government action was taken. Studies estimate the total long term costs of these wars at $3 trillion. Yet to have *every year* fifteen times that number of people die and a million more go bankrupt was simply, they told us, a sacrifice that needed to be made on the altar of small government, or something we could not afford, even though the Congressional Budget Office itself determined the Obama plan would save $109 billion over 10 years compared to continuing business as usual with health care, and sent a letter to Republican Speaker of the House John Boehner detailing this when the Republican-majority House of Representatives tried to repeal the Act in 2012.

Conservatives ideologically opposed to using national action to secure people's access to health care managed to whip up opposition to the Act with hysterical charges about invented evils like "death panels." These succeeded in scaring a lot of people and eroding public support for the overall plan, though surveys showed continued strong support for all the individual components of Obamacare. Knowing their political futures were at risk, numerous congressional Democrats in swing districts still voted for these health reforms in March 2010, and many of them went down to defeat in the election that November, as Republicans picked up 62 seats and regained the majority in the House. This was an act of political courage not often seen in recent congresses, and liberals are proud of it. Hundreds of thousands will now live who would have died. Millions will not go bankrupt who otherwise would have. It's a great example of acting as a community and "putting people first."

Liberals are open to other innovative steps, such as Single Payer health insurance, which would be like going to Medicare for all. Another attractive idea is phasing in an outcomes based health system, something Obamacare hopes to foster. Currently, doctors and medical providers get paid for patient visits, exams, tests and surgical procedures. This practice increases the incentive for doctors, HMOs and so on to perform these costly services. In an outcomes-based system they are paid for outcomes or results. Providers get compensated for their patients losing weight, quitting smoking, lowering blood pressure, getting involved with exercise programs, and the like. If say, diet and exercise would correct a condition as well as surgery, everyone would win. The patient would improve, often at less risk, the doctor would get compensated for that and the payer, be it Medicare, Medicaid, an insurance company or the individual, would save money.

There's one more trend we need to discuss regarding health. Liberals like the idea of putting taxes on unhealthy stuff. In the health world that takes the shape of wanting to raise taxes on things like cigarettes, alcohol, sugar and fat. Alcohol has had substantial taxes for quite a while. Taxes on cigarettes began getting hiked after the Surgeon General's 1964 report tied smoking to cancer and a host of other health problems. There have been proposals in some states and localities to tax sugary soda drinks and in New York Mayor Michael Bloomberg tried to limit the size of sugared drinks that could be sold.

So, why is there a liberal inclination to levy taxes on unhealthy commodities? There are two reasons, really. One is to make it marginally more costly and thus apply a deterrent against the unhealthy behavior. The other stems from the liberal principle of responsibility. If you do something that injures only you then that is your business. But if it harms other people, that's different. It's your responsibility to either cease harming other people or to compensate them for their losses. In the case of items like sugared sodas, the principle applies because it costs all of us, not just those who overindulge. The idea is to make people pay the real costs up front instead of providing an incentive with subsidized costs (such as price supports for sugar) for unhealthful behaviors that cost others.

Here are some facts on one problem of obesity that might put things into perspective. In the last 50 years, from 1963 until today, the adult percentage of the population that is obese has gone from 13% to 34%. The "morbidly obese" percentage was then 0.9% and is now 6%. Obesity saddles America with an estimated $190 billion a year in direct costs, and the average overweight person rings up an additional $1850 a year in health expenses. That's a remarkable amount, almost $600 per year higher than the extra $1274 a year that health care for smokers averages more than non-smokers! *Nature* Magazine reported that those figures are just the tip of the iceberg. Direct costs are only a little more than half (51.6%) of the total. These include treatment for the additional risk component of those suffering from obesity-related diseases. An amazing 63% of that $190 billion goes to treat diabetes. The next highest direct cost is 14% for coronary heart disease. An estimated 300,000 deaths a year are attributable to these preventable conditions.

Add in the indirect costs and America's bill for the excess weight comes in at nearly $400 billion a year. If our obesity rates could be returned to what they were 50 years ago, when they were 62% lower, it would save America $247 billion of that. For instance, computed from the higher absentee rates among the obese, the national economy loses an annual 39 million work days. It's been calculated companies lose $1,026 per year due to absenteeism for a very heavy male worker and $1,262 for a female. Airlines are paying an extra $5 billion for jet fuel to move those heavier passengers compared to 1960s weights, and drivers have to shell out $4 billion more a year for gasoline. It's estimated that 8.5% of our $500 billion annual Medicare budget is attributable to obesity, along with 11.8% of our $260 billion in Medicaid costs, and 12.9% of the outlays paid by private insurers.

That's a lot of money. So when people succumb to the advertising and the addictive properties of sugar, salt and fat, load up on the chips, cookies and soda and pack on those pounds, they aren't just hurting themselves. They're adding to the costs of their employer, thus leaving less money for pay and benefits for everyone at the firm. They are making everyone who buys an airplane ticket pay more, everyone who buys insurance pay more, and everyone who pays taxes pay more.

That's why the tax-the-sugar plan makes sense to liberals. When diabetes sets in everybody has to pay for it through higher insurance premiums and taxes for social insurance programs. It's a cost to society of the overconsumption of sugar. So, if we can deter some of that by increasing the cost of the commodity to reflect what it costs society in lost productivity and medical expense, we can cut those costs by providing an effective incentive. Instead of making everyone indiscriminately pay for the excess through higher taxes and insurance premiums, doesn't it seem more fair to make the people who are buying a lot of ice cream and soda pop, the ones who are going to be needing more medical help in the future, pay a relatively larger share of the cost than others, and use part of the proceeds for education campaigns on better health practices? This is already common practice with tobacco, with many states and the federal government assessing high taxes and using the money for smoking cessation and prevention programs that have succeeded in bringing the smoking rate down dramatically in the past forty years. In my home state of California it's gone from 42% to 12% of the adult population.

It is normal for life and health insurers to charge higher premiums to smokers based on the same principle. The statistical probabilities say they will cost the company more. Consequently, the company charges them more.

Another interesting approach has been pioneered in South Africa. There, a private insurer has teamed up with supermarkets to provide rebates for customers who buy healthy foods. The rebates range from 10% up to 25% on the foods purchased. The program, begun in 2009, covers 800 supermarkets and includes 260,000 households. Figures indicate it is resulting in an 8 to 9 % increase in healthy food purchases and a 7% reduction in sales for unhealthy foods. This will pay off in reduced medical claims against the company in the years ahead. More importantly, the consumers will enjoy longer and healthier lives. Australia is one country studying South Africa's example and contemplating instituting a similar plan.

To sum up, the liberal view is that everyone deserves good health care, and the United States of America is rich and advanced enough to make sure it is a reality. This is a moral imperative and an achievable goal. Other countries far less wealthy are able to do so. America has good health care for most, but it doesn't truly rank with the very top nations. Too many have been excluded from the system and have had to rely on expensive emergency room visits. What's more, the cost of the American health care system is very high, and as the large bloc of baby boomers reach retirement age over the next fifteen years, health care costs will certainly go up even more. The question is what to do.

Conservatives say the solution is to restrict coverage even more by repealing President Obama's Affordable Care Act and telling more people, "You're on your own." Rep. Paul Ryan's budget, passed in the Republican-controlled House of Representatives, would have capped Medicare and given seniors "vouchers" to try to buy coverage on the private market. These approaches would mean going back to more bankruptcies, fewer people covered, an unhealthier population and more preventable deaths.

The liberal solution is to cover everyone because health care is a human right. The problem is how to pay for it. Here are some of the factors that will address that need. Give the Affordable Care Act's cost containment provisions a chance to work, by making sure the young and healthy are in the pool, setting up its competitive insurance exchanges, mandating an electronic data sharing system and moving to an outcomes based payment system. It is noteworthy that since the passage of Obamacare, despite hysterical conservative charges that the program would result in out of control health cost increases, the actual annual increases have been cut nearly in half, from an average of 7.8 percent a year for the twenty years before Obamacare to just 4 percent a year since. Keep fighting the drug monopolies by permitting price negotiation on prescription medicine. Step up education of the public in best practices that will improve their health through positive living choices on diet. Reform the system so that those making the unhealthy choices will individually pay a greater share of the expenses of their choices up front at the point of purchase rather than foisting them on society at large in the form of higher medical costs when they get sick. As our experience with smoking shows, this can have major long term beneficial effects on behavior and health over time. Finally, keep up with and adopt promising innovations like South Africa's supermarket-insurance initiative.

Liberals dream of the day when every human being can expect sustaining health care structured in such a way that society can afford it. With these and other reforms, they will not rest until it is a reality for all.

CHAPTER 9:
Education and Opportunity

Education is the key to unlock the golden door of freedom.
George Washington Carver

Liberals believe in an opportunity society. Creating such a society begins with a value system that fosters personal responsibility. Starting from this foundation, liberals are dedicated to providing the community support essential to success and removing the obstacles that hold people back. The liberal ideal is to give every American, irrespective of the advantages or debilities of their life circumstances, a real shot at achieving their goals and dreams. Education is central to opportunity, for study after study shows how strongly not only income, but social and family stability are related to the level of educational achievement a person attains. Here are some recent figures, provided by the U.S. Bureau of Labor Statistics.

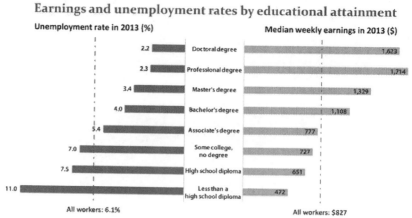

Earnings and unemployment rates by educational attainment

Unemployment rate in 2013 (%)		Median weekly earnings in 2013 ($)
2.2	Doctoral degree	1,623
2.3	Professional degree	1,714
3.4	Master's degree	1,329
4.0	Bachelor's degree	1,108
5.4	Associate's degree	777
7.0	Some college, no degree	727
7.5	High school diploma	651
11.0	Less than a high school diploma	472
All workers: 6.1%		All workers: $827

Note: Data are for persons age 25 and over. Earnings are for full-time wage and salary workers.
Source: Current Population Survey, U.S. Bureau of Labor Statistics, U.S. Department of Labor

The differences are enormous. As the chart shows, the unemployment rate for a typical high school graduate is nearly twice as high as for a bachelor's degree holder, and the college grad earns $57,616 compared to $33,852 for the worker with just a high school diploma. Over the course of a 40-year working career the person with the college degree earns nearly *a million dollars more!*

A study by the Alliance for Excellent Education details a similarly immense impact educational attainment has on crime. The 2013 report, *Saving Futures, Saving Dollars*, compared crime rates among citizens of differing educational levels and found that if the high school graduation rate for males was improved by just five percent America could save $18.5 billion a year in crime costs. More findings include:

"In addition to examining total crime savings, the report projects the number of individual crimes that could be prevented by increasing the male high school graduation rate by 5 percentage points, and finds that such an increase would decrease overall annual incidences of assault by nearly 60,000; larceny by more than 37,000; motor vehicle theft by more than 31,000; and burglaries by more than 17,000. It would also prevent nearly 1,300 murders, more than 3,800 occurrences of rape, and more than 1,500 robberies."

The average amount spent to educate a student for a year is $12,643, compared to the average annual cost of $28,323 to house a prison inmate for a year. As the study notes, "If the nation made a comparable investment in effort and dollars in schools as it does in jails and prisons, the return would be decreased levels of criminal activity and incarceration as well as significant and life-changing impacts on the individual." Benjamin Franklin once wrote, "An investment in knowledge pays the best interest." Liberals could not agree more.

Liberals favor a robust public education system that is well funded and high quality for all. And one of the very wisest investments our society can make is in early childhood education, that is, pre-school before kindergarten. A coalition of law enforcement leaders called Fight Crime: Invest in Kids cited a study showing that at-risk children who were never enrolled in preschool were *five times* more likely to be habitual offenders by age 27 than those who had a pre-school experience. Programs like Head Start and child nutrition are proven ways to close the achievement gap for kids raised in poverty, and liberals oppose conservative attempts to "save" money by cutting or eliminating them. It winds up costing a lot more money in the long run to pay the increased costs of crime and incarceration that inevitably result, not to mention the preventable ruined lives of victims and offenders.

In school, liberals advocate a broad, wide-ranging, liberal arts education. We feel the conservative-led "back to basics" thrust that surged through the American educational system in the 1980s and after was completely wrong-headed. Yes, it is essential that the basics of reading, writing and arithmetic are mastered, but there is much more to education than that. Education is not just the absorption of facts but learning how to think. As Sydney Harris said, "The whole purpose of education is to turn mirrors into windows."

When I first entered college, I in my almost eighteen-year-old naivety and conservative mindset thought my professors would teach me all the answers; after all, they were brilliant people with PhD's. I also expected that since they were so knowledgeable they would mostly agree on everything. I was soon to learn that there were a great many differing perspectives among them. I had one International Relations professor who was an arch-conservative militarist and another who was an idealistic pacifist. I was exposed to a conservative in Constitutional Law and a liberal in California Politics. One military historian thought the United States could do no wrong and one scholar of the Middle East seemed to think America was at least partly responsible for almost everything that went wrong in that turbulent region. The conventional viewpoints of my moderate Economics professor were balanced by the radical notions of my Sociology professor.

The process at first mystified me, but before long came to intrigue me. I began to perceive that a good education didn't teach me *what* to think but exposed me to the world of ideas in all their plentitude. It opened my mind to the diversity of human perspectives and then equipped me with the research and analytical tools to first, detect and eliminate nonsense, and then, to reason my way to *my own* conclusions on things. I now realize that this epiphany was the first step on my journey to liberalism. Pre-packaged answers and unexamined groupthink "certainties" are catnip for the conservative world view. Most people do not take the trouble to examine multiple sources and consider alternative explanations or solutions to things. Without strong critical thinking skills or a wide information base some easily swallow the dark intimations of crackpot conspiracy theory. Others just as easily accept the platitudes proffered by those whose interests lie in preserving the *status quo*, often those with a vested financial interest to see to it that their position on any matter in question is accepted without close scrutiny. As the poet William Butler Yeats put it, "Education is not the filling of a pail but the lighting of a fire."

Liberals believe that rather than paring back schooling to the three r's, and testing people *ad infinitum*, students should be exposed to a very wide range of learning experiences. The junior high or middle school curriculum should have a variety of elective offerings to interest and challenge the students. A good comprehensive high school needs to include social sciences and the arts, including subjects like music, drama and dance. There should be plenty of vocational offerings and lots of activities and clubs in addition to sports. That's because research shows a very high correlation between student involvement and success in later life. Another reason is it allows young people to discover their passion. I well remember getting to Glen A. Wilson High School in Hacienda Heights, California every morning and always seeing a group of young men waiting outside the Industrial Arts building. They wore black leather jackets with *Thee Seventh Dimensions* in bright gold letters across the back. They were the auto shop club guys. Most of them were not very academic but they came to school and made the effort to pass English and Math so they could do what they loved, which was work on cars. A lot of kids on the drill team, band, or sports did the same. That's how they learn the English, Math, History and Science that broaden their skills and interests. Just as importantly, they become the informed citizens a democracy depends on. The surest safeguard for our freedoms is an informed citizenry who can think for themselves. As Thomas Jefferson once said, "An educated citizenry is a vital requisite for our survival as a free people."

Liberals also believe in and fight for universal access and generous support for college education. After World War II, thanks to the GI Bill and increased state and federal support for scholarships and university expansion, tuition and costs were kept low to make the opportunity of a college education possible for qualified students of limited economic means. The number of American college and university graduates increased from 5 percent of the adult population in 1940 to 20 percent in 1990 and over 30 percent today. The U.S. became the most educated nation on earth, and led the world in innovation. Even so, since 1978 college expenses have gone up at over three times the rate of inflation. College tuitions and fees have risen as states, especially under conservative governments, have cut taxes on corporations and the wealthy and tried to balance their budgets by shifting more and more costs to the average citizen. States once paid three-fourths of the cost to send a student to a public university. Now they pay only one-fourth. One serious result has been the exclusion of growing numbers of qualified students from a fair shot at a university degree. Another is burdening young graduates with huge student loan debts to pay off. Since 1999 the amount of student debt owed in the United States has increased by 500 times. In the same period, beginning salaries for new graduates have not increased at all. The ripple effect across the economy is severe. Data show that millennials are delaying getting and having children, and putting off buying cars and homes. Student debt is a big reason behind this. As the Huffington Post highlighted, "According to a report by the One Wisconsin Institute, the impact of student debt translates into over $6 billion in lost automotive sales each year. General Motors is also taking note. Recently, Dr. G. Mustafa Mohatarem, the chief economist for General Motors, cited student loan debt as one of the major reasons why millennials are not purchasing cars."

Federal student loans have also perversely been set up with the priority of making a profit rather than making it easy for all qualified students to get a college education. They turn a profit of $50 billion a year, $5 billion more than the yearly net of Exxon Mobil, the most profitable company in the world. Today, forty million Americans owe a total of $1.2 trillion in student loans, a massive drag on the economy and a major disincentive for people who are qualified but not rich to continue their educations past high school. Liberal Senator Elizabeth Warren of Massachusetts has made it a special focus of hers to reverse these trends. She says, "Just the little slice of loans that were issued between 2007 and 2012 are projected to produce $66 billion in profits to the federal government. Think about that. The role of government has to be helping young people, instead of taxing them for making the effort." She has introduced such measures as allowing students to refinance loans the same way homeowners do when interest rates go down, to allow the student borrowers to refinance all loans at the current new borrowing rate of 3.86% that she recently got passed, or even to offer the loans at zero interest and pay the difference by removing tax loopholes for millionaires and billionaires. That's an approach liberals can emphatically agree with. The measure got the vote of every Democrat, both independents and three Republicans in the Senate, but fell just short of the 60-vote threshold needed to overcome a conservative filibuster.

Even better would be the policies of such countries as Germany, France, Argentina, Brazil and Turkey, where college tuition is free for students who are admitted to college and pass their classes. A nation that wants a vibrant and expanding middle class and wants to be internationally competitive ought to be making things as easy as possible for qualified and motivated young people to get the training they need to excel. The entire nation will benefit from the increased earnings, taxes, and all the social benefits connected with having a highly educated workforce.

About Teaching

The whole art of teaching is only the art of awakening the natural curiosity of the mind for the purpose of satisfying it afterwards.

Anatole France

I've been teaching long enough-over 30 years at various levels-to have seen that different teachers are effective with different styles. Some are strict, some looser, some more interactive and some hands-on, some serious and others humorous. A teacher has to be true to the personality and gifts that he or she has. In my view, the indispensable attributes a teacher at any level must have are a love for learning or at least their subject, and a respect for others, including students, administrators and, in pre-college grades, parents. There is no one "right way to teach," and while teachers are always on the lookout for good, effective ideas from others in the profession, what works for one may not work as well for another. Cookie-cutter prescriptions and educational fads come and go, and good teachers adopt what works for them among the innovations. But nothing works universally well for every teacher and with every group of students in every classroom. If it were that simple the formula would have been set in concrete centuries ago.

A great deal of controversy is engendered over proscriptive education directives and by such issues as teacher tenure. In my long experience, only an extremely small percentage of teachers are incompetent or lack dedication. The best policy to keep education strong is to hire good people, provide helpful staff development and a good, experienced mentor teacher to show them the ropes, and then get out of their way and let them teach. Plenty of support for good salaries and benefits will draw better people, as it does in any profession, and plenty of support for diverse programs is best for the students. Having a strong school-wide handle on student conduct is also essential, both to the learning environment and to teacher retention. But good teachers will excel in even quite difficult situations, while bad ones will fail or burn out even in fairly ideal environments. The National Center for Educational Statistics finds, for example that half the new teachers leave the profession in the first five years. The teaching profession is largely self-selecting; it's not for everyone.

The tenure issue is overblown by conservatives. Tenure just means that the teacher has due process and can't be fired solely on the principal's say so. People deserve to be protected from arbitrary disfavor which could stem from personal animus, rejection of an administrator's sexual advances, or who knows what. There needs to be a documented pattern of incompetence or negligence. That means the administration actually needs to spend some time observing the teacher and offering constructive direction and assistance for improvement. As with any other just practice relating to employees, it should be possible to get rid of really bad teachers. Performance evaluations ought to let them know they are not measuring up and reasonable support should be given to help them improve and rectify their deficiencies. After that point dismissal should be the necessary end for those who still don't make the necessary remediation. The teaching profession is demanding in so many ways, and it doesn't help the students, the school or teachers themselves to be in positions they really aren't cut out for.

That's all well and good, but we cannot lose sight of the fact that teachers are overwhelmingly competent and dedicated. Nobody goes into teaching to get rich. People become teachers because they like kids and want to dedicate their lives to helping them learn and grow. So, what gives? Why aren't the achievement levels higher? Well, the correlation between parental income level and their children's academic achievement is nearly absolute. The larger the poverty-level population grows the greater the societal and educational dysfunction that mirrors it. We must tackle income inequality in a serious way if we want this to improve. A reform like the "Common Core" is fine and liberals tend to like it because it encourages critical thinking instead of simple rote memorization, but we need to remember it's not teachers unions or the latest educational theory or fad that is to blame or is the solution. Parents who value learning, model responsible life choices and insist on achievement are the solution. And parents and students who have hope are the ones who are emotionally equipped to fill those roles: That, and a helping hand when it's needed spell the path to true opportunity.

So, how do we start going about improving student achievement in American education? One important step would be to address income inequality. According to a 2012 study of 4,500 children from low-income families published in *The American Economic Review*, a $1,000 increase in family income raises math and reading test scores by about 6 percent. That's a big part of the reason liberals support an increase in the minimum wage to a true "living wage." When it comes to political approaches, the educational gimmicks and attacks on teachers unions are often no more than the fallout from the latest round of partisan culture wars. Kids are not political footballs and education is far too important a priority to be left to the control of ideological extremists. To address what ails society we have to treat what is holding back people's lives, and all too often it is financial need. And in this regard, the remarkable efforts of one Florida entrepreneur point the way.

Harris Rosen was born in New York but moved to Orlando, Florida and made a fortune in the hotel business. Harris decided to share some of his success to make a difference in people's lives.

He selected the impoverished Orlando neighborhood of Tangelo Park, a low-income, high-crime community of about 3,000 people that was infested with drug houses and where only 25 percent of the kids graduated from high school. Harris started by offering to pay for day care for any kid in Tangelo Park. This gave parents the wherewithal to get a job or go back to school. When the original group of kids got to high school he started a scholarship program that would pay full tuition for every Tangelo Park student at any Florida state college. As the *Today Show* reported, "In the two decades since starting the programs, Rosen has donated nearly $10 million, and the results have been remarkable. The high school graduation rate is now nearly 100 percent, and some property values have quadrupled. The crime rate has been cut in half, according to a study by the University of Central Florida." How can you explain such an amazing turnaround? We've given them hope,'' Rosen said. "We've given these kids hope, and given the families hope. And hope is an amazing thing."

Harris Rosen's imagination and generosity show what can happen when obstacles are removed and people feel their dreams can actually be realized. Liberals applaud efforts like Harris Rosen's and believe such opportunities should not be up to the private philanthropy of one person here and one person there in scattered communities around the country. Rosen's annual investment in the people of Tangelo Park comes to about $167 per person. An equivalent investment in the people of the entire USA would come to about $5.2 billion a year. The estimated total education spending at all levels for 2015 in America is $1055 trillion. With results like these, wouldn't it make sense to spend an extra $5.2 billion a year—half of one percent of our national education spending—on a nationwide program of universal child care and free college tuition for every American kid who can get admitted to a state college or university? Liberals emphatically say yes!

I'll close this section with three blogs I wrote about the topic of education, based on my own experience as an educator for over thirty years, and with reference to the best information I could find. The first is about the need for more education spending and progress on income inequality, the second highlights some of the personal impediments my own community college students face in their everyday lives, and the third is about some of my thoughts on the kinds of classes our young people need. The common denominator is that in education, you have to put people first.

"U.S. Kids Losing Ground"
from Bravegnuwhirled.blogspot.com: April 30, 2013:

Neglect has its consequences, as do the ideologies and policies that foster it. A new study ranks the well-being of American children at number 26 out of 29 Western countries researched, ahead of only Lithuania, Latvia and Romania, and behind such places as Spain, Slovenia, Slovakia and Greece.

The United Nations Children's Fund (UNICEF) report compared kids in 29 developed and "emerging" Western countries in five categories: material well-being, health and safety, behaviors and risks, housing and environment, and education. The U.S. was in the bottom third on all five counts, lagging worst in education and poverty. The Netherlands came in first, followed by Norway, Iceland, Finland, Sweden and Germany.

The report found that the countries with the best child well-being were also the ones that invest most heavily in social safety nets, into which the Scandinavian countries contribute "nearly 7% of their GDP." Meanwhile, budget cuts for education and sequesters for programs for the needy have become the order of the day in the United States over the past few years.

With a per capita GDP of more than $48,000 in 2012, the U.S. is by far the richest nation in the study, but its priorities do not match its resources. The study finds that "income inequality has increased the population of children who grow up in poverty" and that the U.S. economy is "one of the most unequal in the Western world." Many American children are "doing great" but so many U.S. kids are "so much worse off than the average Greek or

Slovakian child as to bring the overall U.S average beneath those less wealthy and developed countries."

Our deterioration into an increasingly two-tiered society, the haves and the have-nots, is clearly underscored in research such as this. Without a restoration of ameliorative spending, programs and help for a burgeoning underclass, these trends will do nothing but worsen. The Republican fixation with slashing spending and leaving those without resources to sink on their own is leading to a looming competitive and social catastrophe. It is imperative that the American people reject this philosophy; it is not only mean-spirited, but a growing body of research also shows that it simply does not work.

"Finals Week" from Bravegnuwhirled.blogspot.com: December 18, 2008

Today ended another Finals Week here at College of the Sequoias. What stands out to me from the results in my classes is the great disparity among the students. Most either did very well or they did poorly, with relatively few in the middling range. They either applied themselves and studied thoroughly or they did not bother to prepare. This suggests some interesting things to muse about.

In my five History classes I distributed study sheets pointing out what they needed to know for their specific final and where to find it. Depending on the various class calendars the students then had either five or seven days to prepare. For the benefit of those who really like to get started early they had also been told for weeks what chapters their final would cover. Since these are all college students who had stuck it out to the end of the semester, one might assume they would all want to make sure their investments of time, effort and money were not in vain.

If so, that assumption would have been disappointed. One of the questions on the test shed some light on the subject. I asked the students to write about an event in their personal history that had an important effect on their subsequent life. That this is a poor area was highlighted by the number of young people who wrote about tragedies very close to them. There seemed to be a disproportionate number of deaths of close family members, imprisonments, and so forth. Family breakups were commonly cited. Parents losing jobs and frequent moves were other themes. Some had such problems or were recovering from health issues and substance abuse difficulties themselves.

It seemed the social problems we have, especially among the less privileged, are truly serious and corrosive in our society. Many have overcome a lot just to be taking classes at a community college at all. Many were the first to go to college in their families; some were the first or second to even make it through high school. Quite a few mentioned how proud their mother would be if they made it through and graduated. Others mentioned a grandfather or a teacher who had inspired them. It is so crucial for parents to offer encouragement and set standards and expectations, and for the rest of us who come into contact with young people to offer them a positive role model and practical wisdom. Too many are not hearing it from many quarters.

Even so, many are just lazy or immature. They simply are not ready or do not get how life operates yet. We will see some of them a few years down the road. We love to see students in their thirties and older come into our classes. They have found out from the school of hard knocks that life without a vocational certificate or degree is usually not a bed of roses. They have been stuck in dead end jobs and are seriously motivated.

At the bottom line, an attitude of pride in one's self, an ethic of achievement and some fear of what life usually metes out to the unprepared would be good cultural traits to pass along. There is also the matter of confidence or belief. Many who do not come from backgrounds that inculcate such values have to fight peer pressure or resentment. Since too many are not getting these ideas at home, they must be communicated at school from the earliest grades. And there also needs to be a more stable financial situation for the working poor. The hand to mouth struggle for existence for many is a major impediment to taking the time or having the resources to succeed. People need to see a realistic way ahead. Just being told about it is not enough for many; they need to see it in their communities.

.

"What Students Need to Learn"
from Bravegnuwhirled.blogspot.com: December 19, 2008
   Following up from yesterday's post about the community colleges, years of familiarity with our students has really settled me on some classes I feel ought to be essential for everyone who goes to school in the United States. I'm not talking just about academics, but about things a person needs to know to live a happy and productive life. With our large and growing underclass, we need to understand that more and more young people are simply not getting these life lessons at home. There is a huge correlation between a single-parent, low-income childhood and incarceration, substance abuse, unwed pregnancy, premature death, in short, all the negative life outcomes that are so strongly associated with poverty.
Here are some of the classes I think everybody needs.
   Health and Wellness. This includes hygiene, nutrition, exercise and first aid. People need to hear that a double cheeseburger and fries every day will kill them before they are 50. Heaven knows they hear and see enough messages every day telling them to scarf down the burgers, beer, soda and candy. We have an obesity/diabetes epidemic? Is anyone surprised? Gigantic benefits for people's lives and for society down the road.
   Human Relations. Members of any society need to understand the rules of common courtesy and expectations. Family dynamics could be improved immensely if people learned how to discuss things in psychologically appropriate ways. Sex, raising children, and all that jazz would be covered in this class too. This class would reduce crime, violence, divorce, child abuse and just a whole lot of human misery in general. The payoff for society would be huge.

Something vocational or domestic. It could be carpentry, cooking, gardening, appliance repair, plumbing, sewing, or the like. Yes, even academic-minded college-prep students could use some of these skills around the house or in their future lives as suburban homeowners. Some would find a path to vocational careers, too. Not everybody needs to get an academic degree, and millions of vocationally-minded teens see little reason to stay in school if white-collar directed courses are all that are taught. Remember, no more than 25% of jobs will require a college degree for the foreseeable future. Serve your customers' needs or you will lose them. This is not a new concept.

Consumer Math. People need to see how much they will wind up paying for things if they run up credit card debt. They should know how much income it takes to afford an apartment or buy a house, how to do their taxes and how much various jobs pay. They need to learn about insurance, including medical, auto, home and life. We need to have savvy consumers who have a realistic appraisal of what they need to do to afford to live in society and are proficient enough not to get scammed by all the predators out there in the market. This shouldn't wait until the senior year of high school. It should be in junior high or the freshman year. The average person does not need fancy abstract math. But they sure as heck need this. Our society is structured so that it depends on them knowing it. But look at the foreclosure rate. So let's see that they do.

CHAPTER 10:

The Environment

Keep close to nature's heart...and break clear away once in awhile, and climb a mountain or spend a week in the woods. Wash your spirit clean.

John Muir

Have you ever been down to the seashore? How do you feel when you first catch sight of the endless blue stretching over the horizon, smell the salt air, hear the crash of surf against sand or cliffs and the high-pitched calls of the circling gulls? Have you ever hiked a forest trail and trod the soft cushion of leaf or needle-padded earth beneath your feet? How do you feel as you wend your way beside a creek now rushing, now gurgling, the pine scent filling the air, as you round a bend and suddenly spot a doe leading a faun through a shaded glen?

No more than a forty-five minute drive from my everyday routine beckons the entrance to Sequoia National Park, home to the Giant Sequoias, the largest living things ever to have existed on our planet. Their majesty is stupefying. Two and a half hours north there is Yosemite Valley, a wonderland of stark granite, falling water and still green meadow under an achingly blue sky. The vista in any direction inspires awe. Or two and a half hours west rest the alternately soothing sands and dizzying cliffs of the Pacific Coast, where the rhythmic washing of the waves under a refreshing sea breeze relaxes all cares while pelicans, sea lions, dolphins, whales and otters provide entertainment.

Liberals love the natural environment. John Muir, the great early twentieth century advocate for preserving wild places, expressed the effect nicely in the quote above. He also said, "Everybody needs beauty as well as bread, places to play in and pray in, where nature may heal and give strength to body and soul." There is something powerfully affecting in unspoiled nature. It connects us with our primal past. Hundreds of thousands of years of survival-focused evolution as hunter-gatherers have attuned us to places bursting with clean water and lush vegetation, for there is abundance, there is sustenance. Our brains are suffused with the warm glow of well-being that tells us, "stop here!" Our minds are at peace because they know our bodies will soon be refreshed and our weary muscles at rest.

Liberals love nature because they tend to be the sort of people who are open to the spiritual, emotional, aesthetic side of being human, including compassion for natural species. But that's only part of the reason. We love it on practical grounds too, for liberals take the long view on meeting human needs. Depleting the resources we require, befouling the air and water we depend on to survive, ruining and building over the arable land we need for farming, indiscriminately introducing untested or harmful chemicals into our food or the means of producing it, interfering with the ecosystem in ways that adversely affect the web of life that we and all species depend on are foolhardy practices. We decry and oppose them not solely because we are "tree huggers" or lovers of small birds, fish or mollusks most people scarcely notice. No, we do this also because we are hard-headed, and as protective as a mother bear is for her cubs.

We don't want species to disappear because medicines are often developed from biological organisms. Drive them to extinction and we may be preventing the introduction of important medicines for human diseases in the future. A particular plant or animal may be a primary food source whose absence could starve other species and cause an entire region's ecology to deteriorate and collapse. That kind of thing can result in a voracious pest multiplying out of control when its natural predators or competitors disappear. These kinds of concerns usually come into sharp focus when the individual interest comes into conflict with or threatens the community interest. Liberals believe the community interest must be considered and given a great deal of weight. As Lincoln said, "I am for those means which will give the greatest good to the greatest number." That is always a prime goal for us. We do not see property rights as absolute. For an example, most communities have noise abatement ordinances. The property owner's right to blare loud music at 3:00 A.M. is superseded by everyone else in the neighborhood's right to several hours of uninterrupted quiet time for needed sleep.

But the conflicts that typically result in environmental disputes pit the profit motive against the common good. If it's cheaper for a manufacturer of a hog farmer to dump waste directly into a river, is that interest overridden by the desire of others to have a clean river for boating, fishing, and drinking water? Liberals say yes. Is it all right for a timber company to buy thousands of acres of forest and chop down every tree for miles in every direction, destroying an entire ecosystem? Liberals say no.

Liberals are not against private property. Liberals are for everyone enjoying maximum rights, but when the rights of one harm the rights of many, we are on the side of the many. One person's rights extend until they impinge upon someone else's rights; that's how we see it. That's why we have not only noise ordinances but traffic signals and pollution control laws. One person's desire to dispose of toxic waste in the most convenient possible way does not outweigh the danger of exposing fellow citizens to sickness and death from lethal poisons.

How do we determine whose rights prevail? We use democracy. When conflicting rights are at issue the people's elected representatives hear testimony from concerned citizens of different viewpoints and examine evidence. They apply factors such as the findings of science, the precepts of the Constitution, the will of the constituents who have elected them, their ethics and their sense of fairness to an issue. Then they pass a law or approve or reject a project, or approve it with specific stipulations designed to promote such considerations as the people's health, the lives of affected plants and animals, or the preservation of resources such as water, air and habitat. That's how. It isn't always easy, or clearly cut and dried. It requires mature judgment applied to weighing the complexity of multiple factors. If new evidence comes up it can be brought up for consideration. But what the process does not need is the influence of campaign cash being dangled in front of officials for the "right" judgment of a situation. As Upton Sinclair wrote, "It is difficult to get a man to understand something, when his salary depends on his not understanding it." Liberals believe the impartial consideration of environmental questions for the good of all parties concerned presents one of the most urgent and compelling reasons to get rid of the influence of private money in political campaigns.

Here are some of the American environmental issues liberals are concerned about.

Fracking

Hydraulic fracturing is a technique to get more oil or natural gas from rock formations deep underground. It involves injecting water and a stew of dissolved volatile chemicals into a well under high pressure. The process fractures rock, freeing hard-to-get-at oil and gas deposits and increasing the production of wells. It's being used in new fields such as North Dakota and Wyoming with geological strata that have been hard to drill up to now, and in old fields such as Pennsylvania to squeeze more hydrocarbons out of formations that had previously been tapped but left a lot of fossil fuel underground that couldn't be recovered using older technologies. California is another state that has large reserves from older fields that will likely become prime industry targets due to fracking. These are primarily in the massive Monterey Shale formation which rests beneath much of the central portion of the state.

Liberals are highly suspicious of fracking for a number of reasons. First, we want to put more emphasis on clean, renewable energy sources such as wind, solar, geothermal and tidal. Fossil fuels are what are putting poison into our breathing air and raising global temperatures through the greenhouse effect of gasses like carbon dioxide and methane. On the whole, we and the earth would be a lot better off phasing out fossil fuels in favor of their clean alternatives rather than finding new ways to produce more of them. Second, we are alarmed about the possibility of toxic chemicals such as solvents being injected into the ground and contaminating the water table we use for irrigation and drinking water. Third, fracking has been associated with earthquake activity in Pennsylvania. To what extent will breaking up subterranean rock formations act to destabilize the crust and set off subsidence and quakes? Is that something we really want to mess with? We need to see a lot more research and provisions for serious safeguards before we're the least bit enthusiastic about opening up this Pandora's box.

Genetically Engineered Foods

Genetically engineered or modified food sources is another issue liberals approach with a maximum of caution. GE or GM crops are touted as means to increase yields or resistance to conditions such as drought or disease. These are potentially good things. But the corporatization of this science raises disquieting questions. It is expensive, often pricing small and third-world subsistence growers out of the market. Part of the reason for this is that it often requires the heavy application of fertilizers and pesticides, often provided by the very same companies that produced the GM varieties in the first place. The interest of these companies is to produce a lack of plant diversity and a dependence on their brands, protected as their intellectual property. They have already successfully sued American farmers, resistant to their crops, whose own fields have become cross-pollinated (contaminated) with the corporate GM crops through no fault or desire of their own. Monocultures of a few varieties of crops make the whole food system more vulnerable to particularly well-adapted pests or disease. And the nutritional value of tinkering with foodstuffs the human body has adapted to for millennia needs much careful study. The industry's absolute resistance to having

GE and GM foods clearly labeled for the consumer is alarming in the extreme. Experience with industries such as tobacco and insurance teaches that people who wish to keep the truth from their customers usually have good reason. Proposition 37, on the California ballot in 2012, went down to a narrow 51-49 percent defeat. It would have required clear labeling of GM foods, but was overwhelmed in the campaign by a $45 million blitz funded by chemical industry heavyweights like Monsanto, Dupont, Dow, Bayer, Syngentia and BASF, and the Grocery Manufacturers Association. A similar initiative was narrowly defeated in Washington State in 2013, thanks to a $22 million campaign there. According to the Seattle *Times,* all but $550 of that came from out-of-state sponsors, headed by the same groups that filled the airwaves in California the year before.

Global Warming/Climate Change

The climate of the earth is heating up, and human-generated greenhouse gasses are the main cause of it. The Intergovernmental Panel on Climate Change (IPPC) was awarded the Nobel Peace Prize in 2007 "for their efforts to build up and disseminate greater knowledge about man-made climate change, and to lay the foundations for the measures that are needed to counteract such change."

In September 2013, IPPC's Approved Summary for Policymakers concluded, *"Observations of the climate system are based on direct measurements and remote sensing from satellites and other platforms. Global-scale observations from the instrumental era began in the mid-19th century for temperature and other variables, with more comprehensive and diverse sets of records dating back hundreds to millions of years. Together, they provide a comprehensive view of the variability and long-term changes in the atmosphere, the ocean, the cryosphere, and the land surface. Warming of the climate system is unequivocal, and since the 1950s, many of the observed changes are unprecedented over decades to millennia. The atmosphere and ocean have warmed, the amounts of snow and ice have diminished, sea level has risen, and the concentrations of greenhouse gases have increased."*

An update released by IPCC in October, based on the efforts of 4,000 contributors and 30,000 climate studies, emphasized that every passing month has done nothing but add additional certainty to the scientific conclusion that pernicious climatic conditions continue to worsen and that the human origin of the observed changes is more definitively certain than ever. Atmospheric scientists overwhelmingly agree that human release of carbon dioxide into the air through the burning of fossil fuels (oil, coal, natural gas) and deforestation are principally to blame for what is happening to Earth's climate. Liberals agree that the science is more compelling than self-serving advertising campaigns paid for by the dirty fuel industry or the politically-driven pronouncements of scientifically ignorant right-wing radio and cable news personalities.

Liberals also keep in mind a few other important principles: This is the only planet we've got. Once a species goes extinct it's gone forever. Carbon dioxide is acidifying the oceans, killing off the coral and the plankton. Coral reefs provide habitat for a multitude of marine species and plankton, through photosynthesis, produces most of the free oxygen in the air we breathe. To pollute the oceans and turn them too acidic to sustain the very organisms we depend on for life on Earth is exceedingly foolish. This isn't about Romanticism, it's about the stark principles of ecological survival.

Liberals and the Environment: Progress and Challenges

Liberals stand strong against proposals to roll back environmental protections. The dishonest, short-sighted and self-serving anti-environmental campaign is pushed most strongly by industries that pollute the air, water and land. It has been over forty years since the establishment of the Environmental Protection

Agency and the passage of the foundational Clean Air, Clean Water and Endangered Species Acts. Hysterical predictions of economic collapse were made at the time and continue to spew from the polluters' propaganda outlets. Yet four decades later those predictions have never been borne out and substantial progress has been made on all fronts. Green energy will produce its own network of jobs, just as earlier transformations did when the economy switched from whale oil lamps to electricity, from firewood to oil and gas, or from the horse and buggy to the automobile.

The banning of chlorofluorocarbons (CFC's) back in 1978 arrested the expansion of the South Polar ozone hole, and now we are finally seeing a reduction in this phenomenon that was destroying the earth's natural shield against harmful ultraviolet solar radiation, a major cause of skin cancer.

As Glen Grunwald reported in *Time Magazine* in 2013, President Barack "Obama has probably done more than anyone in the history of the planet to reduce carbon emissions. He doubled fuel efficiency standards for cars and trucks, which by 2025 should erase an entire year worth of U.S. emissions. He enacted a series of new efficiency standards for dishwashers, refrigerators and other appliances, which by 2030 should save enough electricity to power every American single-family home for two years. He approved 45 renewable electricity projects on federal land, producing 10 gigawatts of clean power; his predecessors approved a grand total of zero. And his 2009 stimulus bill launched a clean energy revolution, with $90 billion worth of unprecedented investments in wind, solar and geothermal power; advanced biofuels; electric vehicles; a smarter grid; cleaner coal; efficiency in every imaginable form; high-concept research into low-emissions technologies; green manufacturing; and much more."

Green energy has therefore doubled in the United States in the past five years with the Obama stimulus investments. Added to the increased vehicle fuel and appliance efficiency standards and incentives for structural insulation, these efforts are beginning to make a difference. The U.S. is importing 1.8 million fewer barrels of oil every day than it did in 2008. In late 2014 he signed an agreement in which, for the first time, China agreed to join the U.S in significantly reducing its emissions over the next several years.

Since the passage of the Clean Air Act in 1970, six common pollutants in the air have been reduced by 72%, including 91% for lead and 83% for carbon monoxide. Acid rain in the eastern U.S. is down by 55%. Current cars and trucks are 99% cleaner than 1970 models. Scientific studies concluded that in 2010, legally mandated protections against air pollution prevented 160,000 deaths and 13 million lost work days in that year alone.

Since the passage of the Clean Water Act in 1972 the percentage of American rivers designated as unsafe for human use has been cut in half. Lake Erie was a particularly ugly example of fouled water. In August, 1969, *Time Magazine* wrote, "Each day, Detroit, Cleveland and 120 other municipalities fill Erie with 1.5 billion gallons of inadequately treated wastes, including nitrates and phosphates ... These chemicals act as fertilizer for growths of algae that suck oxygen from the lower depths and rise to the surface as odoriferous green scum ... Commercial and game fish—blue pike, whitefish, sturgeon, northern pike—have nearly vanished, yielding the waters to trash fish that need less oxygen. Weeds proliferate, turning water frontage into swamp. In short, Lake Erie is in danger of dying by suffocation." Today it is a remarkable success story. Commercial and recreational fishing are back, thanks to the CWA and the 1978 Great Lakes Water Quality Agreement with Canada. Together these efforts keep those 1.5 billion gallons of pollution out of the lake every day.

Endangered species can be saved. Since the Endangered Species Act was passed in 1973, more than 1,300 hundred species have been listed and only 10 have gone extinct. A 2012 study of 110 specific species found that "90 percent of species are recovering at the rate specified by their federal recovery plan." The 2013 report *Back from the Brink: Ten Success Stories Celebrating the Endangered Species Act at 40* highlighted some exemplary results, including America's national symbol, the bald eagle, which had once all but disappeared from the contiguous U.S. states. These signature saves "include the nēnē goose, American peregrine falcon, El Segundo blue butterfly, Robbins' cinquefoil, bald eagle, southern sea otter, humpback whale, American alligator, brown pelican and the green sea turtle."

Yet even with such heartening results, there is still much work to do. Greenhouse gases, particularly carbon dioxide but also methane, continue to drive anthropogenic climate change. With CO_2 concentrations now over 450 parts per million the earth's average temperature has already warmed over 1 degree, resulting in ice cap melting, sea level rise, severe droughts in some places and more powerful storms in others, such as Super Storm Sandy that struck New Jersey and New York in 2012. Projections indicate that five-sixths of the Miami strip is likely to be underwater by the end of the century, even if emissions are held at present levels.

The exhaustive 2014 Audubon Society bird survey projects that 314 North American bird species will be endangered by the end of the century due to loss of habitat caused by the warming climate.

The International Union for Conservation and Nature now has 41,415 global species of plants and animals on its endangered Red List, and 16,306 of these are listed as "threatened with extinction." This is up from 16,118 last year.

The World Health Organization estimates that in 2014, 7 million people worldwide died prematurely as a result of air pollution. That is about one in eight of all human deaths. Tropical diseases such as dengue fever and malaria are creeping northward as temperature warms.

The World Health Organization and UNICEF estimate that "36 per cent of the world's population – 2.5 billion people – lack improved sanitation facilities, and 768 million people still use unsafe drinking water sources." The prevalence of these conditions "kills and sickens thousands of children every day, and leads to impoverishment and diminished opportunities for thousands more."

Liberals should be galvanized by these alarming developments, and should not be disheartened by the perception that the public at large does not realize the importance of what is happening or understand the true causes. Despite all the money the fossil fuel industry has spent on advertising trying to mislead people and despite the highly publicized gatherings of conservatives who chant, "Drill, baby drill," the sensible, factual, scientific-based liberal position is getting out and is persuasive. In 2011 a Pew Research Poll found that 71% of Americans believe "This country should do whatever it takes to protect the environment." And 59% believe that "strongly." 63% agreed that "EPA needs to do more to hold polluters accountable and protect the air and water." When asked about energy production, 63% of Americans said the priority should be to develop renewables like wind, solar and hydrogen and only 29% said the priority should be to expand production of oil, coal and natural gas. Most people get it, and liberals should not be dissuaded from persevering simply because the few who don't are the ones who yell the loudest.

Liberals remain committed to people's safety and freedom from sea level rise, increasingly destructive storms, agricultural decline and preventable disease through the preservation of our planet's natural biosphere. Only by protecting the healthy processes of the Earth can we hope to provide the necessary food, energy, and even oxygen essential to sustaining 7 billion people and the estimated 8.7 million species that coexist with us. Liberals never forget that we depend on a healthy environment that sustains all life on Earth, including our own.

CHAPTER 11:
Defense, War and Peace

"Those who would give up essential liberty, to obtain a little temporary safety, deserve neither liberty nor safety."

Benjamin Franklin

Most liberals believe in America's legitimate right of self-defense. After U. S. troops were attacked by the forces of internal rebellion the great liberal President Abraham Lincoln led America through a terrible Civil War to preserve the Union and secure "a new birth of freedom" to an entire people cruelly and unjustly enslaved. It should not be forgotten that two of the twentieth century's great liberal presidents, Woodrow Wilson and Franklin Roosevelt, led the nation and the free world to victory in the two World Wars. The future great liberal president John F. Kennedy served heroically as a PT boat captain in World War II and future liberal presidential candidate George McGovern flew perilous missions over Nazi Germany as a bomber pilot in that same conflict.

Liberal President Harry Truman, a World War I veteran, put America on a "Cold War" footing with respect to the Soviet Union, augmenting U. S. military forces and forming alliances against the threat he perceived presented by the totalitarian and aggressive Soviet Union. He sent American forces to defend South Korea against invasion by North Korea. Liberal President Lyndon Johnson sent a large American army to fight in Vietnam. Liberal President Barack Obama completed a war he inherited in Iraq and has prosecuted a war he inherited in Afghanistan and ordered drone missile strikes and daring special operations missions against anti-American extremists, including the incursion that killed terrorist leader Osama Bin Laden in Pakistan in 2011.

The point is that most liberals and liberal leaders understand we live in a dangerous world and feel we must have strong military capabilities at the ready. Most liberals grant that there are circumstances in which war is justified. Liberal citizens have served with gallantry in all the nation's wars and liberal leaders have proven themselves effective as commanders in chief. But what characterizes most liberals on matters of defense is their reluctance to turn to war in the first place, based on their conviction that it must be employed sparingly as a last resort to protect Americans, U.S. allies, innocent victims or vital American interests from conquest, death, or loss of freedom. Liberals feel that war and excessive militarism also tend to erode the very constitutional liberties our armed forces exist to protect. That is what the quote from Benjamin Franklin at the beginning of this section refers to. Excessive secrecy, suspicion of dissent and the invasion of constitutional privacy guarantees have all taken place in American history during times of war. And while liberals support a strong defense, they oppose wasteful and unneeded military expenditures that could more productively be spent on other priorities.

There are also some completely pacifistic liberals who oppose taking up arms for any reason. Theirs is a long and respectable tradition in America, one strain of which goes back to such religious groups as the Society of Friends, or Quakers. Another goes back to the nineteenth century Transcendentalist author Henry David Thoreau, who popularized pacifistic views in his book *Civil Disobedience*. Thoreau's ideas were later influential with such non-violent human rights leaders as India's Mahatma Gandhi and America's Martin Luther King. The first American woman in Congress, Representative Jeannette Rankin of Wyoming, was a liberal pacifist who voted against the motions to declare war against Germany in1917 and Japan in 1941. Hers was the only no vote in the latter instance.

The point here is that some liberals are committed pacifists. Most Americans and indeed most liberals are not pacifists, though. Most are willing to support a strong military defense and the sending of our armed forces into combat for what they judge to be urgent and compelling reasons. It is all right for liberals to have differing viewpoints on this, and each can respect the sincerity and motives of the other. What unites liberals, particularly as compared to defense conservatives, as you will see in Chapter 17, is their aversion to using deadly force as a first resort to try to solve problems. It is to be used only after peaceful efforts have been exhausted and innocent lives are in imminent danger, not as a seemingly convenient and quick way to try to eliminate rivals or those who might potentially someday constitute a threat.

This is for a number of reasons. First, the notion that war offers a quick solution to difficult problems is usually illusory. Things almost never go as expected. Let's use the War in Iraq as an instructive example. The Bush Administration confidently predicted all sorts of outcomes prior to launching its War in Iraq in 2003. The people would "greet us as liberators." The Iraqis would be overwhelmed and intimidated by "shock and awe." The fighting would be over in "weeks, not months." The existence of weapons of mass destruction was a "slam dunk." American casualties would be "insignificant." The war would cost "less than $50 billion" or even nothing to the American taxpayer because it would all be "paid for by Iraqi oil revenues." Iraq would turn into a "strong American ally in the heart of the Middle East."

The reality, as we painfully know, was quite different. The war began on March 20, 2003. Less than six weeks later President Bush delivered a victory speech on board the aircraft carrier *USS Abraham Lincoln* under a banner declaring "Mission Accomplished." But his crowing was a bit premature. Instead of greeting us as liberators, many Iraqis took exception to our invasion of their country. Rather than being over in weeks, the fighting continued to rage and American forces did not leave until December 18, 2011, eight years and eight months later. No weapons of mass destruction, the purported reason for the war, were ever found. American casualties ultimately totaled 4,488 military personnel and 3,900 civilian contractors dead and a reported 32,226 wounded. Most people would consider those numbers "significant." Estimates of Iraqi dead range from 109,000 to 162,000 killed, 70 percent of whom were civilians. There were also 319 coalition troops killed.

Financially, the war cost America $845 billion in direct expenses, or $1.7 trillion including indirect costs, according to the Watson Institute of Strategic Studies at Brown University, or up to $3 trillion by the calculations of prominent economist Joseph Stiglitz when all impacts on the economy are taken into account. It's hard to quantify the monetary effect of such war-related phenomena as Post-Traumatic Stress Disorder (PTSD). According to the Veterans Administration it affects 171,423 Iraq and Afghanistan veterans, and has been associated with increased dangerous drinking, drug abuse, suicide, domestic abuse, crime and unemployment. Such effects that negatively impact veterans and society at large for many years after a war are another good reason not to get into one lightly. And Iraq has not become a strong American ally. At the time of this writing the regime installed by American power is allowing Iran to fly arms over its territory to resupply the tyrannical Assad regime in Syria and Hezbollah terrorists in Lebanon, and much of Iraq's own territory has been taken over by extremists.

By any measure the United States of America is well-defended. The American armed forces possess over 8,000 nuclear warheads, which assure that the nation will never be successfully invaded. In the words of former Secretary of State Hillary Clinton, if a rogue state like Iran or North Korea ever dared to launch a nuclear weapon against us or anyone else, they would "cease to exist." In terms of projecting power around the globe, the U.S. Navy operates 10 of the world's 20 aircraft carriers, and the giant American ships carry three times as many carrier-based planes as the rest of the world's navies put together. And the numbers alone do not tell the whole story. American technological air superiority is so advanced that no American soldier has been killed or wounded by enemy air action since World War II. The U.S. defense budget of $690 billion represents 40% of the world total and exceeds that of the next 20 largest military spenders combined. And the majority of those next twenty are America's strongest allies, such as Britain, Germany, France, Italy and Japan.

Liberals tend to question the need for so much military spending and so much military intervention around the world. There comes a point where additional spending and capabilities become overkill. Dwight Eisenhower, Supreme Commander in the European Theater of Operations in World War II, knew as much about war and defense issues as any American ever has. He went on to serve two terms as a moderate Republican president. He spoke the thoughts of most liberals with these words: "Every gun that is made, every warship launched, every rocket fired signifies in the final sense, a theft from those who hunger and are not fed, those who are cold and are not clothed. This world in arms is not spending money alone. It is spending the sweat of its laborers, the genius of its scientists, the hopes of its children. This is not a way of life at all in any true sense. Under the clouds of war, it is humanity hanging on a cross of iron."

Liberals agree. If say, $50 billion of the defense budget could be saved, that could build 500,000 homes a year, or 10,000 elementary schools, or feed 20 million people. Building tanks and bombs does create jobs. But so does building roads, rapid transit lines and houses; so does installing solar panels and repairing our decaying infrastructure, so does sponsoring scientific and medical research.And unlike a bomb, once these assets are built or maintained, or once a cure for cancer is found, the dividends of the expenditure continue to benefit the prosperity and well-being of society for years to come. Liberals question whether we need a military presence in 150 countries around the world. We have 21 separate bases in Germany alone, 70 years after the end of the war there. We need as much military protection as we need, but we do not need more than that, especially when urgent human needs at home are going unmet.

In his farewell address before leaving office in 1961, Eisenhower had more thoughtful words of warning for his country.

He said, "In the councils of government, we must guard against the acquisition of unwarranted influence, whether sought or unsought, by the military industrial complex. The potential for the disastrous rise of misplaced power exists and will persist. We must never let the weight of this combination endanger our liberties or democratic processes. We should take nothing for granted. Only an alert and knowledgeable citizenry can compel the proper meshing of the huge industrial and military machinery of defense with our peaceful methods and goals, so that security and liberty may prosper together."

There is a revolving door between the military officer cadre and the defense industries. Air Force procurement officers who push their service to adopt certain planes or systems find lucrative jobs as lobbyists waiting for them when their time in uniform is over. The same is true of Army, Navy, Marine and Coast Guard brass. The famous case of onetime Navy fighter pilot and later Congressman Randy "Duke" Cunningham highlights the abuses that can occur. Cunningham pleaded guilty to accepting $2.4 million in bribes from defense contractors in exchange for steering millions of dollars of defense and intelligence contracts their way. Cunningham was sentenced to eight years in prison. He was released in 2013.

But even without such overt criminality, the enticements of the revolving door itself, specifically the lure of a lucrative post-military corporate position, makes serious conflicts of interest an everyday occurrence. Eisenhower was also mindful of the basic incentive structure inherent to such contracting businesses. Those who provide military hardware do more business when the nation is at war. Combat and operational losses of equipment, and consumption of ammunition, fuel, food, medicine, and all the other goods and services necessary to keep forces in the field or at sea are increased during wartime. It is therefore in the financial interest of such contractors and suppliers for the United States to be at war. In all the ways lobbyists work to influence policy, therefore, one can expect them to exert their influence on the military, congress, the executive branch and the public at large to seek "strong" (i.e. belligerent military) solutions to international issues.

James Madison, often called the "Father of the Constitution," similarly saw the dangers to a free republic of protracted war. Liberals are mindful of his observation that, "No nation could preserve its freedom in the midst of continual warfare." President Obama echoed this perspective in May, 2013 when he called for an end to this condition. He invited a national discussion on the need to readjust to a more normal peacetime footing following nearly twelve years of a potentially perpetual "war on terror."

Since terrorism is a tactic and not an enemy, we could be at war with it forever. Obama brought up several concerns. Does that mean the President should continue to have the authority to order deadly drone missile strikes anywhere in the world at any time of his choosing? Should the National Security Agency (NSA) continue to keep compiling a record of all telephone communications and internet communications and searches without limit? They are inarguably of potential use in discovering who terrorists have been in contact with once they are identified, and with who may be a dangerous person based on who is frequenting jihadi web sites. But must all citizens be included in this effort? What about the privacy guarantees of the Fourth Amendment? Remember, the Fourth Amendment states, *"The right of the people to be secure in their persons, houses, papers, and effects, against unreasonable searches and seizures, shall not be violated, and no Warrants shall issue, but upon probable cause, supported by Oath or affirmation, and particularly describing the place to be searched, and the persons or things to be seized."* In the normal course of law enforcement a person who arouses suspicion can be searched or surveyed only after a court-issued warrant pertaining specifically to them has been obtained.

It is true that the surveillance process was codified by congress in 2006. The President is responsible through the Executive Branch for carrying out the data collection. The NSA is the agency that actually does the work. There is a FISA (Foreign Intelligence

Surveillance Act) Court that secretly rules on requests brought to it. Congressional leaders of both parties are briefed on the progress of the program, which has to be regularly reviewed and reauthorized by congress as a whole. But the entire process is secret, and has been implemented absent the kind of public debate necessary to the conduct of a democratic governmental system. Liberals are uncomfortable with this. As Madison so presciently warned over 200 years ago, "If Tyranny and Oppression come to this land, it will be in the guise of fighting a foreign enemy."

To sum up, most liberals view war as a ghastly business. Unlike Bush Administration "Neoconservative" war hawks like Dick Cheney and Paul Wolfowitz and militarist political figures such as Senators John McCain and Lindsey Graham, liberals do not view war as a desirable first option for rearranging the world to suit one's current desires. War kills Americans and innocent civilians. It scars returning veterans with psychological conditions that will afflict and debilitate many of them for years afterward. It is incredibly expensive in monetary terms, therefore taking resources away from many other pressing human needs. It almost never goes as quickly and smoothly as envisioned; the excitement of "war fever" early in a struggle is soon replaced by public disillusionment and war weariness. It arouses the hatred of people around the world against us and multiplies resentments and enemies bent on vengeance. And finally, a long period of war poses real threats to our free and open society itself, as security preoccupations begin to encroach on precious civil liberties.

For these reasons liberals, though they may support strong military forces for use if necessary, have a high threshold for what is necessary. The lessons of Vietnam, Afghanistan and the first and second Iraq Wars, all of which enjoyed high levels of popular support at first, paint a cautionary picture of the real effectiveness of wars in faraway places. The human and material price of war is enormous and wasteful. Many of our best young citizens are killed and maimed, and many are spiritually or emotionally scarred for life. The gigantic monetary cost of an un-necessarily large military crowds out essential domestic priorities. The military-industrial complex is an incentive to corruption and to profit-driven bellicosity in our foreign policy. Intervention in foreign lands inspires resentment against America and multiplies our enemies. Preoccupation with security leads to an expanding national security state that endangers our constitutional liberties. For all these reasons, liberals are skeptical of war and those who are eager to initiate it. They stand with Vietnam combat veteran, liberal senator and Secretary of State John Kerry who said, "We need to be looked up to and not just feared." Most of all, they share the ultimate goal and vision of World War II combat veteran, senator and President John Kennedy who said, "Mankind must put an end to war or war will put an end to mankind."

CHAPTER 12:

The U.S. Constitution

"The liberties of none are safe unless the liberties of all are protected."

William O. Douglas

"The law must be stable, but it must not stand still."

Roscoe Pound

The writing and ratification of the U. S. Constitution marked a great step forward for liberal principles by establishing a truly national government with the power to act decisively. The earlier "Articles of Confederation," which the Constitution replaced, was less a constitution than an alliance between thirteen separate mini-nations. The Articles declared, "Each state retains its sovereignty, freedom, and independence, and every power, jurisdiction and right," not expressly given to the national government. The states were united only in a "firm league of friendship with each other," without the power to tax or establish national policies on much of anything besides declaring war, making peace, running a postal service, and establishing a uniform system of weights and measures. Consequently, the new nation was riven by disputes between the states, had no coherent national trade or economic plan and no way to pay its bills. The infant United States was becoming a laughingstock.

The Constitution changed all that. Conservatives like to say the Constitution was written to limit the powers of the federal government, but nothing is further from the truth. The principal problem under the Articles was a government too weak to unify the states and too weak to get anything done. The Constitution vested the U.S. government with expansive powers, far beyond those in the Articles. The Preamble lays out the six major areas of federal responsibility: "to form a more perfect union, establish justice, ensure domestic tranquility, provide for the common defense, promote the general welfare, and secure the blessings of liberty to ourselves and our posterity…"

Article 1, Section 8, the section on the powers of congress, enumerates a wealth of responsibilities in addition to war and peace, of which these are only a few: to "regulate commerce," "lay and collect taxes," "pay all debts," establish and regulate the armed forces, determine copyright and patent law, set up a federal court system, and legislate immigration and naturalization. But in case these specific powers are not enough, it goes on to add, "To make all Laws which shall be necessary and proper for carrying into Execution the foregoing Powers, and all other Powers vested by this Constitution in the Government of the United States, or in any Department or Officer thereof." This last sentence is known as the "elastic clause" because it stretches congressional powers. It grants plenty of authority to carry out the six purposes of the Preamble beyond the means of the powers named in the specific list, as long as they are "necessary and proper." In the modern era, for instance, we can have an air force even though the Constitution's wording only mentions the establishment of an army and navy. It is considered part of the overall mandate of the Preamble to "provide for the common defense."

The Framers of the Constitution were wise enough to anticipate that new ideas, practices, needs and technologies would arise. Rather than restricting the national government from taking essential steps to deal with problems they could not foresee when the Constitution was written in 1787, they granted wide scope for action, because they had seen the consequences of the lack of authority in the impotent operation of congress under the old Articles of Confederation.

Liberals down through the years have used the powers granted in the Constitution to humanize and improve conditions in the country. The power to regulate interstate commerce was cited in such advances as the elimination of child labor, the minimum wage and the Pure Food and Drug Act. Programs like Social Security,

Medicare and the Center for Disease Control are covered under the mandate to "promote the general welfare." This is just as the original Framers of the Constitution intended when they opened with the general principles the new government was to pursue, specifically enumerated certain powers and then went even further by adding the elastic clause.

Conservatives in general and libertarians in particular, like former Congressman Ron Paul of Texas and his son Senator Rand Paul of Kentucky do not like the idea of government acting to help the needy or secure the safety and well-being of working people. They rant and rail against laws and programs that do so, and call for a "return to constitutional government." What they mean, of course, is a do-nothing government that lets discrimination run unchecked, the afflicted wallow in misery and the powerful act with impunity. They say the Constitution does not mention a Federal Reserve Board, for instance, so we cannot have one. But Article I Section 8 gives Congress the authority to "provide for the general welfare" of the nation and to "coin money, regulate the value thereof." The Federal Reserve was therefore established to enhance the country's economic "general welfare" by controlling the money supply and thereby to "regulate the value thereof." By their reasoning, not only would there be no air force, but neither could we have a space program, air traffic controllers, electronic civil defense alert system or Social Security, and there could be no program to develop immunizations against communicable diseases. We could not have done the Human Genome Project and the military could never have developed the Internet. Each of these modern innovations would have required a constitutional amendment to enact. The Preamble and Article I Section 8, including the elastic clause, clearly show how clueless these ideologues are.

Liberals read a right to privacy in the Constitution, something constitutional conservatives strongly deny. The liberal view comes from the Fourth Amendment's restrictions against unwarranted search and seizure. The Fourth Amendment states, "The right of the people to be secure in their persons, houses, papers, and effects, against unreasonable searches and seizures, shall not be violated, and no Warrants shall issue, but upon probable cause, supported by Oath or affirmation, and particularly describing the place to be searched, and the persons or things to be seized."

So, if the authorities cannot enter your home or examine your papers or anything that belongs to you without clear probable cause of a crime, or a warrant procured from a court based on evidence that there is probable likelihood of securing criminal evidence, then it follows there is a private sphere of life safe from intrusion absent some good reason to think otherwise. To the liberal way of thinking, if there is no "right to privacy" then there is no security for liberty at all and we are not a free country.

This is particularly an issue since the beginning of the "War on Terror." The Bush Administration felt the need to be able to intercept and snoop on everyone's electronic communications, for instance, which liberals felt strongly violated the Fourth Amendment's safeguards. If someone is suspected, let law enforcement present their reasons for surveillance or a search and get it approved by a court, as the Constitution directs. It also comes into play with issues like contraception and abortion rights. Liberals feel conservative attempts to legislate controls on personal behaviors and require invasive procedures like the insertion of vaginal probes into women's bodies in attempts to shame or inconvenience them from terminating a pregnancy are egregious violations of the right to personal privacy implied by the Fourth Amendment.

Liberals also take very seriously the constitutional principles requiring fair treatment and trials for those in custody. One such civil liberty mentioned in the original text of the Constitution in Article 1, Section 9 is the right of *habeas corpus*, the principle that a person cannot be held indefinitely without being formally charged with a crime. In addition, the first ten Amendments, the Bill of Rights, were approved for good reasons. The first is that most people's memories of unfair treatment at the hands of the

British were still fresh. The second is that the new United States wished to stand as an example of liberty and humane principles in the world.

The Fifth Amendment protects the accused from being forced to provide testimony against themselves. They can simply decline to answer, requiring the prosecution to find other evidence or testimony. The Sixth Amendment guarantees "the right to a speedy and public trial, by an impartial jury..." It also says the accused shall be "confronted with the witnesses against him; to have compulsory processes for obtaining witnesses in his favor and to have the Assistance of Counsel..." The Eighth Amendment includes the prohibition against "cruel and unusual punishments," in other words, torture. I bring these up because these basic principles have been so recently challenged, and even ignored. In the Bush Administration's "War on Terror" suspects were detained indefinitely without trial, or denied jury trials. Counsel was denied, or prevented from calling witnesses or subpoenaing evidence. Some suspects were tortured.

Former Vice President Dick Cheney has gone on tours defending "enhanced interrogation" techniques. It is common to hear conservatives in casual conversation express contempt for the accused or for the American judicial process that insists on proper treatment of suspects, guarantees them a legal defense in court and considers them innocent until proven guilty. Congress has prevented the Obama Administration from closing the Guantanamo prison and bringing terror suspects to the United States for constitutional jury trials. Some have sat there for more than a decade without charges. Others were ordered released five years ago but are still detained. This is not to say liberals take terrorism lightly. We have powerful security, intelligence and legal tools for dealing with menaces, and the full weight of these must be brought to bear on those who threaten our citizens' lives.

Yet the principles of civilization are important to liberals. If we do not follow our own constitutional processes and respect our own enshrined civil liberties, if due to fear we would give up the very freedoms we are supposedly trying to defend, then the terrorists have already won. Liberals consider it all the more important to stand for these crucial principles, to show that freedom under law is the superior system and the world's best hope for justice. And if we give up these rights, then where are we? If the government can spy on you at will, arrest you without charges, hold you without trial, and torture you until you confess, then how free are you?

CHAPTER: 13
Gun Issues

I think after Sandy Hook, when Obama went out, and he talked a lot about gun control and met with the parents, there was a sense that something was going to happen. But then, I guess, the power of special interests was greater than the public sentiment.

Doris Kearns Goodwin

The United States has a major problem with gun violence, and liberals support concrete action to reduce the death and injury tolls from these lethal weapons. A Gallup survey in 2103 found that 72% of liberals wanted to see stricter gun laws, though only 35% favored a total ban on handguns. Historian Goodwin's quote above refers to the aftermath of the horrific slaughter of twenty little children and six school workers by a deranged gunman at Sandy Hook Elementary School in Newtown, Connecticut on December 14, 2012. Despite overwhelming public backing for common sense measures, even the mildest gun control proposals were unable to overcome filibusters in the U.S. Senate. Gun safety advocates, including many liberals, continue to press for measures to stem the mayhem.

How serious is the problem? On August 4, 2009 a man who had trouble getting girlfriends went into a fitness center in Pennsylvania and randomly shot twelve women, three of whom died, before turning the gun on himself. After a couple of days the story subsided. It was just another day in what passes for normal in the U.S.A. I was interested to know how common this kind of thing is around the world. Not counting war and terroristic murders perpetrated for some political end, were other societies having this kind of problem with homicidal individuals going over the edge and the American press just isn't reporting about it here, or what? I googled the issue and it seems we really are in a class by ourselves in terms of serial and mass killers. The United States has 76% of these kinds of murders. We have 4.6% of the world's population but 76% of the world's deaths at the hands of maniacal mass murderers. Does that sound healthy to you? Not to me either. We lost 4,486 service members in Iraq and 2,187 in Afghanistan. Yet these figures are dwarfed by the losses here at home to our own guns. Every year American gun deaths top 30,000. Over 105,000 are shot every year, an average of 289 a day. Of these 86 die: 30 of them murdered, 53 by suicide, 2 by accident and 1 at the hands of police. Between 2000 and 2010 335,609 Americans died after being shot by guns. That is more people than live in St. Louis or Pittsburgh. By the end of 2013 the number surpassed 400,000, more Americans than died in World War II. So, what can be done? Here's what I wrote three days after Sandy Hook.

"Mass Murder: No More Excuses, It's Time to Act"
from Bravegnuwhirled.blogspot.com: December 17, 2012

It already seems like more than three days since Sandy Hook Elementary School and the hamlet of Newtown, Connecticut first entered our consciousness. This most recent in our nightmare series of massacres, the thirtieth since Colorado's Columbine High School in 1999, is just one more, just the latest. And yet it isn't. This time it's different. We have watched the growing frequency of these rampages, but now a line has been crossed with the slaughter of twenty little children. Now, finally, the ground seems to have shifted. Now, at last, there is a sense that action will be taken. The question is: what?

The problem is complex. There isn't just one reason the United States has fifteen times the per capita gun deaths of the other industrialized countries. No one solution will solve the carnage on its own. And make no mistake, no matter what we do there will be more of these mass murders in the future. But the fact that we cannot eliminate the problem completely does not mean we should do nothing and put up with the evil as it gets steadily worse. We haven't eliminated road fatalities either, and yet actions we have taken--seat belts, air bags, reinforcement bars, cars designed with crumple zones, better road engineering, lighting, signage, and a societal sea change against drunk driving to name some--have resulted in cutting the number of fatalities significantly over the years.

Major voices are speaking out again. It started in the New York Times with Nicholas Kristof. Mayor Bloomberg added his voice. President Obama's remarks yesterday at Newtown's interfaith memorial service, that "We can't tolerate this anymore. We aren't doing enough and we will have to change," made it clear that business as usual is not acceptable, and that the weight of the presidency will soon be engaged. The consensus for action is spreading. This morning conservative Republican television host Joe Scarborough repudiated his previous thinking and spoke at length about the imperative need to take action. Here's what needs to be done. First, we have to re-impose the assault weapons ban, that is, we must get rid of automatic and semiautomatic rapid fire weapons. That includes a program to buy back as many as we can that are already out there. We have to restrict rounds in magazines and clips to some reasonable number such as 9 or 10. A massacre is only possible when the killer has a weapon capable of perpetrating one. Along with that, we have to make sure everyone who buys a gun has a background check. Currently forty percent of gun sales (at gun shows) need not be screened. That has to stop. We don't excuse 40% of drivers from having to take the tests necessary to get a driver's license. We don't neglect to screen 40% of the passengers getting on a plane. Next, all the security lists have to be coordinated, brought up to date and put online for all dealers and law enforcement agencies to see. A person on a terrorist watch list who is not allowed to get on a plane should not be allowed to buy explosives or a gun, either. As these things are done, gun owners have to be included and have a say in the conversation at the table. They must be reassured that no one's hunting rifle or target or personal protection pistol is being taken away. The vast majority of gun owners are decent and law-abiding citizens. They don't want criminals with military assault weapons either. They don't go dove, quail or deer hunting with AK-47s and AR-15s.

We also have to do a much better job of identifying and treating people with dangerous psychological conditions. I recently read a woman's chilling account of trying to control her violently delusional son. Mental health services have been cut too much. Too many people are not getting the help they need. Too many families are overwhelmed and have nowhere to turn until crimes are committed and the justice system is left to deal with the wreckage. Yes, people have rights. But society has a right to be protected, too. Where is the line? There needs to be one.

Finally, what in society is fostering a climate of death and mayhem? Is there an eroticism of the power of violence? Are violent video games, movies and music contributing? If so, to what extent? Who is vulnerable? Are we making things worse by publicizing the names and pictures of the authors of these heinous atrocities? Can the social climate itself be changed? Look at what has happened over the years to the former acceptability of such practices as drunk driving, smoking and racial and gender discrimination. When society decides that something is not cool, but contemptuous, real changes in behavior, changes for the good, can take place. It's time to engage the findings of the behavioral sciences to sort these things out. Let's get to work.

Four months later, the strong views of Americans notwithstanding, the attempt to reform the worst shortcomings of our gun regulations fell short of passage in the United States Senate. The following blog shows just how overwhelming public opinion was for change, and how the will of the people was thwarted by the gun lobby.

"Senate Gun Vote Exposes Democracy in Crisis"
from Bravegnuwhirled.blogspot.com: April 18, 2013
The word "dysfunctional" barely begins to describe the operations of congressional government in Washington, D.C. these

days. Yesterday's defeat in the Senate of simple and reasonable proposals to reduce the nation's gun carnage are but the latest demonstration of the sham our democracy has, in many ways, become. A series of massacres in recent months were not enough to spur action from what some have styled the world's greatest deliberative body. It may once have been so, but those days have long since receded into the distant past.

The first point of dysfunction is that the representatives do not represent. That is, they refuse to enact the wishes of the great majority of the American people. Let me reprise a paragraph from my January 16 blog on the people's views.

According to the ABC News/Washington Post Poll and the Pew Research Survey the people are with the President on his ideas, often overwhelmingly so. Universal background checks are favored by an average of 85% in the two surveys. 76% support background checks on even ammo purchases in the ABC Poll. An average of 69% are for a federal gun database. Banning assault weapons is favored by a margin of 17%, and banning the high capacity magazines is favored by an average of 22% in the two surveys.

Even the smallest of these margins, the 17% majority for banning assault rifles, would be considered a landslide in an election contest. It only got 40 votes. 46 senators voted for limiting magazines to reasonable levels to make a mass murder more difficult. One could understand a Senate that voted against the people's preferences when they were, say, 55-45. But 85-10? 76-18? 69-25? In what sense is a nation to be considered a democracy when eight to one and three to one majorities of the popular will are ignored?

The second point of dysfunction is the "filibuster." The background check provision got 55 votes in the 100-member body. That is a majority, as required by the Constitution for the passage of legislation. Yet the Senate has its own rule that it takes 60 votes to bring something to the floor. This tactic by the minority to derail a vote on something they didn't like used to be employed only rarely. But the Republicans in the Senate have used this tactic 109 times in the last two and a half years of the Obama presidency, stopping virtually all action. By what principle of democracy does the will of the 41 prevail over the will of the 59, or the 45 over the 55, as happened yesterday? A government that cannot act is a government in name only.

The third point of dysfunction is the reason why the overwhelming will of the American people was thwarted. Everyone understands what happened, and that it is emblematic of how Washington operates in contemporary times. The countervailing power strong enough to outweigh the will of the voters was a wealthy industry, the firearm manufacturers, and their lobby, the National Rifle Association. Legislation favored by 260 million Americans was stopped by an organization of 4 million members backed by an interest group that spends $3 million a year on 29 full-time Washington lobbyists, 14 of whom have previously worked in government jobs, and threw $20.5 million into political campaigns in 2012. It was fear of losing their contributions, and fear of those same contributions being given to others to spend against them, that motivated the senators' votes.

So long as our politicians and their campaigns are funded by private interests intent on their own profit we will continue to get the best government that money can buy. There has never been a starker example of that principle in operation than the votes taken yesterday on the floor of the United States Senate.

My frustration with the congressional inaction is clearly evident in the previous blog, but liberals should not give up hope on the issue. For one thing, the opinion surveys show us the American people share the liberal view on gun safety issues, particularly when another of our recurring mass shootings brings the continuing cost of inaction clearly to their attention. Second, an eventual re-institution of sensible laws, including the overturning of *Citizens United*, the end of "corporate personhood," together with limited and public financing of campaigns in a new Progressive Era may one day take away the clout that lets the moneyed interests overcome the popular will. That root cause should certainly be a major objective of every liberal. And third, is the realization that even the conservative-led 5-4 Supreme Court decision that definitively declared it a right to possess firearms independently of the Second Amendment's language about a "well-regulated militia" still upheld the propriety of regulating this right stringently in the service of public safety.

The majority opinion written by the very conservative Justice Antonin Scalia in June, 2008 says that individuals can own guns whether or not as part of a militia. Scalia wrote, "The Second Amendment protects an individual right to possess a firearm unconnected with a militia..." However, he qualified this some by continuing, "Like most rights, the Second Amendment right is not unlimited. It is not a right to keep and carry any weapons whatsoever in any manner whatsoever and for whatever purpose." He went on to clarify, "nothing in our opinion should be taken to cast doubt on longstanding prohibitions on the possession of firearms by felons and the mentally ill, or laws forbidding the carrying of firearms in sensitive places such as schools and government buildings, or laws imposing conditions on the commercial sale of arms."

Even in the absence of federal action, under these guidelines states can enact many protections. For instance, the following set of laws was passed by the California legislature, signed by Governor Jerry Brown, and took effect in the Golden State on January 1, 2014.

• The Department of Justice is keeping records of long-gun purchases. Previously those documents were destroyed within five days.

• Conversion kits can no longer be sold if they allow a gun to shoot more than 10 rounds.

• Purchasers of long guns have to pass a written safety test like the one which had already been in effect for handguns.

• People found guilty of making violent threats will have to wait five years to own a firearm.

• Gun owners who do not keep their weapons securely stored can face criminal penalties if the gun is used in a shooting involving a child.

• Hunters cannot use lead ammunition. This goes into effect no later than July 1, 2019, but likely much earlier, as soon as Fish and Wildlife writes the regulations.

In Connecticut, legislation passed in 2013 in the aftermath of Sandy Hook forbids the sale of gun magazines that can hold more than 10 rounds and requires background checks on owners who buy guns through private sales. It also added many new models to the state's list of assault weapons, all of which are banned, and allocated a $15 million fund to improve school security.

In honor of the victims of gun violence, I'd like to conclude this section with a proposal a friend of mine made. Here's how I wrote it up in my blog in June of 2014.

"Time for a New Memorial Day"
from Bravegnuwhirled.blogspot.com: June 10, 2014

The drumbeat of killings goes on. In the past few days we have seen random shootings take place in Santa Barbara, California, Las Vegas and Troutdale, Oregon. If this seems to be practically a weekly occurrence, that's because it is. In just the case of school shootings, for instance, there have been 74 in the 18 months since the horrific massacre of first graders and staff at Newtown, Connecticut.

These deaths are tolerable, even necessary we are told by gun enthusiasts, as part of the price we pay for the right to bear arms. A friend of mine has an admirable idea about this. Louie Campos proposes we celebrate a new Memorial Day. Just as we reserve the last Monday of May to honor members of the armed services who have given their lives in defense of our country and constitutional rights, we should set aside April 20 or December 14 to honor those who have lost their lives to gun violence so that others can enjoy their right to guns. As Louie put it: "If that unfettered "right" is their idea of freedom then they need to recognize the individuals who are making the sacrifice for their freedom." Well said.

The April 20 date would commemorate the mass murder at Columbine High School on April 20, 1999. The December 14 date would do the same for the Sandy Hook Elementary rampage of December 14, 2012. But of course the sacrifice is ongoing, and the remembrance would be for those and for the many who give their lives every day so that others will have the crucial right of unhindered access to machines that fire lethal projectiles. It is only fitting that the hundreds of thousands of Americans whose lives have been forfeited for the rights of others should be remembered. That's the American way.

CHAPTER 14:

Clean Elections and Controlling Special Interests

We can have democracy in this country, or we can have great wealth concentrated in the hands of a few, but we can't have both.
Louis Brandeis

Liberals want to take the private money out of political campaigning because it buys influence and all too often drowns out the voices of the people. Liberals favor a system where the playing field is level, and where qualified candidates and electoral issue campaigns have an equal opportunity to get their messages out. Public financing is the solution to the problem. It had already been implemented in several states and localities, and there were some laws requiring at least a modicum of openness and restraint in federal elections until President George W. Bush was able to replace two retiring members of the Supreme Court with two extreme conservative justices. With John Roberts as Chief Justice and Sam Alito on the bench, suddenly, in a series of 5-4 votes, what had been constitutional for years became unconstitutional.

From time immemorial the wealthy and well-connected in all societies have sought to control the levers of power to serve their private interest against the interests of the people at large. American society is no different. The interest of the one percent of any society is served by a belligerent and militaristic foreign policy that grabs the resources they want from around the globe. They want to be able to form cartels and monopolies without restriction to minimize competition and maximize profits, to be able to pollute the air, water and land without cost or fear of penalty, and to pay their workers as little as possible with as few benefits as possible. They want to be able to hide their incomes and profits to keep their taxes as low as they can, and don't want to pay for things that don't benefit them directly. For instance, they don't like paying for schools or student aid because their kids go to private schools and don't need scholarships for college. They don't need food stamps to make ends meet on a $10 an hour job. They don't need health care support when they're working or Medicare when they're old. They don't need Social Security in retirement, either. All of these issues are things decided by government, a government they feel they can dominate by electing politicians who will do their bidding.

Plutocrats try to game the system so they can control it, and this is how they do it. Their aim is to make politicians dependent for their election on the campaign cash provided by the one-percent. They feel their best chance to get the majority of the public to vote against their own interests-in well-funded schools, higher wages, retirement assistance-is by overwhelming the people's advocates with massive and slick advertising campaigns. Their strategy is to turn an election, which is supposed to be a contest of votes, where they are weak, into a contest of money, where they are strong. If they can flood all media with ten times the messaging of their opponents, people will have only one side's arguments in mind when they vote. To do this, they are working to declare that corporations have the same rights as human people, and to remove all restrictions on political expenses and requirements for identifying contributors, so people won't know whose special interest is behind the advertising they see or the candidates who are running. The campaign to get rid of these protections is couched in terms of "freedom," as in the freedom to be the kingmakers the politicians depend on to keep their jobs. It is really about power, the power to control policy in the service of pauperizing the working public, creating environmental havoc and removing the safeguards that provide security to the average person.

Over the next few pages I've included a series of blogs I wrote over a period of five and a half years. They chronicle the issue and show how the interests of corporations and the wealthy have gained the upper hand over the overall interest of average Americans. Thus far, President Obama has been unable to change the majority on the Supreme Court, replacing two retiring liberal justices with two newer liberal justices. This makes it all the more important to elect a liberal president in 2016 who will have the opportunity to nominate liberal jurists when new vacancies on the High Court (and lower federal courts) appear. This first entry lays out the basic case against the fat cat campaign finance system and highlights some of the progress that was being made to rein it in.

"Campaign Finance: Democracy for Sale"
from Bravegnuwhirled.blogspot.com: December 27, 2007

Congress doles out eight billion dollars in tax breaks and incentives to oil companies even as the price of oil rises to record levels and industry profits reach all-time highs. A three hundred million dollar "bridge to nowhere" is appropriated to link an Alaskan island-population fifty persons, with regular ferry service-to the mainland. The capital gains tax is reduced to 15%, assuring multibillionaire brokers and hedge fund managers a lower tax rate than average working folks and causing Warren Buffett, the second wealthiest man in America, to famously observe that his secretary pays a higher tax rate than he does. The Administration scoffs at report after report from the scientific community detailing the catastrophic warming of the global climate caused by the release of millions of tons of carbon dioxide and other heat-trapping gases into the atmosphere. Instead it shelves the Kyoto Treaty, orders government scientists to remain mum and sends political hacks to rewrite their findings. Piratical energy brokers manipulate the market to create phantom electrical shortages in California, costing its citizens fifteen billion dollars. The Administration protects the criminals rather than the citizens.

What is going on here? Almost everyone knows the answer. Politicians want big money for their election campaigns, and big-money donors expect something for their contributions. In a myriad of ways large and small the money of special interests stands opposed to the interests of the majority of Americans and the national interest as a whole. All too often in the present system money counts more than votes, both for its own sake and because with enough money politicians feel they can control public opinion and gain the people's votes anyway with a blizzard of campaign advertising. In a fundamental way then, American democracy is for sale.

The recent cases of congressmen Cunningham, Delay and Jefferson and lobbyist Abramoff demonstrate the criminal temptations inherent in the system. But they obscure the actuality that most of the damage is done fully within the law. The idea that a few people with a lot of money should get their interests served at the expense of the many without it makes a mockery of the very word "democracy." The practice spawns incredible waste, both in terms of the counterproductive uses to which government money is applied and to the opportunity cost of it not being applied to things that make sense, be they actually useful projects, the reduction of debt, or back into the pockets of the people themselves. It also wastes enormous amounts of time. Congressmen report spending up to half their time fundraising instead of doing the job they were elected to do: provide constituent service, study issues and prepare legislation. This corrupt system of legalized bribery is intolerable and must be stopped. The solution is public financing of campaigns.

The American people already support the concept. A 2006 poll of 1,000 voters with an error margin of 3.1% conducted by Lake Research Partners found that 74% favored a "voluntary system of publicly financed campaigns," 57% of them "strongly." 10% had no opinion and only 16% were opposed. This support was broad-based, including 80% of Democrats, 65% of Republicans and 78% of independents. The survey found that 82% of respondents felt it would make candidates more likely to win on their ideas rather than their money. 81% said it would make politicians more accountable to the voters. 79% believed it would allow citizens with good ideas to have a chance against the rich and powerful. 79% agreed special interests would not get as many favors.

Several states have already adopted "clean elections." Ten states have a system in place for governor and seven for their legislatures. Two major cities, Albuquerque and Portland, use it for their mayoral races, and Rhode Island requires broadcasters to provide free air time for candidates.

How does a clean election system work? First, a candidate demonstrates viability by gathering a reasonable number of small contributions. The formula to be raised is based on the population of the district or state in question. Upon qualifying, candidates receive equal amounts for the primary. Those who win the primaries get equal amounts for the general election. General election amounts are larger than for primaries. As an example, Connecticut State Senate candidates have to raise $15,000 in contributions of $100 or less. They then get $35,000 for the primary and $85,000 if they win the primary and compete in the general. Keep in mind Connecticut is a small state and these are small districts. Strict accountability must be in place to make sure the funds are actually spent for election purposes. It's pretty much as simple as that.

Several questions usually come up and I'll do my best to answer them. One concerns the "voluntary" nature of such systems. Isn't that a huge loophole? Can't a wealthy person or a person serving wealthy backers spend much more and still get a big advantage? Indeed that can be. But the expenditures can't be limited because the Supreme Court ruled in the 1974 case Buckley v. Valero that mandatory limits on campaign spending were an abridgement of the First Amendment rights of freedom of speech and the press. For example, the Presidential campaign funding system we now have was established after the Nixon scandals of 1972 that led to his resignation. Because of the escalating cost of campaigns and the ability of political organizations to raise ever larger amounts, the funds it provides are no longer considered competitive. In 2008 it is expected that both major party candidates will refuse public financing and will raise as much money as they can privately. This, of course, defeats the purpose of the system. The way to restore the integrity of the system, "matching," is rather ingenious. Suppose a congressional election will be funded at $500,000. One candidate signs on for the clean money process. The other does not, figuring he can raise more. But as soon as he does, the clean money candidate receives a matching supplement from the elections commission. Nobody's ability to buy extra commercials is limited, but nobody gets an advantage by doing so either. Over 80% of Arizona's serving legislators have been elected by clean money under the system, even though it's voluntary. It's become a campaign advantage there for candidates to say they take only "clean" money and aren't beholden to special interests.

Another big question is the cost. Won't the taxpayers be taken to the cleaners by such a plan? Isn't it better just to let the fat cats pony up at no cost to the citizens? Well, actually the price tag is quite modest. Experience in the states having these types of systems figures out to a cost of between $2 and $6 for each voting age resident. In addition, the price of letting the special interests "pay for us" is immense. To cite from two examples I mentioned in the first paragraph, the oil industry contributed a little over $3 million to President Bush's 2000 campaign. They got the aforementioned $8 billion in tax breaks. That's a handsome return on investment of $26,666.66 to one. Not bad, and it goes further. They've also been able to raise the price of oil from $26 a barrel to $98 today. Through their friend in the White House and their allies in Congress they've been able to fight off all attempts at regulation and defeat every effort to assess an excess profits tax on the windfall. Meanwhile the price of gasoline has gone from $1.38 to $3.20 per gallon. That's certainly costing the consumer a lot more than would have been paid in public financing. How much more? The cost of the 2004 presidential election was about $500 million. That's $1.67 for each American citizen. In the other example, Enron and other energy giants spread $4 million around the California legislature to achieve deregulation. With no one guarding the hen house the crooks then robbed Californians of $15 billion. Once criminality was evidenced the perpetrators wound up paying back about 3 cents on the dollar. For a political investment of $4 million they made off with $14.5 billion. Good work if you can get it.

A last question, will this put an end to lobbyists? No, there will still be lobbyists, as there should be. After all, the First Amendment protects the people's right to "petition" their government and there is nothing against their organizing to do so. But the nature of lobbying will change. Their political currency will no longer be money, but votes, as befits a democracy. An organization will have clout because it represents thousands or millions of voters concerned about an issue, not because it has a handful of voters with millions of dollars to dangle.

Taken together with my earlier proposals for redistricting, the adoption of public campaign financing will eliminate hundreds of billions of dollars in government waste at all levels and restore fairness and a strong measure of genuine accountability to the American political system. We deserve a political system we can be proud of instead of one that is unworthy of us, an embarrassment geared to serve the few over the many and the narrow over the national interest. A good first step is the Fair Elections Now Act, co-sponsored in the U.S. Senate by Democrat Richard Durbin of Illinois and Republican Arlen Specter of Pennsylvania. Check it out. Isn't it time to put an end to the nonsense?

*Notes: I would start this blog today with this sentence: Despite polls showing 90% of the American people in favor of universal background checks for gun purchases and wide majorities in favor of banning assault rifles and massive magazine clips, the U.S. Senate votes them all down.

In the last paragraph of the blog I mention redistricting reform. Most liberals favor reforming the way most election districts are currently drawn, which entails the politicians themselves drawing their own district boundaries. This blatant conflict of interest leads to "gerrymandering," the practice of devising district boundaries specifically drawn to maximize the incumbents' chances for re-election or preserving the power of the ruling party. They do this by packing all the other party's supporters into very few districts and giving their own party a less decisive but safe majority in the vast majority of the rest of the districts. For better ideas on how this can be done fairly, more on this see my post "Redistricting: Democracy Subverted" online at (http://bravegnuwhirled.blogspot.-com/2007/12/redistricting-democracy-subverted.html). For another worthwhile read on what the current corrupt system leads to, see my blog post "Democrats Get More Votes But Republicans Win House of Representatives" at12/11/democrats-get-more-votes-(http://bravegnuwhirled.blogspot.com/20but.html). One excellent alternative is the example of California. The voters passed a proposition that set up a citizen's commission to draw the legislative and congressional boundaries in the state. It produced excellent results in 2012, both in terms of fairness (more districts were close) and in terms of electing more liberal candidates to office.

Even so, it's saddening to look back and see the progress that was being made at the time I wrote "Democracy for Sale." Much of it was about to be swept away by conservative court rulings, as you will see in some of the entries below. Eventually, with new liberal members on the court or with a more liberal congress to pass new laws, liberals still look forward to reducing the inordinate influence of big money and returning the balance of political power to the votes of America's working people instead of the checkbooks of international corporations and the super-rich.

"Plutocracy Gets Another Boost"
from Bravegnuwhirled.blogspot.com: June 27, 2008
A U.S. Supreme Court ruling on the 2002 McCain-Feingold campaign finance law gives yet another boost to plutocracy in

America. The ruling makes it more difficult for congressional candidates of modest personal means to match money contributed by the wealthy to their own campaigns. This gutting of the "millionaire's amendment" will tilt elections even more heavily toward the wealthiest candidates.

The "millionaire's amendment" to McCain-Feingold says that the amount a candidate can raise from each individual contributor can be increased if an opposing candidate contributes more than $350,000 to his or her own campaign. Since there are no limits on self-funding, this amendment was passed in order to give less wealthy candidates a more realistic chance to match the war chest of a millionaire opponent. The Roberts Court has instead ruled that while no limits can be set on self-funding, they can and indeed must be imposed on those who have to solicit funding from others.

The ruling is yet another example that elections have consequences. George W. Bush's Supreme Court appointees, Sam Alito and John Roberts, have swung the court toward the conservative perspective of granting carte blanche to the richest corporations and persons and constricting the ways and means by which effective challenges can be mounted against them.

The Supreme Court decision in 2000 declaring Bush the winner in Florida and thus the nation has made an enormous difference in American life. As this latest Supreme Court ruling shows, a consistent bias in favor of plutocracy is but one of the results.

This was the opening indicator of what was to follow. The floodgates were really opened up with the *Citizens United* ruling in 2010. Read below to understand this crucial attack on election fairness. "Plutocracy" means rule by the wealthiest in society.

"Ominous Decision"
from Bravegnuwhirled.blogspot.com: January 25, 2010

The recent Supreme Court ruling on corporations, political advertising and free speech is highly troubling. Overturning decades of precedent and the McCain-Feingold law, the court in

Citizens United v. Federal Elections Commission decided that corporations can spend unlimited amounts of funds for speech in favor or opposition to political candidates and may do so at any time, overturning McCain-Feingold's previous 30-day before an election rule. The 5-4 decision split along familiar lines, with conservatives in the majority and liberals in dissent.

Many rulings in the past have affirmed the ability to restrict money as opposed to speech. This ruling appears to equate the two. Justice Anthony Kennedy's majority opinion also seems to consider corporations people, saying, "By taking the right to speech from some and giving it to others, the government deprives the disadvantaged person or class of the right to use speech..." The language thereby puts a corporate entity in the same legal class as a human person. Presumably this applies even if the corporation is primarily owned by foreign investors such as BP or even a foreign government, as with many Chinese companies. That's a cheery thought.

Imagine Chinese Communist front corporations given unlimited power to run advertising for U.S. politicians who support their agendas and unlimited funds to slam those with whom they disagree.

The decision does uphold the principle of requiring the financial backers to identify themselves. But I wonder whether the ads will have to say, "Paid for by Exxon Corporation" or can run as many now do as sponsored by, "Citizens for a Better Tomorrow" or some other such innocuous-sounding group serving as cover for the real backers.

Of course the ruling will increase even further the power and influence of corporate interests over the political process. Corporate resources dwarf those of unions. But I would expect first the mud to come from activist groups like the Swift Boaters.

In a best case scenario there could be a backlash against too much corporate interference and manipulation, but recent history offers little encouragement to believe in that scenario. In a worst case scenario the actual public interest could become practically without advocacy in the major media. President Obama warns it could lead to a "stampede" of special interest government and is calling on Congress to pass some new restrictions. Of course he is right but it is hard to see that they can do much good other than to require the utmost transparency of commercial funding sources.

If not overturned in the future this further unleashing of corporate power could have far-reaching and extremely pernicious effects on the fabric of American democracy. Hopefully there will be a proliferation of media-monitoring groups like Accuracy in Media to at least try to keep the public informed about who is trying to influence them and why.

Indeed, *Citizens United* has not resulted in honest disclosure. Groups like Karl Rove's American Crossroads run ads under their own names, refusing to identify the names of their donors or the sources of their funds. And corporate political spending truly does dwarf union spending, especially after *Citizens United*. Expenditures by political action committees is at least three to one to the corporations' advantage, and "soft money" is as much as seventeen to one in their favor!

The next ruling shows how far into nonsensical reasoning the majority of this Supreme Court will go to try to justify a position so long as it serves their political preferences.

"Supreme Court Blocks Arizona Clean Money Campaign"
from Bravegnuwhirled.blogspot.com: June 10, 2010

It was bad enough when the U.S. Supreme Court recently ruled that corporate money could be spent on political speech without limits. But now it has really gone over the line in issuing an immediate stay against Arizona's 10-year-old campaign finance system.

Though I don't agree with the first ruling, I can understand it. If you grant that a corporation is a "person" entitled to First Amendment protection and that society has no interest in trying to maintain fairness in political campaigns (two very big ifs) then I can see where the conservative court majority is coming from. They say you can't restrict advertising from any quarter.

Yesterday's intervention in Arizona's clean money system is a different animal altogether. Before even hearing the case, they issued an emergency order to prevent the state from disbursing matching funds to candidates already entitled to it under existing law in the middle of a campaign. Somehow they seem to feel that "First Amendment free speech rights of wealthy or well-heeled candidates are violated when extra money flows to their opponents." The Arizona system results in a greater amount and more balanced speech, not less. And talk about "judicial activism." Governor Jan Brewer, who had $1.4 million in matching funding pulled from her by the ruling after her primary opponent Buz Mills had already spent over $2 million, lamented, "It is extremely unusual for the judicial branch to change the rules of an election while it is being held."

The current court is more and more brazenly favoring corporations and the wealthy over any and all attempts to level the playing field. This shows how crucial appointments to the high court truly are. Without a countervailing check soon, America is headed ever more inexorably toward an unabashed plutocracy.

The Court's reasoning is ridiculously flawed. It does not reduce a rich or corporate-sponsored candidate's speech one scintilla by giving his or her opponent an equal chance to also get their message out. They can still message as much as they want and can afford. What has been reduced is their advantage. The winners in a system like Arizona had were the voters, who until this ruling were getting equal instead of one-sided opportunities to compare the candidates' views. That, of course, is precisely what the corporate and super-rich candidates want to prevent.

Big money's stranglehold on the political process has a terrible effect on the public interest. The lust for campaign cash can warp elected officials' judgment so greatly that they are induced to oppose the overwhelming desires of the American people. Many lawmakers on this and other issues are reduced to serving as puppets of special interest. As you saw in the previous section on gun issues, in the case of the defeat of the 2013 gun control proposals, this terrible effect will result in the deaths of untold thousands of Americans. Let me restate those words to emphasize the liberal view of the corrosive influence of special interest money in the political system: "So long as our politicians and their campaigns are funded by private interests intent on their own profit we will continue to get the best government that money can buy."

There is no greater single victory more important to the liberal cause than the reform of this "pay to play" system of campaign finance. The interests of the great majority of working Americans can only be thwarted when the people are misled to oppose those very interests, often by being bombarded with immense quantities of slick publicity that drowns out the voices of regular folks with limited means. Low wages, poor education, lack of access to health care, the shredding of retirement benefits, wrecking the ecological balance of the earth and exposing workers and consumers to weakened health and safety protections do not serve the needs of the vast majority of people. They serve the interests of a few who are wealthy enough not to have to worry about these issues or who wish to make greater profits even at the cost of hurting others.

On July 1, 2013 the Oregon legislature made it the sixteenth state to call for a constitutional amendment to repeal *Citizens United.* The vote was 48-11 in the state house (including a majority of Republicans) and 17-13 in the state senate (including 1 Republican). The other states that have called for an amendment to overturn *Citizens United* are California, Hawaii, Massachusetts, New Jersey, New Mexico, Rhode Island, Vermont, Connecticut, Maryland, Colorado, Delaware, Illinois, Maine, West Virginia and Montana. The Washington, D.C., Council has called for an amendment as well.

Similar resolutions have been passed in 403 localities around the nation by city councils, county boards of supervisors or directly by the voters. For instance, on October 8, 2013 the voters in normally conservative Salt Lake City approved an Opinion Question by a margin of 89.6% to 10.4% asking for an amendment stating that "Artificial entities are not persons and can be regulated" and that "Money is not speech and can be regulated." This is a movement that liberals can get behind wholeheartedly. If your state hasn't gotten on board, contact your state legislators and let them know how important this issue is to you. We can have clean, honest government that actually represents the people, or we can have the best government that money can buy. There is no disagreement among liberals about which we want.

CHAPTER 15:
Social Issues

Human kindness has never weakened the stamina or softened the fiber of a free people. A nation does not have to be cruel to be tough.

Franklin D. Roosevelt

The liberal approach to social issues is based on a consistent set of values. We start from the premise that human needs come first, and that they should be met ethically and practically. We ground that premise in our reverence for liberty and equality, bearing in mind society's needs for safety and security. We recognize that many such issues are complex and multifaceted, requiring thoughtful consideration. We therefore welcome the use of data from good research to help us find the best ways to meet people's needs and help provide the tools they need to realize their highest dreams and potential. In simplest terms, the question we ask is "how can we help make people's lives better?"

We well understand that matters under the heading of "social issues" tend to be sensitive and controversial. They are often the fodder of the "culture wars" that have proven so divisive in the political arena. We do want to be considerate of various views and people's sensitivities on these issues. However, in the final analysis, we have to place highest priority on our most important principles, principles that lie at the heart of American life. These are freedom and practical effectiveness. The first comes from the basic ideal that consistent with the needs of safety, people in the land of liberty should be free to live their lives as they wish. The second comes from the perspective that facts and the findings of empirical research should take precedence over lore and dogma when it comes to developing law and policy in America.

While there are more than enough social issues to fill several books, the eight we're going to be looking at here are Separation of Church and State, Reproductive Rights, LBGT Issues, Science Education, Immigration, the War on Drugs, Capital Punishment and Homelessness. The idea is to give you a brief explanation of what most liberals believe on these matters and why they see them the way they do.

Separation of Church and State

The Constitution of the U.S. forbids everything like an establishment of a national religion.

James Madison

Liberals believe in the separation of church and state. They support the essential principle of liberty that everyone should be able to follow the religious inclinations of their choice, whether that's an established religious organization, a belief system of their own device, or none at all. Liberals also feel strongly that government, which represents all people in our pluralistic society, must take no part in encouraging or discouraging religious belief, and certainly must refrain from endorsing any particular faith or any denomination or sect of any religion. In short, government should stay out of religion altogether.

Liberals feel this way for a number of reasons, the first of which is because we believe religion is a matter of conscience and personal belief. It's none of anyone else's business. Another is that the United States is a pluralistic nation, as reflected in the motto *E Pluribus Unum*. We are a people of many different backgrounds and traditions, and a major part of America's social peace is due to our trait of religious toleration. For a third reason, look at the history of Europe and the Middle East, where kings, dictators and even republics have tried to impose religious conformity on people down through the ages. The result has been a tragic cavalcade of religious wars, persecutions, inquisitions, purges, pogroms and genocides.

Yes, liberals believe in the separation of church and state. As the quote that begins this section makes clear, they are perfectly in line with how James Madison, father of the Constitution, saw it himself. The First Amendment in the Bill of Rights begins, "Congress shall make no law respecting an establishment of religion, or prohibiting the free exercise thereof;" This says two things, first that the government is not to set up or establish a favored or official religion, and second, that everyone is free to practice whatever religious beliefs they choose, if any. And as Madison and the other constitutional Framers knew, the one is indispensable to the other. Early colonists who came to the New World seeking freedom of religion did not come here with the goal of living under a system where the government or the majority determined what everyone had to believe. That's exactly what they left Europe to get away from!

Thomas Jefferson made it even clearer when he wrote,

I contemplate with sovereign reverence that act of the whole American people which declared that their legislature should "make no law respecting an establishment of religion, or prohibiting the free exercise thereof," thus building a wall of separation between Church & State.

The preamble to a treaty of friendship with the North African state of Tripoli, all the way back in 1797, declared:

As the Government of the United States of America is not, in any sense, founded on the Christian religion,—as it has in itself no character of enmity against the laws, religion, or tranquility, of Mussulmen (Muslims),—and as the said States never entered into any war or act of hostility against any Mahometan (Mohammedan) nation, it is declared by the parties that no pretext arising from religious opinions shall ever produce an interruption of the harmony existing between the two countries.

So as you can see, people who say that the United States "was founded as a Christian nation," and that our government is supposed to enforce this, don't know what they are talking about. The treaty above was ratified by the U.S. Senate just nine years after the Constitution was adopted. The senators had a very clear and recent memory of what the Constitution was all about, and the vote for this treaty was **unanimous**.

I'm religious myself, but like most liberals, I see faith as a personal matter. We need to keep government out of the religion business. As Madison wrote, governmental intermeddling with and attempts to dictate religion in the Old World had produced "torrents of blood." Controversies about whether cities should do things like putting up manger scenes at Christmas and the like are pretty obvious to most liberals. Of course they shouldn't. Religious observance needs to be left up to our churches, temples, mosques and all our other faith congregations. No good can come from using the official power of the state to try to tell people what to believe about religion, and it's not healthy for the religious bodies either. In countries with official religions, the favored faith group is drawn into partisan politics as an adjunct to the government, and other groups feel persecuted or disrespected. A strong separation of church and state thus not only keeps people free to believe as they wish, but also keeps religion independent, as it should be.

Reproductive Rights

No woman can call herself free who does not control her own body.

Margaret Sanger

In the very personal realm of reproductive rights liberals are motivated by their strong commitment to individual freedom. Liberals believe such matters as contraception, parental notification and abortion need to be left up to the people concerned, not dictated by legal restrictions.

It was almost beyond belief in the 2012 election cycle to see social conservative politicians like Rick Santorum trying to roll the clock back on the issue of contraception, and to see some churches and conservative employers like Hobby Lobby bring lawsuits against Obamacare on the grounds that its requirement to cover birth control somehow violated their freedom of religion. The conservative 5-4 Supreme Court decision that ruled in 2014 that the Hobby Lobby retail chain could refuse women's contraception coverage was hard for liberals to even believe. This was an issue most people considered settled in the 1960s, and according to research by the Guttmacher Institute, 99 percent of American women have used contraception. Liberals agree it should be up to the patient what medical care she uses, not her employer. Should a Jehovah's Witness employer be able to deny you a blood transfusion or coverage for it in medical insurance because he doesn't believe in it? Should a Christian Scientist boss have the power to deny you access to antibiotics because she doesn't believe in them? We find the concept medieval. As President Obama has said, "No, you can't deny women their basic rights and pretend it's about your 'religious freedom.' If you don't like birth control, don't use it. Religious freedom doesn't mean you can force others to live by your own beliefs." Let a person's church, employer or brother-in-law give whatever medical advice they like, but give the person directly concerned every option and leave their medical decisions up to them and their doctor.

Another touchy issue in reproductive rights is parental notification or parental consent for a minor to get an abortion. Twenty-six states have laws requiring parental consent for their minor daughter to get an abortion. Twelve states require that at least one parent or guardian be notified before a minor can have an abortion. The U.S. Supreme Court has ruled that parents cannot have an absolute veto over their daughter's decision, so most of these states also have a "judicial bypass" system that can allow a minor to pursue a ruling from a judge permitting her to get an abortion without notifying her parents or having to obtain their consent. That presumes, of course, that she is aware of or is informed that such a process exists.

Liberals oppose such parental notification and consent requirements for a number of reasons. Abortion is a constitutional right as ruled by the U.S. Supreme Court. In what other case is a citizen required to get a parent's permission to exercise a constitutional right? In circumstances where a girl has an open and honest relationship with her parents, she will naturally discuss the fact of her pregnancy and choices she is contemplating with them. When she does not want to, it is indicative of potential red flags such as incest, abuse, or other threats. Thus one tendency in states with these requirements has been an increased incidence among one-third of pregnant 17-year-olds to wait until they are 18 in order to avoid the notification. This means more later-term abortions, which are a greater risk to the mother. On the other hand, in quite a few states abortions have been banned after 20 weeks. Notification and consent mandates, or having to resort to the judicial bypass provision can waste time and take matters past the deadline, which is precisely the intention of many of such states. That is really the bottom line here. Conservatives who disagree with abortion have been trying to chip away at the right by imposing as many obstacles as they can. For their part, liberals stand with individual freedom on the subject.

That leads us to the biggest reproductive rights social issue, abortion itself. Liberals stand again with individual freedom in support of a woman's right to make this choice herself. In the famous *Roe v Wade* case in 1973 the Supreme Court defined abortion as a constitutional right. That puts it on the same level as freedom of speech or religion. We think women contemplating ending a pregnancy weigh matters carefully and do not make the decision lightly. It is, as it should be, up to them.

The American people largely agree. The 2013 Gallup Poll found that 53 percent of Americans favored retaining *Roe v Wade* and only 29 percent supported overturning it. Now keep in mind the number who called themselves "pro-choice" in 2014 was 47 percent and "pro-life" was 46 percent, almost a tie. But a closer look at the results finds that 50 percent believed abortion should be legal under certain circumstances, 28 percent legal under all circumstances and only 21 percent felt it should be illegal.

These findings seem to demonstrate that many Americans are certainly ambivalent on the subject of abortion. They agree by a substantial margin that it should be legal and available to a woman, but many would like to see fewer. There are a lot of liberals who agree. In fact, I would say the overwhelming majority do. That is why liberals favor all the measures that would reduce the number of unwanted pregnancies and make it easier for more women to make the decision to carry their pregnancies to term. Liberals support easy access to effective contraception of all kinds. Liberals support universal health care, which would remove that factor for women who now have no prenatal care or who worry that they will not be able to afford medical care for their children. Liberals support liberalized adoption, including to LGBT parents. Liberals are for paid maternity, paternity and family leave provisions of the kind that are common in most other advanced countries. They support adequate minimum wages and generous food stamp and education policies that would all combine to make it much easier for many women, especially the poor and single, to have confidence they could financially support a child. It is highly ironic and deeply frustrating to us that conservatives, the very people most concerned about reducing the number of abortions, stand in the way in opposition to every one of these measures. As Progress Texas, fighting an uphill struggle against the regressive views and policies of that state put it, "If you want to prevent abortions you make sure everyone has health care, a high school education and birth control. Not the exact opposite." Most liberals would agree with Christine Northrup, who wrote, "If we lived in a culture that valued women's autonomy and in which men and women practiced cooperative birth control, the abortion issue would be moot."

A final reason liberals support abortion rights is that trying to ban them doesn't work. Abortion was legal from the founding of the country until the 1880s.Advertisements for abortion services appeared regularly in newspapers. During the time it was illegal, from the 1880s until 1973, it is estimated that up to 1.2 million abortions a year were performed anyway, illegally and frequently under inadequate and unsanitary conditions. As the National Abortion Federation summarizes of those years, "Many women died or suffered serious medical problems after attempting to self-induce their abortions or going to untrained practitioners who performed abortions with primitive methods or in unsanitary conditions. During this time, hospital emergency room staff treated thousands of women who either died or were suffering terrible effects of abortions provided without adequate skill and care." There is every reason to expect that if abortion were banned these realities would return. Liberals agree it is far better to take proactive measures through contraception and support to reduce the demand for abortions and leave the legal choice in the hands of the mother. These common-sense steps are the only ones that would make abortion, as Bill Clinton often said, "safe, legal and rare."

LGBT (Lesbian, Gay, Bisexual, Transgender) Issues

All men are created equal. No matter how hard they try, they can never erase those words. That is what America is about.

Harvey Milk

Liberals stand solidly in support of full rights, freedoms, legal and social equality for every person regardless of sexual orientation. That means liberals supported repealing the "Don't ask don't tell" policy and permitting open service by LBGT members of the military. We support full marriage equality and all the rights and prerogatives that come with it, such as community property, inheritance, filing joint tax returns, survivor benefits, power of attorney, family leave and hospital visitation. We support adoption rights for LGBT individuals and couples. We support protecting victims from threat and violent assault motivated by animus against their orientation by classifying such acts as hate crimes. Liberals support the passage of the Employment Non Discrimination Act (ENDA).

The main reason for this perspective is simple: equality. Liberals take the Declaration of Independence at its word. Liberals have always been the strongest supporters of equality throughout American history, standing up for blacks, women, Native Americans, the handicapped and immigrants, for every ethnic and religious minority that bigots decided would be next in their seemingly unending quest to try to make themselves feel superior by denigrating someone else, someone different. The other reason liberals feel so strongly about this issue is their temperamental disposition to favor the underdog. Liberals see the LGBT rights movement as the contemporary civil rights movement. Just as our forebears fought to end slavery and Jim Crow or to grant women the vote, this is the equality issue of our day, the chance to extend the Declaration's ethos closer to the ideal it has called us toward for over 230 years.

On May 19, 2014 the nation received word that Pennsylvania had joined what were then 18 other states and the District of Columbia in embracing Marriage Equality. In his ruling striking down Pennsylvania's ban on Marriage Equality, U.S. District Court Judge John E. Jones III wrote the following passage:

"The issue we resolve today is a divisive one. Some of our citizens are made deeply uncomfortable by the notion of same-sex marriage. However, that same-sex marriage causes discomfort in some does not make its prohibition constitutional. Nor can past tradition trump the bedrock constitutional guarantees of due process and equal protection. Were that not so, ours would still be a racially segregated nation according to the now rightfully discarded doctrine of 'separate but equal.' ... In the sixty years since Brown v. Board of Education was decided, 'separate' has thankfully faded into history, and only "equal" remains. Similarly, in future generations the label same-sex marriage will be abandoned, to be replaced simply by marriage."

He continued:

"We are a better people than what these laws represent, and it is time to discard them into the ash heap of history."

Liberals are in complete accord. We do not see different sexual orientations as abnormal. There have been gay, lesbian and transgender people from earliest times. Sappho wrote erotic lesbian poetry in the sixth century B.C. It is normal for lesbian and gay people to be attracted to people of the same sex. People do not "choose" to be gay any more than they choose to be heterosexual. People do not "catch" homosexuality or heterosexuality from hanging around people of a different orientation. The American Psychological Association agrees and stopped classifying LGBT orientations as diseases more than forty years ago.

Longstanding attempts to change people's sexual orientation through such means as "reparative therapy" have never succeeded. Liberals oppose these schemes. Probably the largest such organization, Exodus International, which called their program "change therapy," announced its closure in June 19, 2013 after 37 years of operation. In his apology, director Alan Chambers wrote, "I am sorry we promoted sexual orientation change efforts and reparative theories about sexual orientation that stigmatized parents." Later, he added, "I hope the changes in my own life, as well as the ones we announce tonight regarding Exodus International, will bring resolution, and show that I am serious in both my regret and my offer of friendship. I pledge that future endeavors will be focused on peace and common good."

Liberals salute people like Alan Chambers for his honesty and humility. We look forward to the day when the sentiments he expressed truly spread from sea to shining sea, when full legal equality is a reality for all our citizens, when the last embers of phobia and bigoted ridicule are extinguished, and when all people are accepted for who they are.

Science Education

I know of no time in human history where ignorance was better than knowledge.

Neil deGrasse Tyson

Liberals like science. Thanks to science we can fly through the air and explore space. Scientific discoveries have given us cures for deadly diseases and increased crop yields. They have led to the wonders of mass industrial production and the communications and computer revolutions whose fruits we see all around us every day. There is no doubt that to compete in today's international economy America must remain at the forefront of scientific knowledge and innovation. Scientific prowess is equally central to national defense. Therefore it is crucially important for our people to be scientifically literate, for our children to be exposed to good science education starting in elementary school and for us to provide plenty of opportunities for our best and brightest in scientific and technological fields to pursue advanced degrees at our universities.

Science involves using observation and experimentation to establish facts, against which tentative hypotheses are tested for validity. The entire process, including those observations and experiments, along with the explanations devised to explain their workings are subjected to open peer review. Others in the field are invited to replicate or devise their own tests and to formulate alternative explanations to account for the results. In common usage a "theory" can mean a wild guess on anyone's part based on anything from a great deal of evidence to none at all. In science, however, an explanation of a natural process or phenomenon is only accorded the status of a theory after the overwhelming consensus of experts in the field agree it presents a valid and comprehensive picture of how something works. It must be conclusive. Scientists speak of the Theory of Gravity, for instance. While they remain open to the possibility of new observation or experimentation changing their view, everything they have seen over the past three centuries confirms the findings and calculations

Isaac Newton provided in the late seventeenth century. It is a *scientific theory*, which in science means it is treated as a Law of Nature unless something dramatic happens to call it into question.

This process of inquiry has been responsible for practically all the material progress humanity has made since the Dark Ages. In this age, when the Scientific Revolution has spread from its cradle in Europe to the rest of the world and competition is fierce, it is all the more essential that America preserves the spirit of inquiry and funds it with investment sufficient for us to maintain our edge. As Fareed Zakaria has said, "What we see today is an American economy that has boomed because of policies and developments of the 1950s and '60s: the interstate-highway system, massive funding for science and technology, a public-education system that was the envy of the world and generous immigration policies."

Liberals agree we must not permit ourselves to fall victim to the modern-day witch-burners, flat-earth enthusiasts and corporate polluters who politicize science and attempt to delegitimize it because some of its findings do not happen to fit their preconceived ideas or vested interests on topics like the Theory of Evolution, reproductive issues, sexual orientation or the human contribution to atmospheric heating. We push back against the censors and inquisitors of the present who try to keep scientific findings out of school texts both because they are wrong and because we see the damage such a mentality has done to human progress in the past. We oppose teaching ideas such as "intelligent design" in science classes because in the absence of evidentiary data supporting them they are fundamentally unscientific.

Now is not the time to be dumbing-down our science education or discarding it for mythology. The well-regarded Programme for the International Assessment of Students results for 2012 found that American 15-year-olds scored below average in science against their international peers from 65 countries. The American kids' scores had remained stagnant over the years while other nations experienced strong improvement. The stakes are high. In an ever more competitive and globalized economic system driven by technological innovation, laggards will increasingly be left behind. As Albert Einstein said, "Great spirits have always found violent opposition from mediocrities. The latter cannot understand it when a man does not thoughtlessly submit to hereditary prejudices but honestly and courageously uses his intelligence."

I'll conclude with another biting but on-point quote from astrophysicist Neil deGrasse Tyson. "People cited violation of the First Amendment when a New Jersey schoolteacher asserted that evolution and the Big Bang are not scientific and that Noah's ark carried dinosaurs. This case is not about the need to separate church and state; it's about the need to separate ignorant, scientifically illiterate people from the ranks of teachers."

Immigration

The U.S. immigration laws are bad - really, really bad. I'd say treatment of immigrants is one of the greatest injustices done in our government's name.

Bill Gates

Liberals support having a reasonable and specific set of policies regarding immigration, often referred to as a "comprehensive immigration policy." Such a system will have to balance a number of important concerns. A good comprehensive set of laws must start with safety, making sure that dangerous people such as criminals and terrorists are not allowed in. It must address the economic needs of the United States by acting to attract and admit people with the kinds of job skills our country needs that native workers are not filling. It must also be sensitive to human needs and realities, recognizing the importance of keeping families together. It must make allowances for people who may have entered outside of the legal process who have been here a long time and demonstrated their responsibility by being law-abiding and self-supporting. It must allow for appropriate human services and needs such as education, health care, driver's licenses, and provide opportunity for children who were brought to America very young and have been brought up as Americans.

Liberals are for a humanitarian and proactive stance on immigration issues. We oppose a system designed to keep millions of people in a shadow status devoid of opportunity and are dismayed by the conservative obsession for exclusion and punishment as applied to these issues. Liberals support the idea of the Dream Act, the principle that those who were brought to America by their family when young should be allowed to stay in the only country they have ever known, particularly if they have avoided serious crime and stayed in school or are productively working. Of course liberals agree with the principle that undocumented immigrants should be able to get driver's licenses. People are going to drive to get to work in any case. Do we want them not to have to learn the rules of the road and not be identifiable in the event of an accident? Of course liberals support access to health care for all, including the un-documented. That's the ethical thing to do, and the practical one as well. We can't just let injured people suffer and die. And do we want untreated sick people spreading infectious disease throughout society? Certainly liberals want to open the doors of college and advanced vocational training available to Dreamers. I am proud that my liberal state, California, has acted to begin implementing all these features of a humane and effective approach to immigration issues.

Here's an overall program for immigration I wrote about in my blog, Brave Gnu Whirled (bravegnuwhirled.blogspot.com), back in 2008. A few of the details have been updated to reflect the changes in the last few years.

"Solving Immigration" from Bravegnuwhirled.blogspot.com: February 14, 2008

There are an approximately 12 million immigrants in the United States who have not been admitted through the normal immigration and naturalization procedures. An estimated 400,000 to 700,000 more arrive every year, compared with about 800,000 who enter legally. Most Americans see this as a problem. Many are even hysterical about it. It should be pointed out that these 12 million represent less than 4% of the U.S. population. By way of comparison, the 1920 census found that 58% of the residents of all American cities of 100,000 or more were foreign-born. So today's figures are in fact very mild by historical standards. Even so, it is an issue of concern and should be dealt with.

The debate over what to do about it has been dominated by extremists on the one hand who would like to see every undocumented immigrant rounded up and deported and extremists on the other hand who feel all who wish to come to America should be welcomed with open arms. Currently the deportation group has by far the upper hand politically, but the welcome group has the upper hand de facto. Both positions are complete nonsense, of course. A reasonable approach based on the national interest and humanitarian morality must take a set of reality-based facts and principles into account. Here are a few of them.

The United States has the right to control its borders and determine who gets in and who does not. The American economy requires the services of these immigrants. It is in the national interest that immigrant labor does not displace citizen labor, that all residents have access to health care and education, that they are identifiable persons, and that they not become a permanent underclass in American society. All these objectives can be met by establishing a set of practical and reasonable processes.

The first goal requires firm security at the borders. This is indeed essential, and it is as far as many of the anti-immigrant extremists go. While this is necessary it must be recognized that no such system will ever be effective by itself. Based on appropriations from congress, the Obama Administration in 2012 spent $18 billion on immigration enforcement, more than for all other federal law enforcement programs combined. But the borders and seacoasts are too long, and they are not the only ways people enter the country. Many enter legally at ports of entry by land, air and sea as tourists, students or on business and simply overstay their visas and never leave. The 9-11 hijackers were all here legally, for instance.

If we are serious about getting a handle on the issue there must be tamper-proof identification cards. These must include those for citizens, legal resident non-citizens and temporary visitors. It must be made impossible for people to function for long in the United States without them. There must be deterrent penalties for those who hire, sell property, extend credit, provide rental cars, book transportation, rent hotel rooms and so on to those who cannot establish a legal right to be in the U.S. Some will cry "police state" at this practice, but the issue cannot be dealt with otherwise. Almost all residents have a government-issued ID already, be a driver's license or a Social Security card and number.

The labor department should compile periodic assessments of how many and what types of workers are needed and must communicate the specifics to immigration authorities. Immigration should then issue that many and type of temporary worker cards with tamper-proof IDs that are valid for a stated time period to that many workers. Here in California's San Joaquin Valley the harvest cannot be brought in without guest workers. It is a fool's game to do as we do now by trying to stop them at the border while leaving agriculture no choice but to hire them if they can make it in. The current system is grossly inefficient, not to mention degrading and sometimes life-threatening to the immigrants. Transportation ought to be furnished to the guest workers to and from their places of employment.

Those non-citizens who are currently in the United States, are self-supporting or dependents of those who are, and have no serious criminal record must be allowed to stay. This, I know, infuriates the anti-immigrant set, but there is no practical alternative. It is simply not possible to locate and deport 12 million people. It's not happening. The antis must come to grips with reality, and politicians have to stand up to them. 75% of the American people agree that a mass deportation of illegal foreigners is impractical. Only 16% think otherwise. Government leaders must find the courage to stand with rationality, common sense and human compassion and not with the 16% who scream the loudest.

For one thing, it is beyond our logistical capacity. For another, to attempt to do so would cripple the American economy which depends on their labor. The oft-repeated myth that they are "all here to get welfare" is patently false. Hispanic males have the highest workforce participation of any subgroup in American society. Finally, it would precipitate a human rights calamity. 12 million people would go underground like hunted animals or like the Jews of World War II Europe. Families would be torn apart and children who are American citizens would be sent to foreign lands they have never lived in. Many of the deported would not be able to find a job in impoverished third-world countries and would likely starve. It's not happening and will never happen. Anti-immigrant extremists are going to have to get over it.

So if they are staying, and they are, they must become eligible for services such as health care, education, driver's licenses, and so on. Public health, preventing the establishment of a caste of helots in an egalitarian society and law enforcement imperatives necessitate it. To do otherwise would also be an egregious moral injustice. Those who are here, self-supporting and law-abiding and want to stay must be issued ID cards with a path to permanent residency and citizenship if they learn English and remain productive members of society. Period. The U.S. Senate passed a bill allowing for permanent residence and a path to citizenship in June 2013 by a 68-32 margin, with all the Democrats and 14 Republicans voting yes. Though it makes people wait far too long, 14 years, it's at least a step in the right direction.

But the Republican-controlled House has refused to act, afraid of the reflexive bigotry of their anti-immigrant base. Even conservative leader Grover Norquist has commented, "Historically, opposition to immigration in the United States has been racially and religiously motivated in the ugliest, nastiest way possible." It's high time to end this ugly, inhumane and emotion-fueled immigration conundrum. With firm border enforcement, a tamper-proof ID, a rational procedure for anticipating and admitting the proper number of immigrants legally, serious penalties for hiring any new undocumented going forward, and the extension of opportunity and dignity to those here working hard in jobs most Americans do not want, a solution is possible.

The War on Drugs
Prohibition has failed; legalization is the least bad solution.
Editorial Board of *The Economist*

Many liberals are coming around to the view that the forty-plus-year "War on Drugs" initiated by the Nixon Administration in the 1970s has been a terrible failure and needs drastic transformation or an outright end. Not only has it failed to reduce the incidence of drug use, but like the Prohibition of alcohol in the 1920s it has resulted in a permanent underground economy dominated by violent criminal gangs involved in murder and corruption on a vast scale. There are examples of successful programs in Europe that have legalized and strictly regulated recreational drugs and expanded compassionate rehab treatment for addicts who want to get clean. The results seem to include the reduction of violence and death, generation of revenue, a reduction in the rates of usage and an increase in rates of rehabilitation and recovery. Such a liberal program should be carefully studied for potential adoption in America.

For instance, Portugal decriminalized the possession and use of all drugs in 2001. A person cited for drug intoxication has to go to a hearing in which they are offered treatment, but they are allowed to go home without it if they refuse. A study found that in the years after personal possession was decriminalized, drug use among teens in Portugal declined 25 percent, heroin use declined 30 percent, rates of HIV infections caused by sharing of dirty needles dropped 17 percent and the number of people seeking treatment for drug addiction more than doubled. The money saved from enforcement more than paid for the increased treatment costs.

Sweden offers a different model that combines strict enforcement against trafficking with light punishments but extensive counseling and rehabilitation for users. Sweden has one of the lowest rates of drug use in Europe.

In the United States, about $51 billion per year is spent trying to enforce the War on Drugs, including aid and combined operations with nations like Colombia. About one and a half million are arrested for use and over 500,000 of these are sentenced to incarceration. In 2012, 52 percent of inmates in federal prisons were there on drug convictions. 20 percent of African-American men spend time in jail at some point in their lives due to drug offenses. In quite a few states people with these histories lose their right to vote. Meanwhile, incidences of drug use have not improved. According to the National Institute on Drug Abuse, the percentage of Americans over the age of 12 who had used an illicit drug in 2002 was 8.3 percent. In 2012 it was 9.2 percent. In 2007 the Institute found that 5.8 percent had used marijuana in the previous month. In 2012 the percentage had grown to 7.3 percent.

The point here is not to argue in any way that drug use or abuse is a good thing. Addiction is responsible for enormous social disruption, many ruined lives, deaths, and negative health outcomes. Even marijuana creates problems for many people. The point instead is to raise the question, as liberals do, about whether the way we are attacking the problem is effective and seems to be working. The data would appear to indicate it is not. Immense resources continue to be committed without perceptible improvement. Meanwhile, approaches being tried in other countries show through hard data that they are making headway. We do not seem to be meeting human needs well in the War on Drugs. Research points the way toward better solutions. Humble practicality seems to indicate there are more effective models we might follow. In the War on Drugs, as with so many other issues, liberals are in tune with the common-sense saying: *If you like what you're getting keep doing what you're doing. If you don't like what you're getting you need to change what you're doing.*

Capital Punishment

It is immoral in principle, and unfair and discriminatory in practice.

American Civil Liberties Union

Liberals are divided on the issue but a majority of liberals are against capital punishment. In a 2013 Gallup Poll 50 percent of liberals opposed the death penalty and 47 percent supported it. Clearly, the more liberal position is to be against the death penalty. Earlier in my life I supported the death penalty, but now am irrevocably against it. There are several reasons why I and the majority of liberals cannot support this practice. The nature of these reasons comprises both moral and practical concerns.

Morally, we begin with the principle that two wrongs don't make a right. To use lethal force against a perpetrator who is actively endangering the lives of innocents may well be justified, but to kill someone in state custody is simply murder. Also, execution ends any possibility of redemption for the criminal. The Dali Lama says, "My overriding belief is that it is always possible for criminals to improve and that by its very finality the death penalty contradicts this." John Dear, a Jesuit Catholic priest, wrote of capital punishment, "Behind it lies an illogical maxim: we kill those who kill to show that killing is wrong. If we really believed that killing was wrong, the state would set an example; official killing would be banished."

In addition, the act of imposing the death penalty does not bring back any victims but only creates more. It is a simple act of vengeance motivated by the emotions of anger and hate. Most liberals see these motives as unworthy of a civilized judicial system and as little more than the vestigial relics of a primitive age of barbarism. In 2013 only 22 countries (out of more than 200) carried out any executions. The top eight were China, Iran, Iraq, North Korea, Saudi Arabia, the USA and Somalia. America is the only advanced constitutional nation among them. It is disgraceful to put ourselves in such company.

The practical reasons against the death penalty are important too. Chief among them are that by its very nature mistakes cannot be fixed, the death penalty is invariably applied unequally, and the record shows it does not deter crime. When someone is wrongly convicted and sentenced to death, once that sentence is carried out there is no way to rectify the mistake. We cannot know how many of the 1,200 Americans executed since 1973 may have been innocent, but according to the Death Penalty Information Center, over that time 144 inmates waiting on death row have been exonerated. That makes it almost certain that some people have been executed erroneously. Police, prosecutors, crime lab technicians, defense attorneys, judges and juries are only human. And when they make a mistake in this arena, people can be put to death as a result. There is nothing that can justify taking a risk like that.

Plenty of studies have shown that the death penalty is applied terribly unequally in our country. Maricopa County, Arizona, for example, has four times the death penalty cases of Los Angeles or Houston on a per capita basis. And thanks to the legacy of our race relations, a much higher percentage of minority defendants, especially African-Americans, are sentenced to death. About 14 percent of murder victims are black, yet over 41 percent of death row inmates are black. A 2011 study in North Carolina found that the chances of a defendant being sentenced to death were 75 percent higher if the victim was white than if the victim was black. This is not equal justice.

One of the most commonly cited justifications for capital punishment is its supposed effectiveness as a deterrent to crime. The actual record, however, does not back up this assertion at all. In fact, states with the death penalty have a higher murder rate than those without it. Over the last twenty years the murder rate for states that have the death penalty averages 31% higher than states that do not. If the deterrent effect were there, one would expect those figures to change, yet there has not been one year in the past 25 in which death penalty states had a lower murder rate.

Given the immorality of capital punishment, the irrevocable nature of its judgment, the caprice and evident bias with which it is applied, and its ineffectiveness in reducing crime, many liberals can echo the sentiments of former liberal Senator Russ Feingold who said, "I oppose the death penalty because it is inconsistent with basic American principles of justice, liberty, and equality."

Homelessness

What shocks me is that so many people leave care and become homeless, and when you're homeless you get into crime, prostitution and drugs, and it is a vicious circle. That's what we need to change.

Samantha Morton

The tragedy of homelessness is visible on the streets, vacant lots and under the bridges in communities all across America. The homeless are increasingly subjected to attempts at criminal control. Ordinances against begging, pushing shopping carts on city sidewalks, sleeping in public, camping within city limits and even "storing belongings in public" have all been passed by various localities who don't want to see homeless people. Measures like these are attempts to deal with the visible symptoms of homelessness but they sadly ignore the deeper underlying causes of our societal homelessness problem. "Respectable" people do not want to have to deal with panhandlers and do not want to have to see them. They often do not, however, want to have to pay anything or go to any trouble to actually do anything to alleviate the problem.

Liberals do not feel the same way. Homelessness is a human problem and liberals are dedicated to solving problems and meeting human needs. Liberals know better than to think addressing the symptoms of a problem while turning a blind eye to the root causes will do much good. At best, it shoos the homeless out of one locality into another nearby. "Let someone else deal with it" is not an acceptable position for a community to take when the quality of human life is at stake. As President Kennedy said, "Our problems are man-made; therefore they may be solved by man. And man can be as big as he wants. No problem of human destiny is beyond human beings."

The sad state of homelessness in America is not something that just has to be endured. The exponential growth of the problem owes much to certain public policy decisions that have made the situation much worse. We can trace things back to Ronald Reagan's terms as governor of California from 1966 to 1974. Reagan, a conservative Republican, felt most people who were "sleeping on the grates, the homeless...are homeless, you might say, by choice." As part of his ideology of cutting government services to the needy, he began a process of shutting down the state's mental hospitals. When he was elected president in 1980 he took this perspective national. Aid to cities was cut. Federal aid accounted for 22 percent of city budgets in 1980 but was down to 6 percent by 1988. Public service jobs, legal services for the poor, Community Development Block Grants and public transit were all rolled back. Schools, libraries, hospitals, clinics, sanitation, police and fire services were slashed. The federal housing budget was cut by half, over $17 billion a year, and the minimum wage was frozen at $3.35 an hour. These actions had predictable effects. In 1970 there had been 6.5 million federally subsidized rental units to serve a population of 6.2 million low-income households. But by 1985 there were only 5.6 million units and the number of poverty renter households had grown to 8.9 million.

Prompted by budget cuts and the Reagan ideology, "de-institutionalization" became a national trend in the 1980s. This closing of psychiatric facilities came at the worst possible time, just as the number of poor in America was growing and soon after the end of the Vietnam War, a ghastly and unnecessary conflict that exposed some two million American servicemen to the effects of what we now know as post-traumatic stress. A study done at the time in Ohio learned that 36 percent of those discharged from Columbus State Hospital were homeless. Our prisons have become warehouses for the mentally ill, and according to the Treatment Advocacy Center 16 percent of prisoners are schizophrenic or psychotic and 30 to 50 percent of the homeless are seriously mentally ill. And now, in more recent years, long and repeated military tours in Iraq and Afghanistan have added hundreds of thousands more veterans to the ranks of those who are susceptible to combat-related stress conditions. This is clearly an important long-term human, financial and societal cost that needs to be considered whenever there is talk of committing American forces to war.

A promising liberal solution to the problem is being pioneered in a state generally known for its strong conservatism. Utah crunched the numbers in 2005 and found it was spending $16,670 a year on emergency room visits and jail and court time per homeless person. They calculated that for $11,000 they could provide an apartment and a social worker instead. With their Housing First program, that's what they have been doing, and they have cut homelessness by 74 percent. They expect to have their problem ended during 2015. Many formerly homeless folks have moved into jobs and self-sufficiency. It's a classic case of following the data to determine on an approach to a human problem that is both compassionate and effective. That is what liberalism is all about.

CHAPTER 16:
The Conservative Record of Failure

"A Conservative is a fellow who is standing athwart history yelling "Stop!""
Conservative publisher and theorist, William F. Buckley

The record of conservatism in the United States is a long and tragic one, if your criteria are the rights and well-being of the American people. Time and again they have been on the wrong side of history, standing up for principles that restrict human rights and pushing policies that have brought suffering to millions and economic hardship to the nation. Here is a partial catalog of their errors and failures. I invite you to take some time to fully absorb their enormity.

Independence and New Nation, 1776-1800
Supported Government-Sponsored State Churches
Protected Slavery in the Constitution
Established Property Qualifications for Voting
Passed Alien and Sedition Acts Punishing Freedom of Speech

The Nineteenth Century, 1801-1899
Abrogated Treaties and Exterminated or Relocated the Indian Nations
Supported Right of States to Nullify National Laws
Opposed the Homestead Act, Land Grant College Act and Pacific Railroad Act
Started, Fought and Lost the Civil War Trying to Preserve Secession and Slavery
Established Racial Segregation
Passed the Chinese Exclusion Act
Opposed the Anti-Monopoly Clayton Anti-Trust Act

Early Twentieth Century, 1900-1928
Opposed Voting Rights for Women
Opposed Child Labor Laws
Opposed the Pure Food and Drug Act, Meat Inspection Act, Zoning Laws, Workplace Safety Laws, Workers' Right to Unionize
Opposed Establishment of the National Park System
Fought Against the 8-hour Work Day

Great Depression and World War II, 1929-1945
Failed to Regulate Stock Market Practices, Helping Precipitate the Great Depression
Refused to Provide Relief to Starving and Homeless Millions during Great Depression
Unsuccessfully Tried to Solve Depression by Offering Loans to Business (Reconstruction Finance Corporation)
Tried to Defeat Franklin Roosevelt's New Deal Recovery Measures Such as Minimum Wage, CCC and WPA Work Programs, TVA Development Program, and Higher Taxes on the Wealthy to Pay for Them
Opposed the Wagner Act Which Protected Workers' Rights to Unionize
Opposed Social Security Retirement Program
Opposed Naval and Military Expansion Just Before World War II
Opposed Sending Lend-Lease Aid to Britain and France during World War II
Opposed Desegregation of Wartime Defense Industries

Mid-20th Century, 1946-1980
Passed Taft-Hartley Act, Taking Away Union Rights
Opposed Allowing Jackie Robinson to Break the Color Barrier in Baseball
Opposed Racial Desegregation of the Armed Forces

Supported Hysterical Anti-Communist Witch Hunts of Sen. Joseph McCarthy

Opposed Desegregation, Voting Rights, Fair Housing and Interracial Marriage during the Civil Rights Era

Opposed Medicare

Opposed Women's Abortion Rights

Defeated the Equal Rights Amendment (Women's Equality)

Opposed Cesar Chavez and UFW Movement for Farm-workers Rights

Late Twentieth Century, 1981-1999

Passed Massive 1981 and 1986 Tax Cuts for Wealthy, Tripling Annual Deficit

Reaganomics Tax Cuts for Rich, Service Cuts Accelerate Wealth Gap: Rich Get Richer, Rest Fall Behind

Supported Policy of Expelling All Gays from the Military

Discontinued Green Energy Initiatives

Stock Market Crash of 1987

Deregulated Banks and Savings and Loans: S & L Crash

Deregulated Investment Banking; Led to Crash of 2008

Early 21st Century, 2000-2014

G. W. Bush Tax Cuts Turned $230 Billion Annual Surplus into $450 Billion Annual Deficit

Opposed Repealing Don't Ask Don't Tell Military Policy

Patriot Act Allows Warrantless Searches in Violation of Fourth Amendment

Tortured Prisoners in Violation of Eighth Amendment

Started War in Iraq under False Pretenses

Proposed Privatizing Social Security

Housing Bubble and Crash

Nominated Sarah Palin for Vice President

Financial and Stock Market Crash of 2008

Great Recession

Responded to Great Recession with Massive Bailout for Banks, Nothing for Citizens
Blocked U.S. Participation in the International Global Warming Kyoto Treaty
Supported *Citizens United* Decision Permitting Unlimited Secret Corporate Campaign Cash
Refused to Raise Debt Ceiling, Downgrading US Credit Rating
Opposed Every Jobs Bill during Great Recession
Instituted Widespread Voter Suppression Efforts in 2012 and 2014 Elections
Opposed Hurricane Sandy Relief for New York and New Jersey
Government Shutdown of 2013

The Present Day
Support Official Government Promotion of Sectarian Religion
Oppose Affordable (Health) Care Act
Oppose Allowing Women to Make Their Own Choices on Contraception
Oppose DREAM Act for Undocumented Immigrants
Oppose Marriage Equality for Lesbians and Gays
Oppose Background Checks for Gun Purchases and Ban on Military Assault Weapons
Support Preserving Corporate, Millionaire and Offshore Tax Loopholes
Support Cutting Social Security and Medicare from Senior Citizens
Support Cutting Medicaid Support for the Poor
Support Repealing Voting Rights Act
Oppose Comprehensive Immigration Policy with a Path to Citizenship
Deny Scientific Evidence for Human-Generated Climate Change (Global Warming)
Support Teaching Creationism as Science

The Records of Republican Presidents

In addition to conservative stances on these issues through American history, there is also the record of presidential administrations during the period when Republicans began embracing ideological conservatism. Staring with Herbert Hoover, here is how their stewardship of the nation's economy has fared. As a reminder, a look back at Chapter 7's charts and explanations on comparative liberal and conservative economic performance might also be helpful.

Herbert Hoover, 1929-1933: Hoover presided over the Great Depression, the greatest economic catastrophe and worst peacetime crisis in U.S. history. 25% of the work force was unemployed and nearly another 25% underemployed by 1933. The Gross National Product, the value of all goods and services produced in the country, was cut nearly in half, plummeting from $103 billion in 1928 to $56 billion in 1933. The Dow Jones Industrial Stock Index stood at $381.17 at its peak in September 1929 and bottomed out at $41.22 in January of 1933, a loss of 89.2% of its value!

While millions lost their jobs, homes and farms to foreclosure and faced starvation, dairymen were pouring milk into the ground and farmers were plowing crops under because the prices for their goods had fallen below the cost of production. Teachers in Chicago and across many states had not been paid in months. As bread riots spread, legions of homeless men jumped trains, riding from place to place in the forlorn hope of finding work elsewhere. Meanwhile, shanty settlements of the dispossessed, dubbed "Hoovervilles," sprang up across the country. Under Hoover's direction, the Army drove desperate World War I veteran "Bonus Marchers," seeking early payment of their service bonus, out of the nation's capital, burning their encampment and killing two.

The conservative preference for deregulation and laissez faire had mightily contributed to the crash, with no controls over the wild speculation, insider trading and margin buying that ushered in the stock market collapse. Hoover's recovery plan was too little, too late, and his attempt to balance the budget during such dire economic straits meant that spending was too low and taxes too high to effect significant recovery. What's more, the passage of the Smoot-Hawley Tariff of 1930, the highest tariff in U. S. history, made things even worse by setting off a trade war that devastated global commerce.

Dwight Eisenhower, 1953-1961: Eisenhower wanted to cut spending and try to balance the budget. There was modest economic growth in the Eisenhower years, averaging about 2.5%.That was down by about half from the 4.8% growth rate of Democrat Harry Truman's second term, and the average unemployment rate edged up by a percent under Eisenhower. The economy was up and down in these years. There were two recessions during Eisenhower's presidency, one in 1958 and another from 1960 into 1961. All in all, the economy declined in 11 of the 32 economic quarters when Ike was president, a decidedly mediocre performance.

Though a Republican, Ike was a moderate when it came to economics. He resisted calls from extreme congressional Republicans to dismantle the New Deal, strongly supported the G.I. Bill's provisions in support of education for veterans and went along with an increase in the minimum wage. He said to his brother, "Any political party that tried to abolish Social Security and eliminate labor laws" would never win another election. He even initiated a massive new federal program, the Interstate Highway System. But he did cut federal spending to try to save money, resulting in the reduced economic growth rate, higher unemployment and more inconsistent results than might have been achieved.

Richard Nixon, 1969-1974. Nixon, of course, is often remembered most for his resignation in disgrace in August 1974 due to the Watergate scandal. During the Nixon administration economic growth was fickle and inflation was high. A new term had to be coined to describe the situation: stagflation. Average annual growth under Nixon averaged 2.7%, normally a "fair" performance, but in his case a relatively weak one considering the outstanding 5.7% and 5.4% average gains he inherited from his immediate predecessors, the liberal Democrats John Kennedy and Lyndon Johnson. During Nixon's five and a half years in office there were eight quarters when the economy actually contracted. Two of these were official recessions, the first from late 1969 into 1970 and the second through most of 1974 and continuing into 1975, past the end of his presidency.

Inflation also became a problem, with prices rising an average 5.9% per year during his time in office, topping out at an abysmal 11% during his last year of 1974. In fairness, a goodly amount of that last year's inflation rate has to be attributed to the first OPEC (Organization of Petroleum Exporting Countries) oil embargo, which began in October of 1973, but even leaving that last year out, inflation averaged 5.0% during the Nixon years, a lousy performance compared to the excellent yearly average 2.3% inflation figure Nixon inherited from Kennedy and Johnson. All in all, it was a bad economic time for the American people, as it always is whenever prices are rising faster than the growth of the economy as a whole.

Gerald Ford, 1974-1976. Taking over from Richard Nixon, after Watergate, was no picnic for Gerry Ford. Inflation was out of control, the economy was going downhill, and lots of people were losing their jobs. The well-meaning Ford clearly inherited a mess. Still, it didn't exactly inspire confidence when his main idea for taming inflation seemed to be to get people to wear a campaign button on their shirts reading "WIN," an abbreviation, he explained, for "Whip inflation now!" The Republican former Minority Leader of the House of Representatives proved unable to right the ship of state. The 2.9% economic growth rate was respectable but it was eaten up by a 7½% inflation rate while unemployment surged to 8.1%. It was another failing performance.

Ronald Reagan, 1981-1988. Ronald Reagan came to the White House with simple ideas about restoring prosperity to an economy reeling from huge increases in the price of oil following the Iranian revolution. In his Inaugural Address he confidently declared, "Government is not the solution to our problem, government *is* the problem," Reagan was sure that big tax cuts, especially to high income earners, slashing social programs, and removing as many regulations as possible would do the trick.

The first thing the big tax cuts did was balloon the annual deficit, which tripled. Reagan did not actually reduce spending, which continued to grow during his tenure. What he did was redirect it away from programs that helped people and into America's largest peacetime military buildup. Consequently, there was some growth, increasing from 2.8% a year under Jimmy Carter to 3.6% in the Reagan years, but cutting taxes on the rich while removing support from the poor and middle class meant that 90% of income gains went to the top 10%. The poor actually got poorer. The main success of "Reaganomics" was that inflation was brought down to a more tolerable 4.7%, but that was still higher than the growth rate. Most people's income continued to fall behind inflation. To make matters worse, the unemployment rate went up a full percent to 7.5%.

The bottom line from the conservative "supply side" policies of the Reagan years is that they worked really well for the wealthy. Census Bureau figures show income for the top five percent grew by 14.8% in the Reagan years but only by 2.7% for the median earner. Income inequality increased and everyone but the rich began a slow slide of falling farther behind. Another outfall of the Reagan years was the Savings and Loan crash, caused mostly by the failure of risky real estate loans recently permitted by financial deregulation. That wound up costing the taxpayers $124 billion in bailout fees when the crisis struck during the George H. W. Bush Administration. Reagan also presided over "Black Monday," October 19, 1987, the Stock Crash of 1987, when the DOW lost 22.6% of its value in a single day.

George H.W. Bush, 1989-1993. Before being selected as Reagan's vice presidential running mate, Bush had famously referred to Reagan's economic prescriptions as "Voodoo Economics." Reagan had made the conservative approach popular, though, and Bush went along with his chief happily enough as vice president and for most of his own single four-year term. The results were not good. Inflation improved a hair from 4.7 to 4.4 percent and unemployment dropped a point to a still-high 6.3%, but economic growth was cut almost in half to 1.9%. The deficit also kept going up, even faster than in the Reagan years.

George W. Bush, 2001-2009. The younger Bush took office under marvelous economic conditions and left with them in catastrophe. Democrat Bill Clinton handed off the longest expansion in American history, marked by the creation of 22 million jobs, a budget surplus, and the highest growth rate and lowest inflation since the days of John Kennedy and Lyndon Johnson. Bush fumbled that into the biggest crash since the Great Depression.

Unlike his father, "W" was a true believer in the Reagan bromide that you could tax-cut and deregulate your way not only to prosperity but to a balanced budget as well. He put the theory to the test with two rounds of substantial tax cuts, weighted again toward the wealthy. And once again, the theory produced disaster. The first thing that happened was that the $230 billion annual surplus turned into a $450 billion annual deficit. Bush further pushed the budget out of whack by fear mongering the nation into a war against Iraq and launching a prescription drug program without devising a funding mechanism for either.

The development of "subprime" and "liar loans," hedge funds and derivatives markets, all without effective standards, regulations, oversight, or even accurate assessment by ratings agencies, was part and parcel of the conservative plan to unleash the power of the unchecked market, unfettered by any effective regulatory restraint. The resulting unchecked greed created an enormous "bubble" in the housing market, inflating prices to unprecedented levels. People without adequate income, assets or creditworthiness were talked into loans for expensive homes, even without verification of their incomes. The lenders did not care; they got paid based on sales, and the loans were then sold to third parties under bogus AAA ratings. The idea that the industry would "self-regulate" and forego these shaky but tempting profits was gospel to pro-business conservatives, but proved illusory in the real world.

When the house of cards collapsed, Lehman Brothers, Washington Mutual and Countrywide were among the big names of finance that collapsed with it. The stock market index plunged from 14,000 to 6,500 and unemployment doubled to 9.3%. 4.5 million Americans lost their jobs in the last year of the George W. Bush Administration and 4.3 million more joined them in the next year before the new Obama Administration could reverse the tide. The losses in values for stocks, homes, savings, retirement and pension accounts meant that $16 trillion of American wealth had disappeared, an amount greater than the entire U.S economy produced in a year. It took five and a half years before rising stock values, home values and employment numbers recovered that lost wealth.

In addition to Bush's terrible economic legacy, as Alex Seitz-Wald summed up in *Salon*, "Add to that the bungled wars in Iraq and Afghanistan, the preventable failure to catch Osama bin Laden at Tora Bora, the absolutely horrendous handling of Hurricane Katrina, the outing of a covert CIA officer in a political vendetta, the illegal wiretapping of Americans' phones, the improper firing of U.S. attorneys for political reasons, the use of taxpayer dollars to pay columnists, and 'misrepresenting and suppressing scientific knowledge for political purposes,' to name a few - and, well, then you know why Dana Perino, Bush's former press secretary, was forced to lead her ode to the ex-president by recounting that he 'shared his peanut butter and honey sandwiches with me.'"

To sum up his disastrous presidency, here is my blog based on W's presidential farewell address.

"Bush's Farewell Address" from Bravegnuwhirled.blogspot.com: January 16, 2009

I think the most fateful decision of the past nine years may well have been George W. Bush's selection of Dick Cheney to head his vice presidential search team once W locked up the Republican nomination in 2000. If he had chosen another of his father's old hands, say somebody like Brent Scowcroft, the history of the past eight years would be considerably different. We would still have had some of Bush's "born again" domestic initiatives. We would still have had a corporate-friendly domestic slant. The fiscal foolishness would have been a bit more benign. Most importantly, the neoconservative foreign policy nonsense would likely never have happened.

Bush ran almost entirely on domestic issues. He had no foreign policy experience whatever. To the extent he spoke of it, he said he opposed "nation building," a reference to Bill Clinton's actions in such places as Bosnia and Kosovo, and talked of conducting a "humble" foreign policy, as he put it. He was about cutting taxes, rolling back environmental protections and expanding faith-based programs: The heck with foreigners.

The Cheney decision changed all that. Before long the veteran bureaucratic infighter informed his less than astute boss that he'd found a superbly qualified running mate--himself. Once the Supreme Court ruled Bush the general election winner, Cheney brought in the whole crew from the Project for a New American Century. Donald Rumsfeld, Paul Wolfowitz, Richard Perle, Dick Cheney, Scooter Libby and company moved into the power vacuum created by Bush's ignorance. They convinced him of their millennial theory and flattered Bush that he was the anointed to carry it out. 9/11 expedited things by providing the useful pretext.

We heard yet another defense of this ridiculous and now demonstrably failed academic construct last night. As Bush would tell it, he had acted to bring democracy and freedom to the Middle East through the barrel of a gun. As a result the region is currently on track to usher in an era of lasting peace. If American constitutional principles had to be abridged, so be it. One could argue with his decisions, but not with the fact that he had the guts to make the tough calls, he told us.

It is astounding how the path of events has failed to disabuse Bush of his illusions. The attempt to occupy Muslim countries in the Middle East has not created stable, friendly, peace-loving nations there. The abandonment of the rule of law has not proven effective in garnering supporters or defeating enemies. People in the region do not like Israel or the United States. When given the vote they tend to elect people like Hamas, Hezbollah and Ahmadinejad and Iraqi Shi'ites, who cozy up to Iran.

This was the vision he sold a frightened American public seven years ago. The majority bought it because they were scared and they presumed a president had to know what he was talking about. Very few people in the rest of the world bought it. The American people themselves stopped believing in it three years ago. Rather pitifully, Bush was still selling it last night in his last speech to the American people as President. These days, no one is buying and few are even listening.

One can foresee him appearing at future Republican conventions, every four years making one more effort to reclaim that day when he stood in the rubble at ground zero with his popularity at 91%. Retiring at the age of 62, Bush will be like Herbert Hoover, who haunted and embarrassed Republican conventions into the 1960s trying to peddle the absurdity that his Depression policy was working and that it had really been Franklin Roosevelt's New Deal that prolonged the suffering.

As a former president, Bush will be shown due respect for the office he held. His reputation, however, will never be rehabilitated. It is not enough to have made tough calls. A president has to get them right. That is his tragedy, and ours.

CHAPTER 17:
What Conservatives Believe

The *Merriam-Webster Dictionary* defines conservatism in three ways:

First, it encompasses a general attitude about politics
a disposition in politics to preserve what is established

Second, it describes conservative political views in more detail:
a political philosophy based on tradition and social stability, stressing established institutions, and preferring gradual development to abrupt change; specifically: such a philosophy calling for lower taxes, limited government regulation of business and investing, a strong national defense, and individual financial responsibility for personal needs (as retirement income or health-care coverage)

Third, it sums up the basic attitude underlying the conservative philosophy: *the tendency to prefer an existing or traditional situation to change*

The very word "conserve" means to preserve or keep something the way it is. That is what the first and third parts of the definition home in on. The basic mindset that gives rise to conservatism is a resistance to change, and that is what motivates the thinking and views of a lot of conservatives. Liberals tend to notice what is unjust or not working well in society. They see important needs not being met and start thinking of ways to improve the situation. In contrast, people with a conservative temperament tend to focus on preserving things in society as they are. They are often skeptical or even suspicious of suggestions for change and frequently jump right into defending the status quo when new ideas are brought to their attention. This affinity for traditional ways and hostility to change as described in the first and third parts of the definition lies at the heart of much of the conservative world view. It is the original temperament that has characterized conservatives throughout history. People with this kind of motivation are the ones pushing for such principles as government support for Religion and resistance to ideas such as marriage equality for gays and lesbians. It is the prime motivation for many who support continuing to use the Electoral College instead of the popular vote for electing the president. Their argument runs, "It's the way it's always been done!"

The second part talks about some specific policy positions modern American conservatives typically hold. If you keep up with political news at all you are certainly well aware of conservative resistance to taxes and their frequent desire to cut them at every opportunity. Many speak often of being "small government conservatives." These modern American conservatives point to "excessive government regulation" as a threat to the economy and to people's happiness. They often propose rolling back labor, environmental and safety protections as what they see as undue government intervention into business and society. For instance, many conservatives opposed such innovations as the Environmental Protection Agency, the Occupational Safety and Health Administration and even civil rights legislation as intrusions of "big government" too far into American life. Some continue to try to get rid of these protections, and many conservatives in congress keep trying to limit their effectiveness by voting to water down the protections themselves, restrict the agencies' regulatory authority or cut their budgets so much they cannot effectively carry out their jobs.

This part of the definition also makes mention of "individual financial responsibility." Many conservatives have always despised the great social insurance programs liberals have instituted. Social Security, Medicare and the Affordable Care Act (Obamacare) stand as prominent examples. They hate the idea of everyone contributing to help those in need; they feel everyone should look out for themselves and if people do not have the wherewithal to do so, then tough luck for them.

If you go back through the "Conservative Record of Failure" and the records of Republican presidents in Chapter 16, you will see these principles and policies consistently put into practice when conservatives were in power. You will also notice their uniformly miserable results. When they were out of power they continued to advocate for the same kinds of principles and policies and fought hard to prevent liberal ideas from prevailing. What are they thinking when they stand against equality or against taking decisive action to combat a bad economy that has millions of people out of work and hungry?

The Three Types of Conservative

Though it can often seem like an unbroken, unified, intransigent wall to progressives, the contemporary conservative movement in the United States is actually a coalition of three different types of conservatives. The three types of conservatives are social conservatives, economic/political conservatives, and defense conservatives. Some conservatives belong to only one group, some to two of them, and some to all three. Understanding this dynamic is key to understanding American conservatism. It is also essential to understanding how to interact with, negotiate with, and find enough common ground to get anything done when trying to work with conservatives. It is also important to knowing how to make inroads politically with conservatives who may be sympathetic or even in full agreement with parts of the progressive message.

Keep in mind that there are aspects of conservatism that liberals can find common ground with. When social conservatives talk about the importance of strong and loving families they find ready agreement among liberals. When libertarian conservatives support women's freedom of choice and oppose unnecessary foreign wars they can be good allies of liberals and liberal principles. When economic conservatives push for efficiency and economy in government and its programs they are in accord with the liberal principles of making sure tax money is well spent and programs are targeted and working effectively to help the people they are intended to. The first idea to take away from this is to remember there can be some accord between liberals and conservatives in the general outcomes we want to see: a safer, freer, more prosperous community, and sometimes even in the means to achieve them. The second factor to realize is that not all conservatives even see eye to eye with each other.

It's easy to think of people with a different political persuasion as a monolithic and obstinate bloc who disagree with us and cannot be reasoned with. But just as some liberals are focused on certain issues more than others, there are different priorities and outlooks among conservatives too. Consider that some liberals are mostly worried about the environment, others are labor union members focused on economic issues, still others are heavily into poverty relief, others are about human rights and some feel most deeply about disarmament and international peace. You could add many more issues to the list. In similar fashion, a number of different preoccupations appeal to different people who congregate under the general heading of "conservatives." And not only do the three groups have three different constellations of issues they care most strongly about, they have two basic approaches to politics and governance that are fundamentally at odds with one another!

Social Conservatives

Social conservatives are the ones liberals are often referring to when they think of what bothers them most about conservatism. Social conservatives take most seriously the literal meaning of the word "conserve." That is, they are strongly devoted to conserving, or keeping, traditional cultural ways. They are adamant that marriage must only be between a man and a woman. They want to criminalize abortion. Social conservatives often want to restrict women's access to contraception, and particularly to women who are under eighteen. They resist sexual education in the schools. In fact, they often take their children out of public schools and home school them or send them to religious schools where they are taught that the universe was created in six days and that climate change is not happening. They tend to feel that certain walks of life are the purview of men, and that women do best when they stay at home and let men run society.

Social conservatives want federal and state government and public institutions such as schools and the military to promote religion. And when they mean religion, the overwhelming majority of American social conservatives mean fundamentalist Christian religion. These are the folks you are likely to see driving around with the bumper stickers and decals on their cars that have a Christian cross superimposed over an American flag. Their churches often fly large American flags out front, as though Jesus preached American nationalism seventeen centuries before America was formed. Church and state are not separate to them, and they are most decidedly not for "small government." In their view, the state exists to enforce their version of religion and their interpretation of religious morality on society and each citizen. Arkansas Governor and ordained Baptist minister Mike Huckabee was the most prominent GOP social conservative candidate in 2008. John McCain chose the social conservative Governor of Alaska Sarah Palin as his running mate to burnish his popularity with this group in 2008. Born-again Minnesota Congresswoman Michele Bachmann and conservative Catholic and former Pennsylvania Senator Rick Santorum were good examples of this perspective among the candidates vying for the Republican nomination for president in 2012. Mitt Romney adopted many of these social conservative views in his own campaign in his race for the nomination and in his general election campaign against President Obama in 2012.

News about social conservatives may dominate the coverage at times, but not all conservatives are of this type. Conservatism is not ten feet tall, and in some ways is an uneasy coalition no less than the Democrats are. Richard Nixon's decision to commit the

Republican Party to a "Southern Strategy" in 1968, an approach cemented by Ronald Reagan in the 1980s, has wedded the GOP to a social conservative agenda that has been dominated by concern over issues like abortion, gay marriage and stem cell research. Those views make it almost impossible for a candidate who can gain the party's nomination to win in the socially liberal Northeast and California.

I was talking to a moderate Republican a few years back, during the 2008 campaign between Barack Obama and John McCain. He was a strong McCain supporter, but was pessimistic about McCain's chances of winning the election that year. We went over the electoral map, trying to figure which states the venerable Arizonan would need to win and whether he could win, and it seemed a very difficult task. "When you can't win California it makes it awfully hard," my friend remarked. His basic thesis was that by putting their eggs in the social conservative basket, the Republicans can't win in hardly any of the Northeast, Pacific Coast and Great Lakes states, and have to take almost everything in the South, Plains, and Mountain West. Slip anywhere and they're through.

That is true, but the strategy has resulted in Republican victories in 7 of the last 12 presidential contests. Their victories are sometimes narrow, but they had been winning the majority of the time, especially from 1968 to 1988, when they won five of six presidential contests. But lately they really appear to be slipping, losing four of the past six presidential elections in the Electoral College and five of the last six in the popular vote.

Economic/Political Conservatives

The conversation with my Republican friend pointed up the fact that not all Republicans agree with those social conservative views. The Republican coalition is made up of social conservatives, economic/political conservatives, and defense conservatives. The middle group has a very different perspective on things than the other two. My friend is one of these economic/political types. His consistent view is that government power, especially federal power, should be limited. Economic and personal liberties should be infringed as little as possible by the government. This was actually the view advocated by the modern father of the conservative movement, Sen. Barry Goldwater of Arizona, in his 1964 presidential race.

Economic/political conservatives are the "small government" conservatives. They are the ones most adamant about low taxes and cutting government spending. As Grover Norquist of the economic/political conservative lobbying group Americans for Tax Reform said, "I'm not in favor of abolishing the government. I just want to shrink it down to the size where we can drown it in the bathtub."

When it comes to economic policy this type of conservative wants as little government intervention as possible. They place little stock in concern for the general good of society as expressed by the people through their elected representatives. Instead, they see the individual property or business owner as, ideally, a completely independent actor. They don't like minimum wages or health, safety and pollution regulations. They have an implicit faith in "the market," that is, the buying and selling decisions made by everyone in society, as a nearly infallible barometer of what is desirable. Tea Party Republicans like Representative Paul Ryan and Senator Ted Cruz, Florida Governor Rick Scott, Ohio Governor John Kasich and Senators Marco Rubio and Rand Paul are good examples of this viewpoint.

In terms of constitutional outlook, this kind of conservative reads the U. S. Constitution restrictively, believing that if a power is not expressly mentioned, the government cannot legitimately exercise it. They often view our government itself as the enemy, or at best a necessary evil. Some, such as Sen. Rand Paul, are not sure the Civil Rights Act is legitimate, since it restricts a private individual's, or business owner's right to discriminate. Supreme Court Justice Antonin Scalia referred to the question of the renewal of the Voting Rights Act, passed to eliminate racial discrimination in voting, as the "perpetuation of racial entitlement." He also does not believe the Fourteenth Amendment outlaws discrimination against women, saying in a 2011 interview:

In 1868, when the 39th Congress was debating and ultimately proposing the 14th Amendment, I don't think anybody would have thought that equal protection applied to sex discrimination, or certainly not to sexual orientation. So does that mean that we've gone off in error by applying the 14th Amendment to both? Yes, yes. Sorry, to tell you that.

Here is the relevant section of the Fourteenth Amendment
"No State shall make or enforce any law which shall abridge the privileges or immunities of citizens of the United States; nor shall any State deprive any person of life, liberty, or property, without due process of law; nor deny to any person within its jurisdiction the equal protection of the laws."

So, to Justice Scalia's way of thinking, even though it is prohibited to "deny to any person...the equal protection of the laws," because the Amendment does not specifically refer to women and because he does not believe women in 1868 were thought of as persons, it should still be legal today to discriminate against them. He does not want to allow government any power or authority that he can conceivably keep from it, no matter how contorted the logic he has to use.

The question of course, is why. Understanding this, you understand all. The explanation lies in the fear of tyranny. The basic premise of the economic/political conservative is that strong government is a potential threat to freedom. They think of governments that have gotten too strong, such as totalitarian states like Soviet Russia and Nazi Germany, and fear that could take place here. Consequently, they try to avoid the "slippery slope." Today's drive to require background checks on all gun purchases to try to keep them out of the hands of terrorists, criminals and the violently insane, they fear, could lead to tomorrow's drive to confiscate all guns from sane and law-abiding citizens.

There is also the simple belief that unfettered economic performance does better too, though the record over the past 80 years, as you've seen in Chapter 7, argues against this. They apparently are not much worried about corporate abuse and special interest control of law and the economy for its own selfish purposes. The magic of the market will correct all. Where the liberal sees government under the people's control as a bulwark against injustice and abuse, and a counterweight to the shortcomings of the market, the economic/political conservative instead sees it as the very source of threat and abuse.

What is interesting is that some of this kind of conservative can be very progressive on social issues. Following the logic that less government is better, conservatives of this stripe may, for instance, raise no objection to marriage equality and may favor legalization of marijuana. They can be quite consistent in their view that less government on any topic is better. Economic/political conservatives are not essentially practical-minded people. They are ideologues, believing that the doctrine of small government must be upheld rather than looking to research or human needs to inform decision-making. That is why Republicans in congress voted to deny people disaster relief in 2012 when the East Coast was devastated by super storm Sandy, and why Senator Tom Coburn of Oklahoma called for withholding aid to the people of his own state in 2013 when it had been devastated by tornadoes, unless the money could first be cut from something else. That is why economic/political conservatives resist regulating guns, food preparation standards or polluting industries that kill people. Less government and less regulation is to them always good. More is always bad. Dogma is more important to them than human needs.

Defense Conservatives

The third type of conservative is the defense conservative. Whenever the question of military power comes up, defense conservatives are for more of it. Whenever an international situation gets complicated, they are the first to call for armed intervention to settle it. It seems they're never happy unless we're at war. And whenever constitutional and individual liberties have to be balanced against security concerns, they are almost always for forgetting about the constitutional liberties and in favor of going ahead with whatever surveillance, data mining, searching, spying, detaining, torturing, invading or drone-striking is proposed as a solution to the security question at hand.

Senators John McCain and Lindsey Graham are good examples of defense conservatives. They were against bringing our troops home from Iraq. They advocated invading Libya. McCain mimicked a Beach Boys song at one rally, singing "Bomb, bomb, bomb! Bomb, bomb Iran!" They want to keep U.S. forces in Afghanistan. They have been talking up getting militarily involved in the Syrian civil war. In late spring of 2013 Graham strongly backed the NSA phone surveillance program.

Disagreement among Conservatives

You can see how the economic/political conservatives are at odds with this. Defense conservatives favor aggrandizing the military power of the country almost without limit. But small-government boosters view this as an extremely dangerous threat to the future of liberty in the country. Wars and military hardware are also very expensive, which economic/political conservatives don't like. Social conservatives too, favor the heavy use of government power, in their case to discourage personal behaviors of which they disapprove or to promote others, such as evangelical religion, which they favor. Political conservatives see these stances as unwarranted infringements by the state into personal liberties and matters of individual choice. So, one group of conservatives wants to limit the government and the other two want to enlarge it. It's an uncomfortable and self-contradictory political alliance racked with internal political fighting among themselves that shows no signs of ending anytime soon. Yet they all need each other's votes to win elections.

Where do the "Tea Party" advocates fit in? Though there is some overlap with defense and social conservatives within their movement, most tea partiers are extreme anti-government advocates. Their main focus is low taxes and spending, thus keeping the government and its impact on society small. Thus, they are philosophically simply the most adamant part of the economic/political conservative group. They don't necessarily have much in common with the social conservatives or defense conservatives; some are one or the other or both, but these views are coincidental to their main thrust which is to reduce taxes and government programs of all kinds. There was a lot of ribbing directed their way when some senior citizen Tea Party supporters, railing against Obamacare, shouted, "No government health care, and don't touch my Medicare!"

When times were good for the conservative movement these differences have often been papered over. In tough political environments for the Republican Party such as now, the coalition can become frayed. It is a truism that alliances suffer their greatest stresses and tend to unravel as they near defeat. My friend's greatest lament was that if McCain lost in 2008, it would discredit the electoral chances of his brand of conservative, the economic/constitutional type, even though the environment created by the social/defense conservative George W. Bush was actually to blame. Ironically, it could pave the way for a new succession of Republican social and defense conservative candidates in the years ahead who would either continue to lose, or who, if they won, would continue increasing the power of the state.

Of course, McCain is also an avid defense conservative, so he didn't fully fit into the small-government mold. Yet when he lost, social conservatives went on to loudly proclaim the reason was his inadequate ardor for their moral issues. The 2008 election was not just a battle between McCain and Barack Obama; it was also a battle for the soul of the Republican Party. Once McCain did go down to defeat, economic/political conservatives once again had to hold their noses in 2012 and vote for Mitt Romney and his positions against women's and gay rights and in favor of military intervention all over the world.

Where Did These Conservative Views Come From?

The historical roots of this view against change go back hundreds of years into medieval Europe, where the aristocratic ruling class resisted any change to the social order that would threaten their position at the top of it. But not all of these policy positions necessarily flow from the general conservative disposition to keep things the way they are. The stringent insistence on such policy views as low taxes, "smaller" government, minimizing regulation, especially on business, an extremely powerful military and getting rid of social and relief programs owe their origins much more recently to the modern American Conservative Movement. It was largely popularized by the advocacy of William F. Buckley and brought into national electoral politics by Barry Goldwater.

Buckley lived from 1925 to 2008. Born to a large wealthy Catholic family, he was educated in Paris, London, Mexico and Yale University. At Yale he studied political science, history and economics, and joined the school's Conservative Party and the Yale Political Union. He excelled as captain of the debate team and chaired the Yale Daily News. In 1955 he founded a magazine called the *National Review*, which served as the most important journal for promoting the new take on conservatism.

Buckley brought together three different strains of conservative thought and presented them as a coherent whole. The first of these was to support traditional views on society and religion. The second was a very libertarian view on the role of government in society and the economy. Libertarians believe that government's function should be as minimal as possible, restricting itself to such services as enforcing contracts and basic law and order. You will sometimes see this principle of minimizing government intervention in the economy referred to as *laissez-faire*, French for "let it be." The third pillar of Buckley's new conservative order during that Cold War period was a strong anti-Communist stance that required, among other things, the maintenance of an extremely powerful military and national intelligence operation. With these three intellectual positions in place, you can see the outline of the modern Conservative Movement that is still with us today.

Besides his magazine and newspaper punditry, Buckley effectively promoted his views by hosting 1,429 shows of the long-running public affairs discussion television program "Firing Line" from 1966 to 1999. If you take the time to watch a recording of a Buckley speech or one of his shows you will immediately be struck by his extreme upper class accent and air of monumental arrogance. At the same time, you may nevertheless be impressed by his vast vocabulary and effective wit. In one discussion he quipped, "I won't insult your intelligence by suggesting that you really believe what you just said."

In addition to the one opening this section, here are a few other choice Buckley quotes: "I mean to live my life an obedient man, but obedient to God, subservient to the wisdom of my ancestors; never to the authority of political truths arrived at yesterday at the voting booth." "Idealism is fine, but as it approaches reality, the costs become prohibitive." "There is an inverse relationship between reliance on the state and self-reliance." "Conservatives should be adamant about the need for the reappearance of Judeo-Christianity in the public square." "It seems to me that the idea traditionally defended of endeavoring to maintain existing ethnic balances simply doesn't work anymore."

Another source of ideas for the Conservative Movement was author Ayn Rand, who lived from 1905 to 1982. Rand immigrated from Russia in 1926 and became an American citizen in 1931. Among her writings was a pair of novels, *The Fountainhead* and *Atlas Shrugged*. Both feature protagonists who reject religion, are uncompromising individualists, and lead their lives based purely on self-interest. In Rand's view, which she called "Objectivism," selfishness is the only true virtue and guide to life, and religion and altruism are contemptible weaknesses. The purpose of truly creative and ambitious people is to get as much for themselves as they can, and leave the inferior multitude with as little as possible. The role of the state is to do as little as possible to interfere with this unbridled acquisitiveness of a few. I can remember my mother plowing through the lengthy *Atlas Shrugged* when I was a boy. Though William F. Buckley certainly agreed with Rand's *laissez-faire* economic ideas, he parted company with her over her atheism. Rand has enjoyed resurgence in conservative circles in recent years. The 2012 Republican nominee for vice president, Paul Ryan, was fond of giving copies of *Atlas Shrugged* to his congressional office staff as Christmas presents, and has been quoted as saying, "[T]he reason I got involved in public service, by and large, if I had to credit one thinker, one person, it would be Ayn Rand."

Arizona Senator Barry Goldwater became the Republican Party standard bearer for this new conservative synthesis of traditionalism, *laissez-faire* economics and a massive defense establishment in his run for the White House in 1964. Goldwater's main opponent for the nomination that year was the moderate Republican governor of New York, Nelson Rockefeller. Goldwater and Rockefeller made the choice a strong referendum on political ideology. In an era when many people voted geographically (most white Southerners voted Democratic and many white Northerners voted Republican based on party loyalties that had been handed down since the Civil War), Goldwater explicitly promised to make the Republican Party "conservative."

By this, of course, he meant the new style of conservatism of limited programs other than a strong national defense. Goldwater wanted to roll back the social insurance programs of the New Deal and greatly escalate the Vietnam War. He even spoke of using nuclear weapons there. Part of Goldwater's idea of reducing government power was to leave more issues to the individual fifty states to handle. He voted against the Civil Rights Act, for example, claiming not that he was for segregation but that he was acting to prevent federal government power from getting too strong.

Rockefeller consistently characterized Goldwater as an extremist who would take away help from people in need and abolish popular programs like Social Security. He also attacked Goldwater as dangerously aggressive in foreign policy. Goldwater fought back by highlighting his strongly contrasting views from the Democrats, compared to Rockefeller's acceptance of much of the New Deal program. One of his slogans was, "A choice, not an echo." The New York Governor put up a spirited fight but fell short, losing the campaign-ending California primary by three points, partly as a result of his controversial divorce and remarriage.

So it was that Barry Goldwater, backed by the true believers of the new Conservative Movement, had defeated the "establishment" Republican candidate. From that point on the Republican Party would more and more be captured by the followers of this Movement. The process of turning the Republican Party into a sharply ideological instrument, bent on slashing government in general and the federal government in particular other than in military and related programs, had begun. As the new nominee, Goldwater unapologetically placed himself in the role of a crusader, famously exclaiming in his acceptance speech to the convention, "I would remind you that extremism in the defense of liberty is no vice! And let me remind you also that moderation in the pursuit of justice is no virtue."

Though Goldwater had turned his own party to the right, he was singularly unsuccessful in doing so with the nation at large. He went on to a crushing defeat in November 1964 against Democrat Lyndon Johnson, losing 61 to 39 percent in the popular vote and carrying only six of the fifty states. Johnson's campaign was highly successful at selling the nation as a whole on the themes Rockefeller had not been able to sell to Republicans only, that Goldwater was an extremist in domestic affairs and a dangerous warmonger abroad. It was clear that most Americans supported New Deal programs like Social Security and government services such as hydroelectric power, aid to education and the interstate highway system.

The one thing it is important to realize is that Goldwater was not a true social conservative. Here is what he later confided about them: "Mark my word, if and when these preachers get control of the [Republican] party, and they're sure trying to do so, it's going to be a terrible damn problem. Frankly, these people frighten me; for, politics and governing demand compromises. But these Christians believe they are acting in the name of God, so they can't and won't compromise. I know; I've tried to deal with them." Their inclusion in the coalition was yet to come.

The next Republican president, Richard Nixon, was much more a political opportunist than a committed conservative. In fact, his predilection to do or say practically anything to get and hold onto power was what led to the Watergate scandal that eventually brought him down. The loser of the 1960 campaign to John F. Kennedy was able to get the Republican nomination in 1968 by keeping up his contacts and campaigning hard for GOP candidates in the 1966 congressional elections. He was then able to narrowly win the White House due to the assassination of the Democrats' strongest potential nominee, Robert Kennedy, and their division over the Vietnam War. For his part, Nixon appealed to both Vietnam "hawks" and "doves" by hinting that he had an unspecified "secret plan" to end the war. Once in office, he kept the war going for another five years. He also capitalized on white fears of the civil rights movement and of the liberal anti-Vietnam War movement by emphasizing his support for "law and order," a coded reference to cracking down on blacks and hippies. Nixon explicitly talked about his "Southern strategy" and once in office tried to seat two Southern and formerly avowedly pro-segregationist judges on the Supreme Court. Fortunately, neither was confirmed by the Senate. Yet Nixon's play for the Southern social conservative vote resulted in the Republican Party's winning seven former slave states and their best performance in the Deep South in a century. Five other such states that year voted for the avowedly segregationist third-party candidacy of Alabama Governor George Wallace. The GOP's growing need for those votes over the decades made the South—and social conservatives—absolutely essential to its chances for victory in congress and the White House, and pushed their views farther and farther to the right.

On the other hand, due to his opportunistic bent, Nixon could see that workplace safety and environmental concerns were gaining popularity, and so went along with the establishment of the Occupational Health and Safety Administration and numerous environmental landmarks, including the Environmental Protection Agency, Clean Air Act and Clean Water Act. Aside from the Vietnam War, in foreign policy, Nixon also reached agreements with the two main Communist powers, China and Soviet Russia. The SALT (Strategic Arms Limitation Treaty) with the Soviet Union capped the nuclear forces of both sides for the first time. For these reasons, it is clear Nixon was not a doctrinaire conservative.

Ronald Reagan, however, was the one who put into place the basic elements we still recognize today as the whole package of conservative views and issues. He overtly spoke to the social conservative perspective on issues like abortion and civil rights, feverishly labored to cut taxes and government help for the economy and the needy, scoffed at environmental concerns, and sought to increase military expenditures almost without limit. His winning coalition cemented these views in the Republican canon as orthodoxy not to be challenged. Indeed, Reagan in practice proved more willing to compromise and make deals than those who have adoringly followed him down to our own day. For example, he famously cut a deal with congressional Democrats on Social Security to keep it solvent. He agreed to let them raise the tax to bring in more revenue and they in turn agreed with his proposal to increase the age for receiving full benefits by two years.

George W. Bush personified the entire conservative perspective. His views on "faith based" government-supported programs, his opposition to LGBT rights, women's reproductive rights, minority rights enforcement and stem cell research marked him as a strong social conservative. His instigation of the unnecessary Iraq War, a massive secret surveillance network and official torture mark him as an extreme defense conservative. His repudiation of environmental concerns, including the scientific consensus on global warming, his eagerness to lower taxes on the rich and privatize government functions while gutting regulations on business and help for the needy put him squarely in the economic conservative camp as well. And as we remember all too vividly, these perspectives led to their typical results: social stagnation, foreign frustration and economic failure.

So, is there anything good about conservatism? Well, when we speak of social conservatives, we should remember there are good things people venerate about the past: things like traditional patriotism, social customs, ways which people relate to one another, traditional manners, lore, humor and food that make up a familiar culture. There are also negative holdovers too, such as exclusionary impulses and outmoded attitudes which liberals and fair-minded people in general are always working to change into a greater acceptance of pluralism. Conservatives temperamentally do venerate the past and tend to resist change while liberals look for what is wrong with it and want to bring in the change they feel will be beneficial. The tension between the two is necessary in some sense to retaining a grounding and yet being open to positive progress. In the economic realm, it is also good to be efficient in operating any agency or program, and cost-conscious conservatives can help serve as watchdogs for this. This underlying view is not in conflict with the liberal desire to see that help gets honestly and efficiently to those who really need it, without waste, fraud or abuse. Their view that people ought to be self-reliant and independent is something liberals can agree with too. Defense conservatives usually go overboard in their militarism, but their perspective needs to be heard. Sometimes we really are dealing with bad actors in the world; with these, it is best to remain wary and not let down our guard.

But it should never be forgotten that in the final analysis, these conservative perspectives are fundamentally at odds with the liberal world view. We strongly disagree with social conservatives who wish to use government to impose their religious views on people and who dismiss the validity of logic, science and fact to inform decision making. We strongly disagree with economic/political conservatives when they act to cede all power in society to the wealthy and corporations and call that "freedom," or when they oppose the wise use of government action to promote jobs, opportunity and security for the people. We strongly disagree with defense conservatives and their basic premise that the best solution to foreign problems almost always involves resorting to bombs and war.

"BRAVE GNU WHIRLED" ARTICLES

To conclude the chapter I've included four of my blog entries dealing with various aspects of conservatism. You can visit my site online to peruse through the hundreds of entries I've made since late 2007 by going to (http://www.bravegnuwhirled.blogspot.com/.

"Sad Appeal to 'Little Guy'"
from Bravegnuwhirled.blogspot.com: October 16, 2010

This morning's paper carried an Associated Press article titled "Palin Says 'little guy' Key in Vote." "Former Alaska Governor Sarah Palin said Friday that the country needs to elect business-minded candidates who will not sell out their principles for the sake of bipartisanship." Oh. And the "regular" Republicans these past two years have been models of the infection of bipartisanship?

She went on, "This election is about the little guy, the common man, independence, and the middle class--those forgotten and ignored for too long, and now they're fighting back." The Tea Party of late and Big Conservatism in general for the past 40 years have done one of the best jobs of ironically effective misdirection of angst in modern times. Notice how she knits together a list of identifiers that describe the majority of society and links it to disaffection and defensive umbrage--yes, she's talking about me, and look how abused we are--and then continues with, "We want those business-oriented folks in Washington not to be there singing 'Kumbaya' with the people who caused the problems in the first place."

And what problems are those that affect the little guy of the middle class so strongly? First would be the Wall Street meltdown and foreclosure crisis, caused by the reckless unregulated practices of big business. Next would be the jobs crisis, caused by big business outsourcing all those middle class jobs overseas. Third might be an opportunity crisis, characterized by such things as the college cost crunch, public school deterioration and infrastructure decline, fueled by the success of big business and the wealthy at getting their tax burdens reduced so that more and more has to be borne by "little guys" who cannot afford it. Now in the wake of the Citizens United court ruling, $50 million in secret contributions from big business is pouring into the election campaign on behalf of the Republican cause. No doubt we are expected to believe their largess is donated not to further GOP support for corporate interests but due to the multinationals' concern for the 'little guy.'

Disaffection in the white working and lower middle class is real and understandable. Their standard of living has been getting inexorably squeezed for the past thirty years. The Koch brothers, Coors family, Rupert Murdoch and a handful of like-minded rightist billionaires have been working assiduously for at least that long to misdirect the chain of causation for that away from themselves for even longer. All the poor, aggrieved little guy has to do is turn ever more authority over to the tycoons who have rigged the system against him and require less and less of a societal contribution from those who have been driving him to desperation and all will be well. It would be laughable if it weren't so tragically sad.

"Hearing the Dog Whistle (The Case for Right-Sized Government)"
from Bravegnuwhirled.blogspot.com: April 25, 2010

As a matter of political philosophy, conservatives say they feel that government should be as small as possible while taking care of basic functions. I recently had a conservative intellectual express his view by quoting what Abraham Lincoln once said, "the legitimate object of government is to do for a community of people, whatever they need to have done, but cannot do at all, or cannot do so well for themselves, in their separate and individual capacities." I certainly have no dispute with that perspective. That is because it reflects a pragmatic rather than an ideological approach to what government ought to do. If it needs to be done, and people can't do it on their own, then government ought to do it. The rub, of course, comes in determining what needs doing, and in assessing whether individuals or other private entities can do it so well on their own.

These days the right is energized in opposition to President Obama and the Democrats in Congress. Tea Party protesters maintain that totalitarianism is on the way that Big Government for its own sake, or for the sake of controlling people, is in the process of being imposed. Well, let's look at the top issues facing the country these days. To rail against big government is truly to blow the dog whistle for these folks. They understand you are one of them and see the world their way. But what is really needed to solve the nation's current many challenges? Is government action or laissez faire required? We ought to take a look on a case by case basis.

Let's start with the economy. When the financial system crashed in late summer 2008, the Bush administration and congressional Republicans and Democrats agreed a massive bailout had to be instituted to save the economy from a Great Depression. It was done and worked. Candidates McCain, Obama and overwhelming majorities of both parties approved TARP. While there is no doubt greater accountability should have been required, to have sat aside and done nothing would have been catastrophic. The (at least) $700 billion infusion will wind up costing, according to current Treasury Secretary Tim Geithner, about $78 billion, as the money is paid back with interest. That saved the national economy for less than the cost of one year of the Iraq War--a bargain.

The Obama-Democratic $787 billion stimulus bill from the spring of 2009 was similar. Anyone who has taken Econ 101 understands Keynesian economics and the need to infuse demand into an economy to head off or alleviate serious recession. It is what every government has done since the Depression. Even the Chinese committed a $586 billion USD stimulus to their economy in November, 2008.

The same goes for financial regulation. Does anyone seriously imagine the outfits that precipitated the meltdown with unsound but immediately profitable subprime loans and unregulated derivatives speculation will be able to avoid the temptations of quick buck schemes in the future without regulations to prevent them? How many times does it take? We had the stock crash of '29 when there were no regulations back then, another in '87 when deregulation was first instituted, then the S & L crisis and now the financial/housing crash after things were loosened up again. Every time the rules come off the system implodes.

How about defense? Do we defend ourselves against terrorism with more government or less? Military and intelligence assets, homeland security practices and equipment, FBI tasking, liaison with foreign nations at all levels, law enforcement assistance, training, covert action, drone strikes in Yemen and Pakistan and such all cost money and require government involvement. Do you know many conservatives against any of these things? Neither do I.

Conservatives are worried about immigration again, since an Arizona rancher was killed, possibly by drug traffickers from across the border. The state legislature just passed a sweeping law allowing police to question anyone they think might be an illegal alien and arrest anyone they so question who does not have evidence of citizenship or permission for legal residency with them. Conservatives in general always seem to favor harsh crackdowns to catch illegal aliens. Does that sound like small government to you? The Archbishop of Los Angeles likens it to Nazi and Communist tactics.

Consider energy independence and climate change. These are essential priorities the market can't solve yet. It is still far cheaper to burn gasoline, diesel and coal than it is to go solar or harness the wind. By the time that changes the carbon dioxide in the atmosphere will be so high the world will face ecological calamity. In the meantime we remain vulnerable to blackmail or delivery interruptions from abroad. Even weak mileage and emissions standards have resulted in a 25% drop in pollution since 1970 though twice as many cars are on the road. Government requirements and incentives are necessary to get this done.

Health care is another example. Conservatives have a surprising blind spot to advocate police state tactics after one person is possibly killed from across the border but turn a blind eye when Harvard Medical School says 45,000 people have been dying yearly from lack of access to health care. This is clearly something events have shown a lot of people "cannot do so well for themselves."

The list could go on and on. We have a lot of issues that have been festering because they have not been adequately addressed. Left to themselves they have been getting progressively worse. Handwringing about the size of government will not solve any of them. We do not need big or small government; we need the right amount-whatever that is in a specific case-to deal with the many serious problems that need solving.

"Once Upon a Time in Freeville"
from Bravegnuwhirled.blogspot.com: April 11, 2009

Once upon a time there was a small town called Freeville. The people of Freeville were the happiest in the world because they were free. They gloried in how free they were, and told visitors and people from other towns about it all the time whenever they met.

Freeville was situated on the east bank of the Swift River in the foothills of the Snowy Mountains. Across the river on the west bank lay most of the good farmland. There the land was flat and the soil was deep and fertile. Wide fields of swaying grain and dense orchards laden with fruit abounded there.

Most of the people of Freeville lived in town on the east side of the Swift River and had to cross it to work in their fields and orchards on the west side. For a long time there had been only two ways to cross the river. One way was to pay Giles the ferryman a bushel of grain or fruit. Then he would take you across in his boat. The other way was to swim.

Everyone thought this was a great system for crossing the river, because everyone was free to make their own choice. The better-off farmers always freely chose to pay Giles and ride the ferry. It cost them but they arrived on the other side safe and dry. The not-so-well-off farmers and the workers who labored for the farmers always freely chose to swim, because they had no extra grain or fruit to trade for a ride. Some died every year, but that was accepted as part of the inevitable price of freedom. Fate acted in strange ways, and who was to question it? At least they had died free, after freely choosing their means of crossing the Swift River.

Then one day a citizen of Freeville named William was telling a visitor about the wonderful freedom the Freevillians enjoyed. But to his surprise the visitor did not marvel. Instead, he laughed derisively. He scoffed, "You besotted oafs have not even a bridge across your river, and many die every year because of it!" William was taken aback. "What is a bridge?" he asked. The conversation became so interesting William invited the stranger home for dinner. Through the evening the two worked together to draw a picture of a bridge. William found out everything he could about how to build one.

After bidding his guest good bye the next morning, William was bursting with enthusiasm to tell everyone in Freeville about the bridge. He showed them the drawing and described how it could be built. It would be the best thing that had happened in Freeville in a long time! All his friends became enthusiastic. Many lives would be saved.

But William had not thought things through. Fortunately, Giles heard of the gathering crowd and came to talk to them. "Whence heard you of this bridge idea?" he asked William. "From a visitor to Freeville," William responded. "From a stranger?" asked Giles incredulously. "From the Unfree people? How can a free idea come from an Unfree stranger?" he asked. No one could think of an answer. Everyone knew that everything about Freeville was the best.

"Such a structure would take away our freedom!" declared Giles. "Now we have the choice to ride the ferry or swim. That is freedom. But with the bridge everyone would take the bridge. Our choice would be taken away. Liberty would be sacrificed for security, and foreign philosophies like Togetherism would rule the land! People would be interfering with the natural order of Fate. The next thing you know, we would all be slaves with no freedom at all!"

Giles' brilliant logic had won the day. All the people admitted the error of their ways, including William. Of what had they been thinking? The people of Freeville went back to being happy and free. The next spring, when William's son died in the Swift current, of course he was sad. But he was also proud, proud that his son had died free.

And they all lived happily ever after. Except the ones who didn't.

"Six Republican Myths"

from Bravegnuwhirled.blogspot.com: August 23, 2008

The Republican Party has won 7 of the last 10 presidential elections due to a consistent message which has crafted a winning reputation in the public mind. But that message is more mythology than reality, slick packaging with shoddy merchandise inside. Here are six of the most prominent of these myths.

Myth #1: Republicans are for small government. This is demonstrably false. The federal government grew substantially under Reagan, the elder Bush and the current Bush. Republicans are for smaller government only when it pertains to things they don't like. For instance they have time and again fought to cut Social Security, health care, public schools, environmental and worker protection, veterans benefits, and programs in general that help everyday people. They consistently expand government for things they do like. This includes such things as prisons, the military, corporate welfare, immigration enforcement, private schooling, religious organizations, spying on citizens and attempts to control people's sexual behavior and choices.

Myth #2: Republicans are prudent fiscal managers. The record shows precisely the opposite. Republican Administrations have been the most fiscally irresponsible in American history. The deficit Reagan inherited from Carter's last year was $59 billion. He increased it to $200 billion. The first Bush increased it to $300 billion. After the Democrat Clinton achieved a $230 billion surplus, the second Bush turned that back around to $480 billion in red ink. This happens because Republicans do not feel they need to collect taxes to pay for all the expensive initiatives they undertake. Instead, they borrow. Over 70% of the entire $10 trillion in national debt amassed since the inception of the country was compiled in just the last three Republican administrations.

Myth #3: Republicans are better on national security. After Iraq, this contention would be laughable were it not for the thousands killed uselessly in an unnecessary war. The national security of the United States was not furthered when only a half-hearted effort was mounted to eliminate the enemies who attacked us on 9-11. The national security of the United States was not furthered when America broke its longstanding tradition, initiated a war and exhausted its army fighting against a nation that posed no threat. Ignoring sound military advice, the Republican president and his congressional majorities then persisted in following a failing strategy for four years before finally changing. The 9-11 Commission's recommendations on terrorism were not followed or funded until Democrats took control of Congress in 2007.

Nor was the nation's security enhanced by denigrating allies and treating them with contempt, thus losing their support. Arousing the world against us through unilateralism does not make us safer. Resorting to posturing and saber-rattling rather than opening negotiations with rival states only ensures their continued enmity. Engaging in torture against suspected enemies does little but increase the numbers of enemies and their determination against us. Hiring a horde of private contractors at 7 times the pay of our soldiers damages morale, wastes our defense dollars and leaves our actual armed forces less prepared. Refusing to encourage alternative energy to break our dependence on some of the most odious, unstable, and in some cases, even hostile nations is another way Republican policies have made us less secure. In a host of ways, the basic defense posture of this party makes us less safe, not more.

Myth #4: Republicans are better for business. Republicans have proven better only for big business, whose profits are up 85%, and for millionaires and billionaires, whose ranks have quadrupled. For small business and the rest of the economy, their policies have failed since 1980. The typical standard of living has not improved in over 30 years other than the 1990s during a Democratic Administration. The stock market gained 8,000 points that decade, but has been flat for the past eight years. The wealthiest 5% of Americans have the greatest proportion of the national wealth since the verge of the Great Depression, when figures were first kept.

Myth 5: Republicans believe in free enterprise. Basing policy on handing out no-bid, unaccountable, cost-plus contracts to favored corporations is not free enterprise. Devising energy, water, highway and commercial policy based on secret meetings with industry representatives, and allowing lobbyists to write preferential regulatory and tax legislation in exchange for hiring party staffers and making campaign contributions is hardly free enterprise. These practices are instead among the defining characteristics of fascism.

Myth #6: Republicans stand for freedom. Not lately, they don't. By suspending habeas corpus, the basis of legal freedoms in Western Civilization for 800 years, refusing to testify before congress, initiating unwarranted surveillance of citizens in violation of the Fourth Amendment and the FISA law, similarly violating the ban on torture and turning suspects over to nations to torture for us, refusing to provide documents for congressional investigations and stifling scientific reports that disagree with their preconceived ideologies, the current Republican Administration and its loyal supporters in congress have shown the greatest contempt for the real freedoms enshrined in the Constitution. This short list is but the tip of the iceberg, as anyone who has kept informed well knows.

If you can be spied on without probable cause, arrested without charges, held without trial and tortured until you confess, how free are you? The fact that such practices exist in the United States of America and are tolerated for one day throws into stark relief the tenuous nature of liberties and the ease with which a government that appeals to fear can take them away.

CHAPTER 18:

Why Conservative Thinking Doesn't Work

During the Great Depression President Herbert Hoover's limousine would often pass families of destitute people begging, holding signs up pleading for work, trying to sell pencils on street corners or camped out in public parks. He reportedly was personally moved by their plight. More than once he gave of his own personal funds to needy individuals and families, sometimes in person and other times through third parties. Over the objections of his staff, Hoover always refused to let his gifts to be publicized in the press.

Yet, despite these impulses, he refused to consider any form of public, governmental action to help them. With millions facing starvation, private philanthropy and the kind act of a wealthy person here and there were simply unequal to the task. The compassion in his heart notwithstanding, President Hoover's response to the economic emergency of his presidency was an utter failure. The man who had gotten relief aid to the people of Belgium after World War I and to American flood victims as Commerce Secretary in the 1920s would not countenance engaging the resources of the United States government in his official capacity as president to alleviate the desperate condition of the American people in their hour of greatest need.

Hoover was bitterly reviled by the destitute Americans of his time; their shantytowns and homeless encampments came to be called "Hoovervilles." Running for re-election, he was subsequently thrown out of office by the largest electoral margin of any incumbent president and spent the rest of his long life as a figure of mockery and derision among his fellow citizens.

The Hoover presidency stands as the greatest object lesson in why conservative thinking doesn't work. The most basic and fundamental reason conservative thinking doesn't work is because it puts ideology ahead of people. The second most common reason conservative thinking doesn't work is because it so often puts ideology ahead of fact. And the third reason conservative thinking doesn't work is because it puts ideology ahead of public opinion.

Why Conservative Thinking Doesn't Work: Putting Ideology Ahead of People

You will notice a common thread here: ideology tends to trump everything else in conservative thought. They have their preconceived beliefs, and they don't let much of anything-necessity, evidence or the popular will-get in the way if they can help it. They call it "standing for principle," but what principles are served when millions remain jobless and hungry, or an unnecessary war is launched that kills tens of thousands and maims and scars many times that number?

The liberal asks, "How do we get good health care to more people," and then starts figuring out how to do it. The conservative asks, "How do we keep government involvement to a minimum and, if possible under those conditions, improve health care?" The liberal asks, "How do we make the air cleaner for people to breathe?" The conservative asks, "How do we avoid enacting any new government regulations and, if it is possible without them, make the air any cleaner?" By putting ideology before human needs the conservative forecloses a whole range of solutions to problems, solutions which sometimes are the best or perhaps even the only reasonable ones that can work.

Medical care for senior citizens stands as a good example. By the 1950s, medical care for senior citizens had reached a crisis stage. There were four times as many seniors as in 1900 and hospital costs were rising at almost seven percent a year. Consequently, only one senior in eight had health insurance. It's easy to see why. What insurance company could make money selling affordable insurance to the oldest and sickest members of society? Health insurance for older Americans was therefore prohibitively expensive and only the wealthiest could afford it.

John Kennedy campaigned in 1960 on doing something about this, but once elected couldn't get a plan through congress. After President Kennedy's assassination he was succeeded by Vice President Lyndon Baines Johnson. LBJ won election to a full term in 1964, and the voters also sent an overwhelmingly Democratic congress into office with him. In 1965 they passed the Medicare program, and basic coverage for senior Americans has never been a problem since. Conservative spokesman and later President Ronald Reagan said Medicare would be, "the end of freedom in America." Instead, it has become one of the most successful and popular programs ever enacted--a true lifesaver to millions of people. Everyone pays into it during their working lives, and it's there for them in their retirement years.

Medicare is a great example of liberal effectiveness at solving human problems contrasted with conservative obsession with ideology. Medicare was and is necessary because the private market cannot make money providing a necessary service to people who need it; and all of us who live to a ripe old age *will* need it. If old folks are to get medical care a government program must either provide it or pay the medical professionals to do so. The alternatives are to bankrupt practically every senior citizen and their family as medical bills mount, or simply to let them die.

Medicare shows the liberal ideal of meeting human needs. Conservative opposition shows their ideological approach. It is more important to them to stop the establishment of government programs than to solve urgent societal necessities. They opposed Medicare before it passed, have attempted to repeal it since, and would currently like to take it away a little at a time until it is no longer effective. That is the intent of the Paul Ryan Budget, passed by the Republican House of Representatives in 2011, 2012 and 2013, which would have turned Medicare into a diminishing voucher program. Fortunately for the well-being of 49.4 million American seniors, the Ryan plan was not passed by the

Democratic-controlled Senate. But the effort illustrates the general point that the conservative ideology of opposing government action is more important to them than meeting urgent human needs and solving the problems people face.

The same prioritization of size-of-government ideology and opposition to society using the democratic process to meet human needs goes well beyond the issue of Medicare, of course. It also includes such matters as job training, scholarships, Social Security, food stamps, immunization programs, Obamacare, and labor, safety and environmental standards. The alternative to government action on these fronts is that people do not get jobs, go broke, go hungry, lose their health, and even die. That is one reason conservative ideas don't work.

Why Conservative Thinking Doesn't Work: Putting Ideology Ahead of Fact

As I've described earlier, one of the main reasons I gave up the views of my conservative upbringing and embraced liberalism was my growing realization that science did not support conservative arguments and that the clear historical record did not back up claims of positive results when conservative policies were followed. Let's look at a few examples.

Take global warming, or climate change. The scientific consensus is near absolute. The immense amount of carbon dioxide and other greenhouse gases being pumped into the atmosphere by the burning of coal, gasoline and natural gas, deforestation and other human activities is causing massive changes in global climate. These include a spike in temperatures unseen in the past 400,000 years, sea level rise, increasing severity in the power of storms and changes in precipitation patterns, such as the spreading drought in the American West. This graph from the National Oceanographic and Atmospheric Administration shows the close correlation between global temperature and the concentration of carbon dioxide in the air.

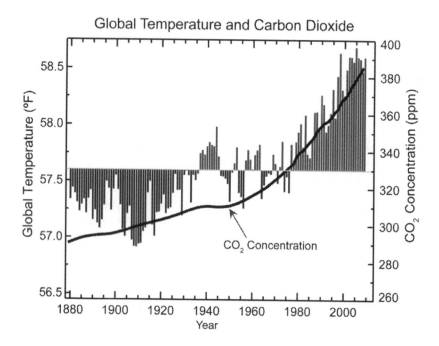

The conservative argument against this is that it must be a conspiracy cooked up by academics eager to get research grants to prove their theory. Most of the publicity campaign making these allegations is funded by oil and coal companies, who spend lavishly to raise questions about the connection between the use of their products and the deterioration of the climate, but who have not been able to refute the data or the correlation between CO2 in the atmosphere and world temperatures. Imagine how much the fossil fuel giants would pay for just one conclusive study showing any truth to their contention that greenhouse gases and temperature are unrelated. There is a conspiracy all right, but not the one that conservatives want to believe in.

The ongoing conservative fight against LGBT rights provides us another example of ideology, or perhaps plain old-fashioned prejudice, trumping not only science but the American egalitarian ethic. Some base their case against gay equality on grounds that same sex attraction is a disordered mental state, even though the American Psychological Association (APA) has been clear since 1975 that it is not. Another justification advanced against equality is that gender identification is a "choice." This, of course, begs the question that even if it *were* a choice why that would justify denying someone their rights. But here again, speaking of all sexual orientations, the APA finds that "most people experience little or no sense of choice about their sexual orientation." Conservatives fought hard to keep the "Don't ask don't tell" policy in force in the military, and predicted all manner of catastrophic morale problems if LGBT personnel were allowed to serve openly. They were certain of this despite the track record of twenty-five militaries around the world, including Australia, Britain and Canada, who were already accepting openly gay members without difficulty. "Don't ask don't tell" was officially ended in the U.S. Armed Forces on September 20, 2011. Have you heard of any serious problems resulting from this? Neither have I.

Conservative economic thinking holds that cutting taxes, regulations and government spending inevitably leads to balanced budgets and prosperity. But the facts do not confirm this. The top income tax rate for the wealthiest taxpayers was only 24% in 1929 under conservative Republican leadership, and that is when the economy cratered and the Great Depression began. It was raised to 79% under liberal Democrat Franklin Roosevelt by 1936, and strong recovery took place. Strong recovery also took place in the conversion back to a peacetime economy after World War II under the liberal Harry Truman. During the prosperous liberal Kennedy and Johnson years of the 1960s, the top rate averaged 77%. It was still 70% when conservative Ronald Reagan came into office in 1981. He cut the top rate to 50% for starters and the deficit tripled. He then chopped it to 28% and slashed spending for social needs. During his tenure the rich got richer, the poor got poorer and the middle class stagnated. In addition, banking deregulation led to the Savings and Loan Crash of the late 80s. Bill Clinton raised the top rate back up to 39.6% in the 1990s. The 90s saw the longest economic expansion in American history and the federal budget was actually running a surplus the last three years of Clinton's administration. Conservative George W. Bush was inaugurated in 2001, removed many regulations and initiated tax cuts back down to a 35% top rate. Once again, contrary to conservative ideological expectations, the budget returned to deficits, and the deregulated financial sector had its worst meltdown since 1929, leading to the Great Recession and the loss of millions of jobs.

To people in a fact-centered reality, the above results speak for themselves. The adoption of conservative economic ideas has produced poor results time and time again, while liberal policies have produced a demonstrably superior record of growth and prosperity. Yet conservative thinking remains impervious to facts. They remain wedded to cutting taxes and reducing spending on human needs. They block or roll back environmental safeguards, mocking the science and human health data that testify to their effectiveness. They repeal consumer protections while protecting corporate welfare, tax dodges and immunities. When the facts and evidence refute their claims they remain unmoved, because they *believe* in them. Putting their pre-set ideological views into practice, regardless of the effect on real people's lives is one of the defining characteristics of conservative ideology. That is what an ideologue is, and the main reason why conservatives do not seem to learn from the record when it comes to matters central to their core beliefs. They consistently put ideology ahead of fact.

Why Conservative Thinking Doesn't Work: Putting Ideology Ahead of Public Opinion

The United States of America justifiably prides itself on being a beacon of democracy for the world. Democracy comes from two Greek words, *demos*, the people, and *kratia*, power or rule. A true democracy is based on the idea that the common people can be trusted to determine what is good for them and the country and that they should have the predominant say in how society is governed.

In our representative system we do give a great deal of latitude to our elected officials. They must make decisions on a diverse array of issues, many of which most members of the public may not know much about. But it is still expected that the people's will needs to be taken into account, especially on matters they feel strongly about. That is the reason the First Amendment includes the right of the people "to petition the Government for the redress of grievances." It's a way of insuring government leaders cannot insulate themselves from the people's concerns. Otherwise, why give the people a say at all? Why not stay with the assumptions of the monarchical system of old, that the people are ignorant and only the king has the wisdom to know what is good for them? One would think that in a vibrant, responsive democracy, when the people have strongly-held views the government leaders would be eager to put them into effect. But that thinking rarely operates when conservative ideology is concerned. On issue after issue, conservatives in office follow their ideological preferences, not only when they run counter to human needs, not only when they fly in the face of fact, but also when they are heavily unpopular with the American people.

Reputable polling organizations find that conservative positions are out of touch with the views of most Americans on a host of issues. Here are some recent examples, as illustrated by the findings of the Gallup Poll.

In 2010 the Dream Act was favored by the American people by a margin of 54 to 42 percent. It would grant legal status to young people who were brought to America as infants or small children, have stayed out of legal trouble and who go to college for two years or serve in the military. It won by 14 votes in the U.S. Senate but conservatives stopped it on a filibuster.

A much larger percentage of Americans are in favor of a "path to citizenship" for illegal immigrants if they have been in the U.S. a "long time, pass a criminal background check, pay back taxes and a penalty, and learn English." A whopping 87 percent agreed in a 2013 Gallup poll. Only 12 percent disagreed. The Senate passed an immigration bill with these provisions by a wide majority with support from both parties, but conservative opposition in the House of Representatives has prevented it from even being brought up for a vote in that chamber.

In 2013, Gallup found 53 percent of Americans were against overturning *Roe v. Wade*, the Supreme Court decision that gave women the right to an abortion. Only 29 percent wanted the decision reversed. The same year found 78 percent in favor of legal abortion under "all" or "certain circumstances" and only 20 percent wanting to be "illegal in all circumstances." Yet that is what conservatives, especially social conservatives, want to enforce. In 2013, over 50 new restrictions on abortion were passed in states where conservative legislatures hold the majority.

Gallup asked Americans in 2013, "Would you vote for or against a law that would require background checks for all gun purchases?" 83 percent said "for" and 17 percent said "against." Conservatives in the U.S. Senate blocked the majority from passing just such legislation with a filibuster.

Conservatives continue to battle against contraception, even though 89 percent of Americans feel contraception is morally acceptable and only 8 percent do not. Even Catholics think so, by a margin of 82 to 15 percent. Conservatives tried to use opposition to contraception to invalidate Obamacare. Meanwhile, 98 percent of American women report using contraception at some point in their lives.

58 percent of Americans were in favor of legalizing marijuana against 38 percent opposed. This is even though just 38 percent said they had ever tried it and only 6 percent said they had used marijuana in the past month. Most, including those who do not use marijuana themselves, seem to think this legal war is an exercise in futility.

In 2014, Gallup found Americans supported same-sex marriage by 55 to 42 percent. In 2013, 52 percent of Americans said they would, if given the chance, vote to make marriage equality the law in all 50 states, versus 42 percent who said they would vote no.

The trend is also noteworthy. From 1996 to 2008 the percentage for marriage equality grew by an average of 1 percent a year and the percentage against fell by 1 percent a year. But since 2009 the momentum has accelerated. In '09 opinion as sampled by Gallup was still 57 to 40 against. In the ensuing four years the liberal view gained 3 percent a year and the conservative view lost three percent a year, producing the current 13-percent margin in favor. Conservatives, of course, continue to ignore the rapidly gathering national consensus and remain against marriage equality.

Conservatives fought for the 2013 "Sequester" budget cuts to public services, even though 56 percent of the American people felt if they were adopted "the economy will get worse." Conservatives instead cast their lot with the 30 percent who disagreed.

Other reputable polling organizations have discovered similar out-of-step conservative views on important topics. During the 2012 election campaign, for example, Pew Research found that the voters opposed Republican Vice President Nominee, Rep. Paul Ryan's plan to turn Medicare into a voucher program by 15 points, 49 percent to 34 percent. Yet support for the "Ryan Budget" was one of the key principles of the Romney campaign.

Conservative congressmen, led by Sen. Ted Cruz of Texas, orchestrated a government shutdown in late 2013 to try to stop the implementation of the Obamacare health program. The Quinnipiac University Poll found that Americans opposed the shutdown idea by an overwhelming margin of 72 percent to 22 percent. The same poll found that that issue was the key in giving Democrats a 9-percent edge at that time in people's preference for voting for congress for the 2014 elections.

In late 2013 prominent defense conservatives such as Senators John McCain and Lindsey Graham decried the idea of negotiations with Iran over its nuclear program. Meanwhile, the CNN Poll found Americans supported direct negotiations with Iran over its nuclear program by 75 percent to 20 percent.

A 2013 Kaiser Family Foundation poll on deficit reduction asked people what they thought ought to be cut "if the president and Congress decide to reduce the deficit by reducing spending." Lopsided majorities were against any cuts to public education, Medicare and Social Security, and strong pluralities were against cuts to Medicaid and health insurance subsidies. Yet education is one of the places where conservatives made major cuts in the recession, and the others are consistently mentioned in conservative proposals to cut, privatize and voucherize.

The people support clean campaign finance practices, and liberals are fighting to overturn the 2010 *Citizens United* Supreme Court ruling. In that case, the court's conservative majority, by a 5-4 vote, threw out forty years of law and held that unlimited corporate political contributions were fine. A 2012 Greenberg Quinlan Rosner poll found that 62% of registered voters disagreed with the *Citizens United* decision. Yet conservative leaders continue to back it.

The issue of income inequality continued to gain greater importance as the prosperity of the wealthy surged in the recovery while pay for most workers lagged behind. President Obama pushed for a major hike in the federal minimum wage, from $7.25 an hour to $10.10. A Quinnipiac survey in January 2014 found the American people solidly in support, by the huge majority of 72 percent to 27 percent. Even Republicans agreed, 52 percent to 45 percent. Nonetheless, conservatives, particularly economic conservatives, and the business community were bitterly opposed.

Income inequality could be a ticking time bomb for conservatives. A Pew poll in early 2014 found 65 percent of Americans felt income inequality had gotten worse in the past ten years, and 69 percent said government should take action to reduce the gap. Only 26 percent said government should do little or nothing about it. A 2013 Gallup poll had found that by a count of 59 percent to 33 percent Americans felt the distribution of wealth in the country is unfair and should be "more evenly distributed among a larger percentage of the people." Another question in the same poll asked, "Do you think our government should or should not redistribute wealth by heavy taxes on the rich?" 52 percent said it should and 45 percent said no, it shouldn't. Don't hold your breath waiting to see if conservatives will act to implement the people's choice on this one.

Time and again conservatives have demonstrated they are little concerned with what the people actually want. The cases you have just read provide plenty of examples on issue after issue where the wishes of two-to-one, three-to-one, even up to ten-to-one majorities of the American people are ignored in favor of following conservative ideology and satisfying a small minority of conservative voters at the behest of an even smaller fraction of wealthy backers. This is a third and foundational weakness that accounts for a good deal of the reason why conservative thinking doesn't work—it so often ignores the needs, the wishes and the plain common sense of the great majority of the very people it purports to serve.

But perhaps the greatest reason why conservative ideas don't work lies in the philosophy that underpins them in the first place, the philosophy of indifference, of "I've got mine, too bad for you." The liberal philosophy is one of concern for the community, of doing that which will help all to move up the ladder, well-expressed by President Kennedy's statement that "a rising tide lifts all boats." As noted economist John Kenneth Galbraith once so cogently observed, "The modern conservative is engaged in one of man's oldest exercises in moral philosophy; that is, the search for a superior moral justification for selfishness." Stripped of its intellectual veneer, that is the crux of conservative morality and the world view it supports. That such a moral foundation stands in direct opposition to every major philosophical, ethical and religious tradition developed in the five thousand years of human civilization before the twentieth century is an indication of just how radical the Ayn Rand-Bill Buckley-Barry Goldwater doctrine is. That it also stands in opposition to the facts and the clear record of experience sadly leads to a great deal of unnecessary suffering for millions of people.

Whose Interests Do Conservative Views Serve?

Conservatives of all stripes, and especially Tea Partiers, fancy themselves saviors of regular Americans from the clutches of big interests. They believe they are standing for freedom against undue restrictions and for economic opportunity. Yet, as we have seen, the results of their efforts have consistently produced precisely the opposite results. Conservative positions and actions have prolonged discrimination against minorities, women and gays for decades. Their economic prescriptions have, as we have also seen, produced poor results for the bulk of the American people over a very long time, the more than eighty years that reliable statistics have been kept. Yet their ideology remains intact and powerful. They are not a national majority, but are a competitive force that dominates the South and Plains states and can win national elections under the right circumstances. They must be serving somebody's interests. Whose?

Corporate Interests:

The greatest beneficiaries of conservative ideas are corporations. Conservatives oppose increasing the minimum wage and fight hard against worker's union rights. Both of these policies keep workers poor and corporate profits high. Conservatives voted against the Lilly Ledbetter law, which allows women to claim discrimination if they are getting less pay for the same work men do. They oppose raising the minimum wage, which has lost 40% of the purchasing power it had in 1968. This has the effect of keeping many full-time workers so poor they qualify for food stamps and health insurance subsidies. In effect, rather than making these hugely profitable companies pay their workers decently, the average American taxpayer subsidizes the labor cost for these corporations so their workers can afford the basic necessities of life. Liberals feel it would be better to require the employer to pay a living wage so working people would not need support from the public.

Under the guise of reducing regulations, conservatives make life easier for polluters who are poisoning the air, land and water. Everyday citizens pay the cost in asthma, cancer and neurological diseases. They preserve offshore tax havens like the Cayman Islands, Cook Islands and Cyprus, where multinational corporations with U.S. operations such as Apple, Google and Microsoft are able to hide profits and shield themselves from contributing their fair share of tax revenue to the U.S. Treasury. A 2013 study by U.S. PIRG found that $150 billion per year was being added to the U.S. deficit as a result. Instead of concentrating on bringing this kind of money back to America where it could do some good for the economy, conservatives look to pare down the deficit by taking food stamp money from the hungry, cancelling unemployment insurance for those out of work and cutting Social Security checks for the elderly.

Conservative ideology serves the corporate interests of privatizers, interest peddlers, and the Military-Industrial Complex. The move to privatize government operations means a lot of money for contractors. For instance, a 2013 study by the Congressional Research Service found that 62% of the personnel in Afghanistan were contractors instead of U.S. troops and civil employees, and that 50% of the personnel in Iraq had been so.

Removing limits on political contributions as with the *Citizens United* decision and gutting such requirements as the McCain-Feingold campaign finance law is a boon to shadowy behind-the-scenes political string pullers. The Koch brothers, Charles and David, for instance, were reportedly able to contribute upwards of $400 million through their network to conservative candidates, state propositions and causes in the 2011-2012 election cycle. Thanks to conservative opposition to "sunshine requirements" much of their and other political funding is now "dark money," funds that the voters may never know the origin of. This strategy is integral to conservative hopes for success.

To see why, you don't have to look any further than California's Proposition 23. This 2010 ballot measure would have largely reversed California's progressive climate change law, AB 32, which mandates progress on reducing air pollution emissions, particularly the ones that contribute to global warming. Two Texas oil companies, Valero and Tesoro, and Koch Industries, which ranks among the top ten polluters in the nation, were the money behind the Proposition 23 effort. The oil companies' pitch was that having to clean up the air would cost jobs. But thanks to California's strong disclosure laws, the environmental community was able to highlight the fact that almost all of the $9.1 million in funding for Prop 23--from gathering the signatures to get it on the ballot to the string of TV commercials touting it--came from oil companies, and armed with that knowledge, the people were not fooled. They knew that oil companies, particularly out of state ones, didn't care about California jobs. They knew that oil companies didn't care about making their product cleaner, and they really knew that oil companies weren't in favor of making cars use less gasoline. The voters could see through the special interest that was against their own interest, and despite the massive campaign to pass it, Proposition 23 was voted down by a margin of over 2.2 million votes.

The Prop 23 story highlights the effect of liberal perspectives. When people are knowledgeable they can be counted on not to toe the corporate line when its interests run counter to their own. Thanks to open politics requirements, the voters in 2010 were able to get a clear picture of who was trying to pull the wool over their eyes and why. The conservative push to allow unlimited political contributions on the grounds of "freedom of speech" and keep them secret on the grounds of privacy flies in the face of the clear public interest. They also mock the American principle of open and honest politics. Some rank-and-file conservatives hold these views sincerely and innocently, while the motivations of corporate boards and manipulators like the Kochs are no doubt quite a bit more cynical and self-serving. But the effect remains the same in either case. The aim of such secrecy is to dupe the voters into believing they are voting for their own or the general public interest when they instead are voting for someone's narrow, selfish interest at the expense of the good of the people as a whole. An election requires the people to have the utmost truthful information at their disposal. Democracy itself depends on it. As Thomas Jefferson said, "If a nation expects to be ignorant and free in a state of civilization, it expects what never was and never will be."

Conservative tax cutting also greatly serves the interests of corporations. Here are some major corporations that paid no income tax in 2012, followed by their revenue figures that year. General Motors $152 billion, Verizon $116 billion, Bank of America $75 billion, AMR (American Airlines) $25 billion, Lear $15 billion, JC Penney $13 billion, Caesars $9 billion, Alpha Natural Resources (Coal and metal mining) $7 billion. In 1951 corporate income tax receipts amounted to 6 ½ percent of GDP. Today they are down to 2 percent. That is over $70 billion less in after-profits revenue being used for the good of the community.

Wealthy People:
Wealthy individuals also draw great benefit from conservative tax ideas. When Ronald Reagan cut income taxes across the board by 25% over three years, that might have meant a $2 million annual bonus for someone pulling in $20 million a year, but only $50 a month to someone who earned an average 1981 wage.

Conservative tax ideology has benefitted a certain type of wealthy person even more: those whose money comes from investments rather than wages. That is why Mitt Romney, reputedly worth about $160 million when he ran for president in 2012, said he paid a tax rate of about 14 percent when the upper income bracket for income taxes was 35 percent and average middle class Americans paid 25 percent on their wages or salaries. Capital gains tax is assessed on the profit one makes when buying something like stocks, bonds, real estate or a company at one price and selling it later at a higher price. The capital gains rate was once as high as 40 percent, but over time the financial industry and its conservative congressional supporters were able, in the George W. Bush years, to chop that down to 15 percent. That's how we have the inequity of a millionaire hedge fund manager or corporate takeover artist paying a smaller percentage of their income in taxes than regular people earning 1/100 of the same income. (President Obama was able to make deals that raised the income tax for those making over $450,000 back up to 39.6 percent and capital gains to 20 percent.) Huge tax breaks for such investors do not produce jobs. They simply provide more profits for the recipients to make more bets on Wall Street, commodities futures, and the like. The reduced revenue, however, means greater pressure for cuts on things the middle class needs, things like infrastructure maintenance, education funding, college scholarship assistance, job training, unemployment insurance and emergency services.

Interest Peddlers:
   The conservative drive to get rid of any meaningful campaign finance reform means that money will continue to play an enormous role in politics. Members of congress report spending up to half their time asking lobbying groups and wealthy individuals for campaign money. So long as this is the case, politicians at all levels will be under strong pressure to do the bidding of their biggest donors rather than the public at large. There is a reason why millionaires and big companies pay a lower tax rate than average people and why food stamps and unemployment insurance continue to get cut but oil and agribusiness subsidies do not. Everyone knows what the reason is. The conservative penchant to support the current campaign money machine makes certain that the shadow "pay for play" system continues.

Fundamentalist Religious Organizations:
   The First Amendment in the Bill of Rights says, "Congress shall make no law respecting an establishment of religion..." There can be no official church of the United States, and the spirit of this

"establishment clause" further means that it's no business of government to support religion or advocate one religion over another. In 2006, conservative congresswoman Michelle Bachmann told a Christian group that public schools "are teaching children that there is separation of church and state, and I am here to tell you that is a myth." In obvious contradiction to their supposed preference for "small government," social conservatives like her want to use government power to support their version of religion and proselytize for it. They want public schools to lead children and governmental entities to lead citizens in sectarian prayers. They want public schools and official agencies to promote statements of their dogma that lack any scientific evidence as though they were proven scientific facts. They also want to keep teenagers ignorant about the fundamental facts of reproductive health. This kind of conservative's interests is served when city councils, schools boards and state legislatures can be turned into enforcement wings or missionary adjuncts of their churches.

Racists, Sexists and Homophobes:
   In 1964 the soon-to-be Republican presidential nominee, Barry Goldwater, voted against the Civil Rights Act. He explained his view that "The two portions of this bill to which I have constantly and consistently voiced objections…are those which would embark the federal government on a regulatory course of action with regard to private enterprise in the area of so-called public accommodations and in the area of employment." In other words, to him the doctrine of small government was more important than ensuring that people would not be racially discriminated against in housing, being served in a restaurant or in getting an equal chance to be hired for a job. The right of the racist to discriminate seemed more important to Goldwater than the right of the citizen to be treated like an equal human being. Kentucky Senator Rand Paul is often mentioned as a possible Republican presidential nominee. In 1998 he said, "A free society will abide unofficial, private discrimination, even when that means allowing hate-filled groups

to exclude people based on the color of their skin." When running for Senator in 2010 Paul appeared on "The Rachel Maddow Show." Maddow asked, "Do you think that a private business has the right to say we don't serve black people?" Paul replied, "Yes." So even though Goldwater said then and Paul and many conservatives like him say now they oppose racism, actual racists understand and enthusiastically approve of philosophical positions like this. They understand the implications of what they would be able to go back to if the federal enforcement of civil rights were to end. It is no coincidence that five of the six states that voted for Goldwater in the 1964 presidential election were in the segregationist South, and that that same region of the country is the most supportive of Senator Paul today. Racists like these conservative political ideas.

Those who stand against equal pay and opportunity for women and gays are also gratified by conservative opposition to equity for those who suffer from discrimination and from conservative efforts to gut enforcement of laws against racial, gender, LGBT and other forms of discrimination. Conservatives opposed and defeated the Equal Rights Amendment for women's rights in the 1970s. More recently, they fought and lost their battle to keep gays in the closet by opposing the repeal of "Don't ask, don't tell" in the military. In early 2014 the conservative Arizona state legislature passed a bill making it legal for businesses to discriminate against gay people based on "religious convictions."

Nationally, conservatives continue to fight against women's rights to contraception and abortion. They also tried to stop women from trying out for military combat roles. The conservative Supreme Court's 5-4 majority overturned the enforcement provisions of the Voting Rights Act in 2013. Until a liberal president and congress once again control the White House and Capitol Hill at the same time and can update the Voting Rights Act, it will be open season for conservative state legislatures to set conditions and draw lines that prevent minorities from electing representatives to represent them.

Republican Party:

One of the primary beneficiaries of conservative positions is, not surprisingly, the Republican Party. The Republican Party is the minority party and needs all the help it can get. According to Gallup in 2013, 47 percent of Americans identify as Democrats or lean Democratic, while 42 percent identify themselves as Republican or lean Republican. At the time of this writing only 19 percent of Americans have a favorable view of the Republican Party and 80 percent have an unfavorable view. Gallup further finds that the Republican Party is 89 percent white and 11 minority. (The Democrats' comparable figures are 60 percent white and 40 percent minority.)

To deal with this problem, there has been a concerted effort in the past few years to restrict the voter pool to conservative advantage. In states politically controlled by Republicans they have moved to limit such practices as early voting and have passed voter identification requirements that mandate the possession of a state-issued photo ID. Tennessee is an example of a Republican-controlled state that lets a handgun carry permit count as voter ID but refuses to accept a college student ID for the same purpose. Of course, gun owners skew Republican and college students tend Democratic. Further, rather than making it the responsibility of the state to make sure each eligible citizen gets such a card, they make it the citizen's responsibility to acquire one. And they know full well that those most likely to not have such a card or be able to easily get one are the poor, the young and minorities, precisely the people most likely to vote Democratic, or the elderly, who vote most strongly to protect Social Security and Medicare. Pennsylvania House Majority Leader Mike Turzai famously admitted in public his view that his Pennsylvania voter suppression legislation would guarantee that Mitt Romney would carry the state in the 2012 presidential election. Turzai was wrong, but his frank admission of intent reveals what the recent conservative preoccupation with "voter fraud" is really all about.

Opposition to the Voting Rights Act also helps Republicans in elections for the same reason, given that the intent and effect of the Voting Rights Act was to make sure minority voters who have historically been subjected to suppression of their voting rights get access to registration and the right to cast a vote. Since minorities tend to vote heavily Democratic, the 2013 Supreme Court ruling by the conservative majority on the bench that took the teeth out of the Voting Rights Act was a conservative dream-come-true.

Many everyday conservatives like the Electoral College method of electing America's president simply because it's always been done that way. They like tradition. But Republican politicos love it for a different reason. They know the undemocratic Electoral College tends to help the Republican presidential candidate in nationwide races. That's because more low-population small states tend to be rural and conservative, and the Electoral College exaggerates the vote for those smaller states. For example, in the last Census, California, with over 37.3 million people, had 66 times more residents than Wyoming, which numbered but 568,000. Yet California only has 18.3 times more electoral votes, 55 to 3. If it was proportional and Wyoming got 3 electoral votes California would receive 198! Viewed from another angle, from the 2000 to the 2010 Census California's population grew by more than 3.4 million, while Arizona's went up by less than 1.3 million. Despite this, Arizona added a congressional seat and an Electoral Vote for the 2012 election while California did not.

The *Citizens United* Supreme Court decision mentioned above supports a conservative position, that of making unlimited and secret special interest money available for political campaigns. The decision is also heavily to the advantage of the Republican Party. Because the GOP backs the corporate legislative agenda of gutting worker, consumer and environmental rights and protections, and because business outspends labor in politics by about twelve to one, *Citizens United* has the potential to drastically increase the Republicans' financial advantage in campaign spending.

It winds up being all of a piece. Rather than moderate their policy positions to win more support from women, minorities, workers and the poor, conservatives have instead gone the route of doubling down on extreme positions and trying to win by gaming the system to their advantage wherever possible. Thus we see voter suppression, gutting of the Voting Rights Act, opposition to electing the President by popular vote, and opening the spigots to unlimited cash from the plutocrats whose economic interests they serve.

Trickle Down

One of the greatest examples of the failure of conservative ideas is the miserable performance of their economic orthodoxies. It certainly played a major role in convincing me that my one-time faith in conservative ideas was badly misplaced.

Some people continue to defend trickle-down theories which assume that economic growth, encouraged by a free market, will inevitably succeed in bringing about greater justice and inclusiveness in the world. This opinion, which has never been confirmed by the facts, expresses a crude and naive trust in the goodness of those wielding economic power and in the sacralized workings of the prevailing economic system. Meanwhile, the excluded are still waiting.

Pope Francis

There is a growing realization throughout the world of the failure of conservative trickle-down economics to provide for the well-being of most people. Indeed, in the places where it has been adopted most recently there has been the clearest evidence of its ill effects in the form of lack of jobs and growing inequality between the income of a few at the top of the economic pile and the great number of most workers.

As we saw in the chapter on the economy, the surest way to widespread prosperity is to make sure average blue and white collar workers have money to spend and confidence their jobs are secure. Liberal thinking has produced greater prosperity because it keeps this in mind and fosters conditions that lead to such a society. A strong minimum wage, protections for union organization, liberal health provisions, a progressive and labor-friendly tax code, realistic immigration policy and good retirement security are some of the pieces that work together to make sure a fair share of earnings go to the workers. When that happens the 70 percent of the economy driven by consumer spending is healthy and the economy runs on all cylinders. The wealthy thrive too under such conditions.

When instead we see the minimum wage failing to keep up with inflation, union rights being compromised and even impeded, people losing health care benefits, tax provisions that give preference to off shoring jobs and that tax workers' wages higher than wheeler-dealer's capital gains, when we see immigrants being denied legal status and kept in the shadows so they dare not speak up for decent pay and treatment, when we see companies being allowed to raid and gut retirement plans, then we see the entire conservative action plan in operation. Its effect is to apply a slowly worsening squeeze to the middle class that leaves it too financially insecure to spend enough to keep the economy healthy. In an economic sense, that is *why* conservative economics doesn't work. The idea that lowering taxes and all restraints from corporations under the idea that they are the "job creators" and that some of the benefits will trickle down to average folks has now been tested several times in our country. It has also been tried overseas, such as the European "austerity policy" that was adopted as a cure for the Great Recession of 2008.

The results are now conclusive. As Pope Francis was bold enough to point out, conservative "supply side" trickle down dogma was nothing more than an "opinion, which has never been confirmed by the facts..." As it turns out, the liberals were right all along. It is the workers with good wages who are the job creators. Their spending provides the sales that drive profits and create the demand that produces more jobs. The economy works from the bottom up, not from the top down

That is the fundamental and fatal flaw in their economic thinking.

Summing Up

Better the occasional faults of a Government that lives in a spirit of charity than the consistent omissions of a Government frozen in the ice of its own indifference.

Franklin D. Roosevelt

We've already seen why conservative thinking doesn't work on a number of levels. It doesn't work in practicality because it puts ideology before people. Over eighty years ago, faced with the Great Depression, Herbert Hoover said, "Economic depression cannot be cured by legislative action or executive pronouncement." Because his mind was already made up he followed this ideology of "hands off" and things got worse. Unfettered by that kind of prejudice, Franklin Roosevelt came into office, took direct action, and made things better. Today the same kind of thinking holds true when conservatives push for the rights of corporations as if they were people but fail to protect the rights of actual human beings to vote, be protected from discrimination or earn a living wage.

Conservative thinking doesn't work because it values pre-ordained ideology over fact, and ignores or dismisses bothersome data that do not fit with conservative presuppositions, such as scientific findings about human-caused climate change. It flagrantly ignores public opinion, as when conservatives blocked common-sense gun registration requirements favored five to one by the American people, and acted instead to make it easier for terrorists, violent felons and the criminally insane to acquire lethal firepower. Social conservatives in particular remain strongly attached to ancient prejudices that deny equality and personal freedom to millions of people. Finally, economic conservatives and

Tea Partiers remain wedded to antiquated and disproven economic nostrums that have reduced economic growth and shifted a bigger and bigger share of the economic pie to a tiny percentage of the population at the very top.

My growing awareness, during the Reagan years, of the beginnings of the developments described in this chapter was a key element in my own conversion from conservative orthodoxy to a liberal perspective. I came to see these conservative precepts as not only morally flawed but also as destructive to the common good when they were applied to society. To be blunt, not only was a philosophy built on selfishness and callous indifference repugnant, but it wasn't even effective in producing the material benefits it promised would make things worth it in the end. I stuck with Reagan and the first Bush for nearly twelve years, but was fortunately open-minded enough to eventually admit the clear truth to myself. I hope people reading this book will not be as stubborn as I was for as long!

CHAPTER 19:
Winning

Liberalism always wins, eventually.

Chris Matthews

We've just finished the section on conservatism, and I hope that hasn't left you pessimistic. Yes, they are well-organized. They have money behind them. They never cease their efforts to whittle away at the rights and protections liberals have won, to surreptitiously insert corporate and millionaire-friendly special-interest schemes into legislation at the expense of everyday Americans, to make it easier for the unscrupulous to poison the environment and cheat consumers, and to reduce the basic support society needs to foster widespread opportunity. They have many intransigent supporters who refuse to be swayed no matter how completely the facts discredit their views nor how disastrously their policies have backfired every time their leaders have had a chance to enact them. But despite this you should never be in doubt about the ultimate vindication of our cause, because in the long run, all liberalism does is win.

We live in a country where women have the right to vote and black people can ride a public bus and go to school with white people. That's what winning looks like. We have Medicare and Social Security to help the elderly when they're too old to work and Head Start and school nutrition programs to help poor children begin the day with a chance. We have safety rules that have reduced workplace deaths by over 90%. Nine-year-olds no longer die in mine cave-ins or have their arms torn off in industrial accidents. Poor workers earn a minimum wage, and women can sue if they do the same work as a man and get paid less. Americans who don't get a health plan at work now get financial help to buy affordable health coverage. The air and water are cleaner than they've been in half a century. Cars have seat belts, air bags and structural crumple zones that have reduced crash fatality rates by 82 percent. Companies that produce unsafe products or engage in shady practices have to undertake expensive recalls or have been fined millions or even billions of dollars for the damage they have caused the public. And that's what winning looks like too.

Conservatives fought bitterly against every one of these liberal ideas and programs, and they lost. They keep on losing and liberals keep on winning by expanding freedom, equality, opportunity and security for everyday Americans. Sometimes change takes a long time and sometimes it happens with breathtaking speed. Sometimes, as with votes for women, the struggle seems to go on with no end in sight, and then victory comes suddenly in the blink of an eye. We are seeing that happen in our own time with marriage equality, social acceptance and the other equal rights and benefits that were denied for so long and are now being won across the nation by LGBT Americans. Even when they win elections conservatives have been unable to roll back these gains. Liberalism is an inexorable force. In the end it always wins. Always. As Victor Hugo put it, "There is nothing more powerful than an idea whose time has come."

The reason liberals win is because the liberal dream grows out of the deepest yearnings of the human heart. Everyone wants love and acceptance. Everyone wants to feel they belong, be afforded respect and be valued for who they are. Everyone wants to be treated equally, to have the chance to express themselves and pursue their dreams in their own way and to contribute to the people around them. Everyone wants material sufficiency, safety from the preventable perils of life, and to be able to look forward to peace of mind in a secure old age. Everyone wants to feel like they matter. These intrinsic needs common to all humanity are the wellsprings of liberalism.

They are also the reason why liberals win specifically in America, because these universal yearnings of the human heart and soul are the roots of the essential virtues and founding principles America has always stood for, that it indeed was founded to achieve: freedom, equality, justice, democracy and opportunity, founded on the spirits of compassion and truth and lived through the creed of liberty under law. Liberals win because we fight for a fair shake, a fair deal and a fair share for those who work hard and play by the rules. We believe all of us as members of society are in this together and that our individualism is not lessened by having a common purpose and the shared goals we can help each other reach by community effort.

Winning the Contest of Ideas

Americans who want to be first to set the agenda need to be quick, and must understand the use of language.

Howard Dean

Liberals want to live in a world where human needs come first, where the air, water and food are pure. In this kind of world people's health needs are guaranteed, as is vocational or college education for everyone willing to make the effort. At times when the private economy does not provide sufficient jobs, we favor community provision of gainful employment. In our view, no one who works full time deserves to live in poverty. We envision a world that lives together in peace, not a world governed by militarism and a society awash in guns and gangs. We continue to pursue the dream of a nation that lives up to the majesty of its creed that all are truly equal before the law and in the eyes of their fellow citizens without respect to color, gender, orientation, faith, or any of the other markers or prejudices that have held back the celebration of human dignity in the past.

We seek a nation that fosters science and research with a view toward bettering the human condition, a view that makes it a priority for each generation to pass along to the next a community, a nation and a world a little bit better than the one it inherited. Above all, liberals continually ask the question, "What kind of society do we want to live in?" Liberals have a huge advantage on this question, because as we saw seen in Chapter 17, the American people support the liberal perspective on practically every important issue. And in the larger sense, looking past the specifics of the particular issues, the bottom line is that Americans prefer a society where human needs come first, not a dog eat dog society where the rich and powerful game the system to serve themselves and cut average people out of a chance for a fair shot and a fair share. Franklin D. Roosevelt spoke out on the challenge of attaining the liberal dream when he said, "The only limit to our realization of tomorrow will be our doubts of today. Let us move forward with strong and active faith." In order to do this we must, as the civil rights marchers of the twentieth century sang, "keep our eyes on the prize." The prize itself is the simple but profound dream FDR enunciated as "…the hope of the world—a decent, secure, peaceful life for men everywhere." And while such a goal may seem self-evident to liberals, our adversaries are adept at convincing people that if only we start another war, if only we allow more poison in the air, if only we can deny equal rights to women and gay people, if only we enact another round of tax breaks for billionaires or regulatory breaks for Wall Street, then finally this time it will trickle down to help the average Joe and Jane.

That's an important principle to keep in mind, because the success of the liberal vision depends on winning the contest of ideas. In a democratic society the vision that ultimately prevails is the one that captures the support of the citizenry. In order to do this, liberals need to know how to employ the methods that win people's support, and this is where most liberals could use some coaching. Liberals are good at explaining what they think about particular issues. When they do their homework liberals are great at presenting facts and data galore to back up their positions. In many ways throughout this book, you've seen me present a lot of facts and evidence to show why and how liberal ideas and policies work and why and how conservative ones don't. This is all well and good. Liberals like logic and tend to be intelligent people. In no way should we abandon these traits and advocate things that are illogical and support them with arguments that are counterfactual. But it is crucial to recognize that in the contest of ideas, facts and logical argument are not enough.

Consider for a moment how frequently it happens in our elections that people vote against their own stated views and their own interests. Many people say they are tired of war and want peace, but then go out and vote for the candidate who is eager to make war. They say they are pro-education and then vote for the candidate who promises to cut it. They work at a non-union, minimum wage job and vote for the candidate who is for abolishing union rights and against raising the minimum wage. They are going to college or supporting their children in college and vote for the candidate who wants to cut scholarship help or wants to cut corporate taxes and reduce state support for the university system, which will necessitate raising their tuition. They are senior citizens kept alive and out of bankruptcy by Medicare but they vote for a candidate pledged to support a budget that would gut and privatize Medicare, likely leading to their financial ruin and possibly even their death. We all know plenty of cases like these. Liberals are often mystified by this phenomenon. What on earth are these voters thinking?

Well, that's the point. People don't vote, or make a lot of life choices, for that matter, based only on thinking. We are humans, not machines, and we make many choices based on feelings and moral perspectives. We also filter factual material and reasoned argument through our own personal moral frames of reference. In this book, for instance, although I have taken pains to present plenty of historical and factual material, you've rarely seen me go into an issue without having first established the moral, ethical or human dimension. People are not often convinced by reason alone, especially on political topics. They have to care, empathize with the approach, and feel in their gut that it's a good thing to do. It will take a lot of hard work to assure the continued advance of liberalism in America. To accomplish this it is necessary that liberals organize, advertise and proselytize tirelessly. But these efforts still won't lead to successful results if our appeals fail to connect with people on a personal, moral level.

Take a look back at Chapter 3. Those are the values that underlie the liberal moral world view, and when making the case for a particular issue it is essential to state the appropriate value or values behind that issue. For instance, when making the case for an increase in the minimum wage, don't just point to data showing reduced unemployment or higher economic growth associated with states and localities that have higher minimum wages. First, introduce the principles being served by the idea, such as fairness, opportunity and prosperity. This immediately activates a positive moral reference in the listener's minds and makes them more receptive to your arguments. Who is against justice, freedom or compassion? Who does not desire prosperity, peace and security?

A prominent linguist and cognitive scientist, named George Lakoff has done a lot of work on this subject. Among his writings are two books, *Don't Think of an Elephant* and *Moral Politics*. I recommend them to anyone interested or involved in carrying the liberal message to others, either on the one-to-one personal level or in public. Consider the title of the first book. When told not to think of an elephant, what is the first thing that comes into your mind? In similar fashion, certain words and concepts are associated with an inherently liberal or conservative mindset. Lakoff refers to these mindsets as "frames." Suppose, for instance, a conservative proposes a tax cut in order to reduce spending for education, health and nutrition. If you allow yourself to get suckered into referring to the tax cut as "tax relief" you are activating a conservative frame. The very way you engage on the issue implies that taxes are something threatening like a disease, from which a person should seek "relief." As Lakoff explains it, "For there to be relief there must be an affliction, an afflicted party, and a reliever who removes the affliction and is therefore a hero. And if people try to stop the hero, those people are villains for trying to prevent relief." So how does a liberal respond to a conservative call for tax "relief?" The liberal does this by reframing the issue into "tax fairness." Everyone needs to *contribute* to the *community* and the *common good.* The liberal reframes the purpose of the taxes into *opportunity* (education), *security* (health) and *love* (nutrition for poor kids).

Learn to activate the liberal frame and take command of any debate. The values liberals believe in are the bases of our message and world view. They are inherent in the American people and in the human heart around the world. The more we use them the more they help people relate to the essential righteousness of our cause and views. Remember, these values include ethics, peace, equality, freedom, and community, opportunity, meeting human needs, democracy, empathy, progress, science, justice, security, practicality, diversity, unity, civil rights, service and love. To these you could add fairness, prosperity, responsibility, health, happiness, beauty, nature, patriotism, togetherness, belonging, compassion, reason and spirit. If you speak of "marriage equality," for example, you emphasize the liberal value behind your view on the matter and evoke the liberal frame underlying it, equality. You have taken the moral high ground in the discussion, and it is not easy for anyone to argue effectively against the morality of equality.

Another part of winning the contest of ideas is how we personally conduct ourselves. To be effective we need to be good personal representatives of the liberal spirit. Our outlook is positive and optimistic. We speak to solutions. We are not loathe by any means to point out the shortcomings and failings of conservative dogma, but we express ourselves civilly, treat all people with respect, and refrain from personal attacks and insults. In debates and public discussions I have been badgered, bullied, insulted and basically treated disrespectfully quite a few times by conservative counterparts. I remind myself to keep my cool, speak to the values and issues in question and avoid personal retaliation. Thanks to that kind of response, I've been told time and again that the meaner they get the better I look. Remember what Martin Luther King said: "hate cannot drive out hate; only love can do that." You're not likely to convince rabid conservatives no matter what you say. But people with open minds are much more likely to identify with a forthright, reasonable person than someone who's mean and nasty.

Liberals win when they sincerely share what they believe in, present a vision that resonates and make a connection with peoples' hearts about the kind of community they'd like to live in. They clinch the win when they then identify the policy, plan, data or history that makes their point. In the bigger picture, liberals win every time rights are expanded, opportunity is increased, peace is furthered and justice is served. We get there by appealing to compassion and interest, the head and the heart, facts and feelings. Liberalism is right in the moral sense, and that's why it also works in the practical sense. Never doubt that as a liberal you are part of something noble and beautiful, something that has stood the test of time and is responsible for practically all the humane progress that's been achieved for centuries. That's a quest and a legacy that makes me proud to be a liberal.

CHAPTER 20:
Getting Involved

Human progress is neither automatic nor inevitable... Every step toward the goal of justice requires sacrifice, suffering, and struggle; the tireless exertions and passionate concern of dedicated individuals.

Martin Luther King, Jr.

You can make a difference in the world and feel part of something bigger than yourself by getting involved. The best way liberal values spread is at the personal level, from people interacting with others. A friend has a lot more influence than an ad someone might see on television or the internet.

There are many ways to have an impact. In your community there are panels and commissions the city council appoints citizens to serve on. Find out what they are; pick one you are interested in and find out how and where to submit your name. Write letters to the editor of your hometown newspaper. Volunteer some time at the local rescue mission, YMCA, church youth group, or food bank. Like most liberals, I believe we are on this earth to do some good in it. When you give back in the service of others you feel fulfilled and good about yourself. Try it and you'll see.

You can give support to groups doing good work with your time, expertise, and/or money. Here are some groups I support. Some I have actually worked with; others I contribute to financially because I believe they are making a difference in positive ways. At the end of the section I've included one of my blog entries from the 2008 election. It highlights the huge impact a relatively few people can make.

Remember, one of the best ways you can help liberalism is by registering people to vote and then encouraging them to exercise this precious right.

Environmental
Nature Conservancy (http://www.nature.org/aboutus/index.htm)

I've belonged to The Nature Conservancy for many years because I like their values and the effective way they go about their business. The mission of The Nature Conservancy is to "conserve the lands and waters on which all life depends," including projects in all 50 states and around the world. They preserve natural habitat in a number of innovative ways. Often, they just buy the land. Then there's no trouble with getting regulations passed. They also negotiate conservation easements with landowners or set up national parks in underdeveloped countries, giving the locals an ecotourism stake in keeping the area unspoiled. They involve the local people in whatever they do, and get buy-in. Members get a very informative magazine, too.

National Parks Conservation Association (http://www.npca.org/)

The NPCA is the top advocate for our precious national parks. In these times of miserly funding they can use all the help they can get. I'm an enthusiastic supporter. They send out a nice quarterly magazine you can use to help plan your visits, too.

Clean Government
Common Cause (http://www.commoncause. org/site/pp.asp? c= dkLNK1MQIwG&b=4741359)

Common Cause is the pre-imminent clean government group. They fight the fight to keep special interest money out of politics. They promote corporate and political ethics. They oppose voter suppression and promote diversity of opinion in the media. They have shined a spotlight on right-wing schemes to hijack state governments through the Koch brothers-sponsored American Legislative Exchange Council. These folks merit your support. They already have mine.

California Clean Money Campaign (http://www.caclean.org/aboutus/)

This group is working for the same ethical principles for California state politics that Common Cause is fighting for on the national level. A particular issue they champion is the California Disclose Act (A.B. 1648 and S.B. 52) which would require individual and corporate contributors' names to be public and the major ones to be disclosed on the political ads you see. It's patterned after H.R. 5175 on the federal level and a reaction against the terrible *Citizens United* Supreme Court ruling that legalized unlimited anonymous corporate political funding.

League of Women Voters (http://www.lwv.org/content/about-us)

There is a lot to like in the League of Women Voters, which has been around since women got the vote in 1920. They are non-partisan and fiercely protective of voting rights. As a result, they have progressive views on things like voter access and suppression, ethical politics, and reducing the influence of big money. They don't endorse parties or candidates, but they do take positions on issues. And because they study the issues and rely on facts rather than prejudices, they often have liberal views on matters like the environment. If you go to their web site be sure to click on the section "Our Work." They also provide a wonderful service called Smart Voter, packed with unbiased election information. Take a look by going to (http://smartvoter.org/).

Citizens Against Citizens United (http://www.citizens-against-citizens-united.com/)

This organization is dedicated to passing legislation or a constitutional amendment against the 2010 Supreme Court ruling giving special interests including corporations the unlimited right to inject untraceable cash in unlimited amounts into the political process.

Party Organizations
Democratic County Central Committees

This is where the rubber meets the road at the grass roots level. Central committees do the basic work of building a political party from the bottom up. You can find active central committee members registering voters and getting them to the polls on Election Day. They organize fundraisers, host candidate appearances, endorse candidates and ballot initiatives, distribute literature, hold politically related events like awards dinners, Labor Day picnics and charter local Democratic clubs. I served on my county central committee for four years. In California it is an elected position, so I had to file and have my name put on the ballot. Often times there may be openings on a central committee between elections, and you may be able to get appointed or serve as an alternate. In my experience, if you have a willing pair of hands they can put you to work.

Here's the url for the Los Angeles County Democratic Central Committee, an example of a huge and well-funded county party organization. (http://www.lacdp.org/). Here's the url for the much smaller Tuscarawas County Democratic Party in Eastern Ohio. (http://www.tuscdems.org/)

Local Democratic Clubs

County central committees charter local clubs of like-minded people who want to get together to make friends, talk issues, spread the liberal message to the community and provide a visible space for activists, elected officials, candidates and regular folks to have a voice. The official central committee, often meeting in the county seat, may be distant from some parts of the county, too formal for some, or the local club may want to focus on certain aspects or issues in particular, such as the environment or gay rights.

The Republican Party is so dominant in my county my wife and I did not even know there was a liberal organization of any kind here until we heard about the meetings of the Visalia Democratic Club. Other clubs that have been chartered by the local central committee in our county over the past few years include the Tulare

Democratic Club, Latino Democratic Club, Porterville Democratic Club, Democratic Women of Tulare County and the College of the Sequoias Young Democrats. I have served as faculty advisor of the COS Young Democrats since their inception in 2008, and several of our dedicated members have already begun careers in public service and liberal activism. Here is their *Facebook* page: (https://www.facebook.com/?ref=tn_tnmn#!/groups/13154159356 6400/).

Official Democratic Party Organizations

Official Democratic Party organizations include the Democratic National Committee (http://www.democrats.org/), Democratic Senatorial Campaign Committee (http://www.dscc.org/) Democratic Congressional Campaign Committee (http://dccc.org/) and Democratic Legislative Campaign Committee (http://dlcc.org/).

The Democratic National Committee is the official national party organization. It's focused on the President's agenda when a Democrat is in the White House. It's a good source for issues and spreading the word, and has links for volunteering.

The Senatorial, Congressional and Legislative Campaign Committees are zeroed in on electing Democratic candidates to the U. S. Senate, House of Representatives and state legislatures, respectively. They can get you involved in campaigns, you can learn what's going on, or just donate money. And the fact is, of course, that the reality of the present electoral system means liberal candidates need money to compete and win. On the down side, I became annoyed with the frequent telephone calls I was getting from the Senatorial and Congressional Committees for fundraising appeals. They are worth supporting, but tell them to "take me off your telephone list" if you don't want to get their calls virtually every month. I send an annual check by mail.

Minor Parties

There are minor political parties that carry the liberal banner in all or most of their perspectives. Here in California we have the Green and Peace and Freedom parties on the ballot. There is no doubt they are quite liberal in outlook. Both favor environmentalism, social justice, a mixed economy and a pacifistic foreign policy. If you want to get involved with either or others around the country of a similar nature, go right ahead. You can advocate for causes and feel the sense of belonging that getting involved provides. But in my view, in terms of effecting real change you will be wasting your time. None of these groups have the electoral appeal to win an election, and are ignored by politicians in office, the media and the public at large. You are far more likely to make a difference by getting active in the Democratic Party and working to keep it faithful to liberal principles.

I'm still upset about Ralph Nader's Green Party presidential candidacy in 2000 that siphoned enough liberal votes away from Al Gore in Florida and New Hampshire that both states fell to George W. Bush. Had Gore taken either one he would have been the forty-third president, not Bush. Without Nader's diversion of those votes we'd have had no Iraq War, no Bush tax cuts that gutted social services and took the money away that Gore was going to use to insure the solvency of Social Security and Medicare, and no "No Child Left Behind Act." We would have had ratification of the climate-friendly Kyoto Treaty and we would be light years ahead of where we are with green energy. I do not endorse folks getting involved with these groups. Whenever they win voters they take them away from the Democrats and thereby help Republicans win.

Liberal Activist Groups

MoveOn.org (http://front.moveon.org/)

The giant internet-based "Democracy in Action" group lives up to its name. By joining you will vote on the issues and campaigns the organization supports, and these member votes determine the positions and action MoveOn takes. There are plenty of opportunities to organize and get into direct action in your community. MoveOn is over 7 million strong.

Organizing for America, Organizing for Action: (http://www.barackobama.com/)

President Obama is trying to do something new in American politics—he is trying to turn his campaign apparatus into an ongoing movement to support his progressive initiatives. The idea is to enlist supporters nationwide to organize and advocate for issues like health care, gun control, marriage equality, comprehensive immigration reform, a balanced approach to fiscal problems, investments in green energy, early childhood education, and so on. The idea is to build up a groundswell of public opinion that will "move the needle" and push congress and state legislatures to act. The idea has merit. A lot of politicians are pretty cynical but they can read a poll or an election result. As an example, notice how congressional Republicans, at least in the Senate, finally started moving on immigration after their dismal performance with Latinos in the 2012 election.

Democracy for America (http://www.democracyforamerica.com/)

This group grew from the 2004 presidential campaign of former Vermont Governor and Democratic National Committee Chairman Howard Dean. DFA is strongly liberal in outlook and the group is proactive. I attended a worthwhile nuts and bolts political training session they provided in Fresno, California a few years ago.

Robin Hood Tax (http://www.robinhoodtax.org/)

Robin Hood Tax is a group advocating a one-half percent tax on all Wall Street transactions. It would raise an estimated $350 billion a year in the U.S. The money would be available to preserve the social safety net, fund education, rebuild infrastructure and create jobs. Legislation to put this into effect was introduced by Rep. Keith Ellison in April 2013. The big banks and brokerages that crashed the economy and got bailed out by the taxpayers are bigger and more prosperous than ever. Meanwhile, federal finances have never fully recovered and too many are still out of work. If you believe it's time the banks and brokerages to pay the American people back, this is a great way to do it. Bill Gates, Warren Buffet, Ban Ki-Moon, Kofi Annan, Desmond Tutu, Pope Francis, Nancy Pelosi, Richard Trumka (AFL-CIO) and Rev. Jesse Jackson are among the prominent supporters.

Non-Commercial Media
Public Broadcasting Service (PBS) (http://www.pbs.org/)
   I like supporting media that isn't beholden to corporate advertising. Public TV is a great service.
National Public Radio (NPR) (http://www.npr.org/)
   There is a wealth of intelligent programming on NPR. Like PBS, it's not beholden to corporate commercial pitchmen for its existence.

Human Rights
Southern Poverty Law Center (http://www.splcenter.org/)
   The SPLC promotes tolerance and keeps tabs on hate groups. It has shut many of them down by filing lawsuits against white supremacist, fascist, racist, sexist and homophobic groups for violating people's civil rights. The resulting judgments against the hate groups have bankrupted several and put them out of business. New ones keep popping up and old ones keep coming back in new forms, especially with the election of the first African-American president and recent rapid gains in LGBT and women's rights. It takes a lot of courage to go after some of these bad actors, and SPLC has it and then some.
Interfaith Alliance (http://www.interfaithalliance.org/)
   The Interfaith Alliance works to protect freedom of religion for all religions. What sets it apart is its insistence on a firm separation between church and state. Interfaith's position is that just as government entities cannot pass laws that interfere with the

practice of religion, neither do they have any business promoting anyone's religion. They file suits to keep taxpayer money, for instance, from being diverted from public school systems into private religious schools.

Human Rights Campaign (http://www.hrc.org/)

HRC is the largest LGBT (Lesbian/Gay/Bisexual/Transgender) advocacy group in America, claiming about 1 million members. They have some thirty regional offices around the country.

Equality California (https://www.facebook.com/Equality California? ref=stream)

Equality California is a very active and dynamic LGBT rights group in my home state. They have been carrying the fight against Proposition 8 and it has been exciting to watch the tide turning in favor of equality these past few years.

American Civil Liberties Union (http://www.aclu.org/)

The American Civil Liberties Union is the best known liberal group carrying on the fight to preserve individual rights and freedoms. It contests censorship and unjust immigration practices. It brings legal action against attacks on reproductive freedom, labor rights, the denial of equality on the basis of gender and orientation, and a lot more. ACLU attorneys are bulldogs!

Americans for Responsible Solutions: (http://americansforresponsiblesolutions.org/

This is the gun control organization formed by former Arizona Rep. Gabby Giffords, who was shot through the head in a horrific mass shooting, and her husband, former astronaut Mark Kelly. They are smart advocates of realistic change that can cut down on the carnage in society caused by too many crooks and crazies with too many, too powerful and too lethal weapons.

Alliance for Retired Americans (http://retiredamericans.org/)

These guys fight to protect Medicare, Social Security and Medicaid from the privatizers and slashers in Congress who want to see the elderly set adrift in their old age to deal with mounting medical needs on their own. This is a group to support if you currently rely on these programs or want to make sure they are there for you when the time comes.

Serving the Needy
Salvation Army:
(http://www.salvationarmyusa.org/usn/www_usn_2.nsf)
This venerable group dedicated to providing physical and spiritual nourishment for the desperate is also one of the best.
Mouth & Foot Painting Artists (http://mfpausa.com/)
The MFPA was formed to help artists who were born without or who have lost the use of their hands to be self-supporting and provide for themselves by marketing their paintings. They have items like cards, paintings and calendars for sale.
Crop Walk:
(https://secure2.convio.net/cws/site/SPageServer?JServSessionIdr0
04=14d43vj8w9.app244b&pagename=chw_about_crop)
Crop Walk is about fundraising to fight hunger. The money goes for food relief and for the means to help needy people around the world better provide for themselves. That could mean such assistance as seeds, tools, and clean water and irrigation systems for Third World communities. Events are held in all fifty states every year.

Registering Voters
Here is a blog I wrote during the 2008 presidential election campaign. It was just after the Republican Convention, and polls showed the convention had given nominee John McCain a bounce that put him nearly neck and neck with Barack Obama. Memories of 2004 were still fresh at that time. In '04 George W. Bush had edged out John Kerry by one percent in Ohio, and a victory there would have given Kerry the presidency. That's how close things can be. It points up the impact a relatively small number of people can make when a great deal is at stake. A lot of people, each doing a little, can accomplish a lot.

"You Have Power"
from Bravegnuwhirled.blogspot.com: September 8, 2008

The election race is tight again. There are about 44-45% for McCain and 44-45% for Obama. That leaves 10-12% undecided. With millions of dollars and millions of voters in play, people typically feel they really can't have much of an impact as individuals. And while that is probably true, those individuals acting in the aggregate can have an enormous impact. Here's a plea for getting involved.

There are always a lot of people unregistered. According to the census bureau, in the last presidential election in 2004, 28% of the people weren't registered as you can see here. There are also always a lot of people who are registered but don't vote. Even in the most high-interest presidential elections that's usually more than 40%. In 2004 again, the same Census Bureau report finds that 63% of the voting age population actually did turn out. And that was the most since 1992.

So, what am I getting at? Well, in the past three weeks I've registered five people to vote. All I had to do was go to the county office, get some forms and have them available. You know, it turns out a lot of people, particularly younger ones, have never been asked to register. They just need someone to invite them to and make it convenient and friendly. I recommended they all register for vote by mail, too. This they all did. That makes it more likely they actually will vote. I've heard that Oregon, which is all VBM, gets turnouts of 86%.

So suppose you are a McCain or Obama fan. The 44% of the people who are for your guy is really only 44% of the likely voters, in other words, 44% of the 63%. Of the total population that works out to about 28% for each candidate and 8% likely to vote but undecided. That leaves a whopping 36% who aren't likely to vote. That's more people than are for either major party candidate! There are a lot of potential voters out there for your guy. In raw numbers that means there are currently 70 million people for McCain, 70 million for Obama, 20 million who will pretty surely vote who are still trying to make up their minds, and 90 million who probably aren't going to vote.

Now suppose just 1% of your candidate's supporters go out and do what I did. That would mean 700,000 people would go out and sign up five family, friends, co-workers, people at the coffee shop, or what have you. That would mean an extra THREE AND A HALF MILLION VOTES for your guy. A close election turns into a clear win with just that much minimum effort by 1% of his supporters.

And I'm not talking about going door to door or setting up a table outside a store and sitting there all day. I'm just talking about maybe wearing a button for your favorite. It's a conversation starter among people who like your guy. You get around to asking if they're registered, you have a few forms in your car, purse, briefcase, tool box or what have you, and bingo. You can even feel like you're getting really involved by taking down their phone number and calling them when the absentees are mailed out, saying, "Hi, remember me?" and reminding them to fill out the ballot and send it in.

I've signed up five in three weeks, and there are still eight weeks to go. What do you think you might be able to do? Want to feel like you're making a difference? Go ahead and give it a try. If you're like me you'll be glad you did.

That post from 2008 points up what can happen when people are energized behind the liberal vision. Obama and the liberal vision went on to win a smashing victory. Today as a result we are greener, freer, more equal, more inclusive, more just and more prosperous than we would otherwise be. Progress never comes as quickly and easily as we wish, and it never comes without work and struggle. But it comes. Indeed, look how far we have come. Though it is easy to dwell on difficulties and give in to frustration, the dream of a world based on peace, love and meeting human needs is too precious to abandon. On taking office in 1961, the great liberal President John F. Kennedy quoted scripture to call upon the American people to remain steadfast, "rejoicing in hope; patient in tribulation." He inspired the nation to take up the "struggle against the common enemies of man: tyranny, poverty, disease, and war itself." We are called to take up the same struggle in our own time and place, to advance the dream a bit further than those who came before. Kennedy's words are as timely now as then. He continued, "All this will not be finished in the first one hundred days. Nor will it be finished in the first one thousand days; nor in the life of this Administration; nor even perhaps in our lifetime on this planet. But let us begin."

INDEX

Made in the USA
Charleston, SC
07 July 2016